The Future of Labour Market Reform in the Gulf Region

The Gulf Research Centre Book Series at Gerlach Press

The Gulf Region: Economic Development and Diversification (4 vols set)
Ed. by L. Luciani, S. Hertog, E. Woertz and R. Youngs
ISBN 9783940924001, 2012

The GCC in the Global Economy
Ed. by Richard Youngs
ISBN 9783940924018, 2012

Resources Blessed: Diversification and the Gulf Development Model
Ed. by Giacomo Luciani
ISBN 9783940924025, 2012

GCC Financial Markets: The World's New Money Centers
Ed. by Eckart Woertz
ISBN 9783940924032, 2012

National Employment, Migration and Education in the GCC
Ed. by Steffen Hertog
ISBN 9783940924049, 2012

Asia-Gulf Economic Relations in the 21st Century: The Local to Global Transformation
Ed. by Tim Niblock with Monica Malik
ISBN 9783940924100, 2013

A New Gulf Security Architecture: Prospects and Challenges for an Asian Role
Ed. by Ranjit Gupta, Abubaker Bagader, Talmiz Ahmad and N. Janardhan
ISBN 9783940924360, 2014

Gulf Charities and Islamic Philanthropy in the 'Age of Terror' and Beyond
Ed. by Robert Lacey and Jonathan Benthall
ISBN 9783940924322, 2014

State-Society Relations in the Arab Gulf States
Ed. by Mazhar Al-Zoby and Birol Baskan
ISBN 9783940924384, 2014

Political Economy of Energy Reform: The Clean Energy-Fossil Fuel Balance in the Gulf
Ed. by Giacomo Luciani and Rabia Ferroukhi
ISBN 9783940924407, 2014

The Silent Revolution: The Arab Spring and the Gulf States
Ed. by May Seikaly and Khawla Mattar
ISBN 9783940924346, 2014

Security Dynamics of East Asia in the Gulf Region
Ed. by Tim Niblock with Yang Guang
ISBN 9783940924483, 2014

Islamic Finance: Political Economy, Performance and Risk
Ed. by Mehmet Asutay and Abdullah Turkistani
ISBN 9783940924124, 3 vols set, 2015

Employment and Career Motivation in the Arab Gulf States: The Rentier Mentality Revisited
Ed. by Annika Kropf and Mohamed Ramady
ISBN 9783940924605, 2015

The Changing Energy Landscape in the Gulf: Strategic Implications
Ed. by Gawdat Bahgat
ISBN 9783940924643, 2015

Gulf Research Centre Cambridge
Knowledge for All

Sustainable Development Challenges in the Arab States of the Gulf
Ed. by David Bryde, Yusra Mouzughi and Turki Al Rasheed
ISBN 9783940924629, 2015

The United States and the Gulf: Shifting Pressures, Strategies and Alignments
Ed. by Steven W. Hook and Tim Niblock
ISBN 9783940924667, 2015

Africa and the Gulf Region: Blurred Boundaries and Shifting Ties
Ed. by Rogaia Mustafa Abusharaf and Dale F. Eickelman
ISBN 9783940924704, 2015

Rebuilding Yemen: Political, Economic and Social Challenges
Ed. by Noel Brehony and Saud Al-Sarhan
ISBN 9783940924681, 2015

Science and Technology Development in the Gulf States: Economic Diversification through Regional Collaboration
Ed. by Afreen Siddiqi and Laura Diaz Anadon
ISBN 9783959940023, 2016

Higher Education Investment in the Arab States of the Gulf: Strategies for Excellence and Diversity
Ed. by Dale F. Eickelman and Rogaia Mustafa Abusharaf
ISBN 9783959940122, 2016

Iran's Relations with the Arab States of the Gulf: Common Interests over Historic Rivalry
Ed. by Maaike Warnaar, Luciano Zaccara and Paul Aarts
ISBN 9783959940047, 2016

Egypt and the Gulf: A Renewed Regional Policy Alliance
Ed. by Robert Mason
ISBN 9783959940061, 2016

Intellectual Property Rights: Development and Enforcement in the Arab States of the Gulf
Ed. by David Price and Alhanoof AlDebasi
ISBN 9783959940108, 2016

The Arab States of the Gulf and BRICS: New Strategic Partnerships in Geopolitcs and Economics
Ed. by Tim Niblock, Alejandra Galindo and Degang Sun
ISBN 9783959940085, 2016

The Arms Trade, Military Services and the Security Market in the Gulf States: Trends and Implications
Ed. by David B. Des Roches and Dania Thafer
ISBN 9783959940160, 2016

Strategies of Knowledge Transfer for Economic Diversification in the Arab States of the Gulf
Ed. by Rasmus Gjedssø Bertelsen, Neema Noori and Jean-Marc Rickli
ISBN 9783959940146, 2018

Yemen and the Gulf States: The Making of a Crisis
Ed. by Helen Lackner and Daniel Martin Varisco
ISBN 9783959940306, 2018

Conflict Resolution and Creation of a Security Community in the Gulf Region
Ed. by Tim Niblock with Talmiz Ahmad and Degang Sun
ISBN 9783959940368, 2018

The Future of Labour Market Reform in the Gulf States: Towards a Multi-Disciplinary, Evidence-Based and Practical Understanding
Ed. by David B. Jones and Sofiane Sahraoui
ISBN 9783959940344, 2018

The Future of Labour Market Reform in the Gulf Region

Towards a Multi-Disciplinary, Evidence-Based and Practical Understanding

Edited by David B. Jones
and Sofiane Sahraoui

Gerlach Press

First published 2018
by Gerlach Press
Berlin, Germany
www.gerlach-press.de

Cover Design: Frauke Schön, Hamburg
Set by Anne Jeschke, Gerlach Press
Printed and bound in Germany

British Library Cataloguing in Publication Data.
A catalogue record for this book is available from the British Library.

Bibliographic data available from Deutsche Nationalbibliothek
http://d-nb.info/1136383549

ISBN: 978-3-95994-034-4 (hardcover)
ISBN: 978-3-95994-035-1 (eBook)

Contents

Introduction

David B. Jones and Sofiane Sahraoui

> "It was the best of times, it was the worst of times, it was the age of wisdom, it was the age of foolishness, it was the epoch of belief, it was the epoch of incredulity, it was the season of Light, it was the season of Darkness, it was the spring of hope, it was the winter of despair, we had everything before us, we had nothing before us, we were all going direct to heaven, we were all going direct the other way."

In terms of GCC labour market reform, it is in many ways the best of times and the worst of times, as described in Dicken's introduction to The Tale of Two Cities. On one hand, the speed, scale and scope of change continues to grow. Public sector pay and benefits have been reduced (then reinstated) by 20%, along with new Nitaqat regulations in Saudi Arabia and new maternity leave benefits and expatriate visa conditions announced in the UAE, along with increased international scrutiny on the fair treatment of expatriates, all since our workshop took place in August 2016. The dynamism of this field is centred on an increased recognition of the urgency and importance of reviving the moribund regional labour markets across the GCC. Private sector employers are clearly placed front and centre as the new frontier for nationalization in particular. On the other hand, the resources to invest in greater productivity and positivity in our region's workplaces are still available and a young, growing and well – educated local workforce could afford the opportunity of a "demographic dividend" as much as a "demographic disaster".

Nonetheless, it is also clear that achieving the shift to the "post – oil", "knowledge – based economies" enshrined in the various visions of governments across the GCC within the next decade or so, will not be straightforward. Changing the nature of nationalization policies, fundamentally alters the social contracts established by ruling elites in regard to the distribution of economic rents gained from development based on the exploitation of fossil fuel resources since the middle of the twentieth century. Whilst it is clear that "nationalization 2.0" will remain at the heart of labour market reforms going forward, changing nationalization also has broader social impacts related to nationalism and national identity well beyond innovations in positive discrimination policies to regulate labour markets. Local labour policies lie at the heart of the loyalty and legitimacy nexus within the GCC and will continue to do so for the foreseeable future.

It is important to note, that beyond the GCC, positive discrimination policies have a mixed record of success in places such as South Africa and Malaysia for instance. Indeed, it could be argued that only in places where there is sufficient and sustained economic growth or economic rents, e.g. in Singapore, can such policies persist. This is the challenge faced by GCC governments – can the targeted transition to "knowledge – based economies" be achieved as economic rents diminish in the region and workers deliver competitive rates of productivity to ensure competitive economies with sustainable employment opportunities during the rest of the twenty – first century and beyond. Ruling elites have not yet answered the question as to how fast can labour reform take place? Changes in employment conditions and the workplace psychological contract are core to the social contracts established across the region in the latter half of the twentieth century. Most recently, less than a year after the launch of Vision 2030 in Saudi Arabia, the reductions in public sector benefits have been reversed and indeed there have been announcements of pay increases for serving military officials in the ongoing conflict in Yemen. The reinstatement of benefits to public employees after six months emphasizes the practical limits of reform in the kingdom in particular and the GCC in general. Ruling families must be seen to provide for their people in order to secure their continued loyalty to the state and compliance with government policies.

Moreover, by implication, changing nationalization policies will mean concomitant changes for the nature of expatriation in the region too. "Expatriation 2.0" may not get as much attention in the region's newspaper headlines but is just as important in understanding the new regional talent landscape lying before us. Expatriates currently dominate private sector labour markets, where virtually all future employment growth is predicted to occur. The current "activist" approach to policy reform currently undertaken regional governments arguably risks "crowding out" action and accountability amongst employers, educational institutions and individuals to innovate in terms of creating more sustainable regional labour markets. Governments across the region are actively driving not only labour market reform but also its implementation by demanding compliance with what must appear as increasingly byzantine regulations by private sector employers. It is debatable whether increasing the complexity of regulation can increase long – term workplace productivity when there is a need for more integrated competition across all segments of the region's labour markets, not less.

Without strong engagement with private sector employers it remains uncertain how successfully changes in government policies will be implemented, especially during the imminent introduction of corporate and sales taxes and continued removal of utilities subsidies across the GCC. Taxation is likely to enhance expectations of representation amongst labour market stakeholders. The prime target audience for the new wave of labour reforms are private sector employers, the majority of them owned and managed by expatriates in many parts of the GCC economy. It remains to be seen whether a lack of a formal consultation framework with employers, and indeed employee's associations, as is still common in a tripartite model of labour policy formulation and reform in many parts of the world, will encourage governments to rely too much on regulation over engagement with the private sector. For many private sector employers, this distance from government can lead to mutual misunderstanding and even fear of engagement with regulators, which will not support effective implementation of new policies.

The question remains: What can GCC nationals do to make themselves more attractive to private sector employers and vice versa, what can the private sector do to make itself more attractive for GCC national job-seekers? Indeed, a recent report by the World Economic Forum (January, 2017) "Accelerating Economic Reforms in the Middle East and North Africa", places "enhancing the efficiency of the labour market", as the top of the list of six priorities for business leaders. Business leaders are seeking more mobility between jobs, greater flexibility in labour regulation and a relaxation of redundancy laws, particularly as they apply to GCC nationals. Arguably, GCC policy – makers are moving in the opposite direction. With recent initiatives such as the "Absher" and "Tawteen" initiatives in the UAE for instance, the language associated with these policies themselves, focuses on "compensating" nationals for the relative hardships and challenges of working in the private sector.

Herein lies the fundamental contradiction in the dual role of regional governments, both as regulators of the labour market and as the prime employers of the local workforce. Whilst we are observing reforms in the former, the terms and conditions, salaries and benefits, working hours and holidays continue to be offered at levels which commercial employers find unsustainable, private sector employment of nationals will continue to be limited. Despite recent changes in Saudi Arabia in terms of reducing and restraining public sector benefits for national employees, this is only an incremental step towards redressing a half century or more of increasing divergence between pay and benefits provision between government and private sector employers.

Clearly, this is a complex and challenging issue. Our view is that many stakeholders and many academic perspectives need to collaborate to both improve our understanding and the odds of success. Hence in this volume, we present papers from our workshop which represent the perspectives of policy – makers, employers and educationalists. Our workshop was attended by economists, psychologists, students of gulf studies and government officials. We have also presented a broad geographical coverage of the distinct labour market issues as they exist across the GCC. It is clear that multidisciplinary approaches are the future of scientific endeavour, particularly in regard to social science, with a broader approach needed to address complex challenges such as the reform of GCC labour markets.

Supporting more efficient labour markets in the region is the major challenge – how can we better match the changing contours of available labour supply and labour demand in our region, not just for today but also to sustain the living standards and development attained by the nations of the GCC in the last 75 years? Herein lies the rub and herein lies the underlying question asked throughout this book.

Several papers provide a regional overview and highlight the distinct nuances of how these issues play out across the GCC. Sophie Olver – Ellis provides a regional overview of the changing landscape of labour market reform across the region, focusing specifically on Saudi Arabia, Kuwait and Qatar. She highlights the differences that exist within and between these 3 nations, for instance highlighting how there are "islands of efficiency" within the Saudi context for instance, with Saudi Aramco and SABIC for instance standing out as competitive and productive employers amongst others in a largely "rentier" economy. She also highlights how the "kafala" system is deployed differently across the 3 nations studied and how Kuwait, and to a slightly lesser extent Qatar, labour market distortions are becoming more entrenched, whilst Saudi Arabia continues to innovate and operate as the region's laboratory labour market reform. Olver – Ellis concludes that this is primarily due to the respective ruling elites having chosen different paths to extending their legitimacy amongst key stakeholders.

Mark Thompson's paper provides an overview into the changing dimensions of the broader social contract within Saudi Arabia, from the perspectives of Saudi male graduates, with a particular focus on the dynamic expectations in regard to employability and navigating the education to employment transition amongst this group. Most interestingly, it is clearly debatable whether the younger generation of Saudi males see traditional networks of contacts and mutual obligation such as "wasta" as creating or limiting opportunities in the labour market and what regional differences exist across the Kingdom as a whole.

McGlade and Ansari highlight the unique nature of youth employment challenges in Oman, with a particular focus on the growing reliance on the SME sector by policy – makers as a source of new employment opportunities going forward. They argue that this will be a challenge as only 14% of Omanis are employed in the private sector, largely amongst large, stable commercial employers. Persuading a significant enough number to take the risk associated with entrepreneurial activity and SME jobs is unlikely to have a major impact on reducing structural unemployment. They also highlight that more highly educated Omanis are more likely to be unemployed and for longer, and less likely to be attracted to the industries targeted by the government as future sources of employment, namely tourism, agriculture, etc. They conclude by highlighting the critical role of effective career guidance for helping improve the efficiency of regional labour markets.

Bajraktari and Salman narrate some of the distinct challenges to employability in Bahrain with some specific recommendations to achieving greater efficiency and sustainability with regard to the Kingdom's labour markets. They provide validated data on wages across segmented labour markets and argue that until reform is able to unify the competitive market rates, Bahrain's talent landscape will remain inherently unsustainable.

Anastasia Nosova focuses on the business community in Kuwait and how their interests are reflected in the pattern of labour market reform, or not. With 81% of Kuwaitis employed in the public sector, she argues that patterns of employment are not only non – productive but are actually counter – productive. Private sector investment and employment is effectively "crowded out" and the role of trades unions and the Kuwaiti parliament tends to focus on short term advantages for their client groups, such as extending wage growth rather than total employment and labour productivity. Established business elites are also able to use social and political institutions, along with informal networks, to limit opportunities for new market entrants, thereby reducing the dynamism and productivity of the economy overall.

The next two chapters focus on changes in the world of learning and how the talent supplied as a product of the region's education and organizational development is striving to keep pace with new technology and changes in the world of work itself. Punshi and Topolskaya provide data – led insights into how the world of corporate learning and talent development in the GCC remains somewhat anachronistic and is struggling to fully benefit from the full efficiency and effectiveness gains from actively adopting new approaches to learning. Whilst highlighting that learning budgets are high, the motivation of individuals and employers to invest effectively in human capital development remains low. Gupta and Lambert then review the impact of positive education practices on character development and employability skills amongst grade 11 students in the UAE. Their data analytics and insights highlight the potential benefits of this innovative approach to enhancing the continued reliance on didactic learning amongst this population and the positive impact on their potential employability and career choices from alternative learning practices.

The final two chapters bring the perspective of employers into the debate. In both cases, they operate in the commercial sphere in the UAE as essentially private sector organisations with government ownership. Wissam Hachem provides a detailed case study of the role of rewards in impacting learning performance amongst cadet pilots at Etihad Airways. Finding that providing recognition for learning progress was more effective than rewards alone, the paper also serves as an interesting case study on how employers are motivated to provide significant resources to develop their own learning facilities to develop local talent in particular. Jonas Harring – Boll's paper takes an evidence – based approach to providing predictive analytics on which behaviours lead to sales and customer service outcomes within one of the largest banks in the GCC. Most interestingly, his statistical analysis demonstrates that qualifications alone are not significant in predicting workplace performance and that general employability skills and behavioural characteristics are far more powerful in comparison. Finally, the increased use of such predictive talent analytics by private sector employers inherently reinforces a corporate culture of equality of opportunity, diversity and meritocracy in the face of increasing positive discrimination policies to support greater representation of GCC nationals in the private sector workforce in particular.

In conclusion, the question remains that with rapidly changing patterns of nationalization, expatriation, automation, productivity and well – being occurring across the region, the question is whether labour market reform can keep up with technological and social change more broadly. Are we designing policy – frameworks which are fundamentally based on a concept of "work" which arguably appeared anachronistic at the end of the twentieth century and not just for the twenty first century? The world of work is changing fundamentally on a global and not just a regional level. It is unrealistic to expect that the region can insulate itself from the impact of international labour arbitrage and technological advances by labour market reforms alone. Changes in the way humans (and their automated avatars) organize themselves to produce goods and services, earn a living and deliver value to customers are rapidly accelerating. A concern for policy – makers in the GCC is that the concentration of nationals in administrative and managerial roles in the government and banking sectors are arguably amongst the most vulnerable jobs, most likely to disappear, as a result of the latest waves of automation.

Indeed, in many ways, the way people create and distribute economic, social and psychological value for each other are predicted to be unrecognizable within a decade. Over the same period, every single month India will add more than a million net new job seekers to its workforce. This directly further decreases the relative per person productivity figures in the GCC and indirectly increasing the potential supply of labour into the gulf region. We are entering an increasingly VUCA (volatile, uncertain, complex and ambiguous) world, where most nations or employing organisations no longer have the stability to be able to cascade strategic imperatives into departmental KPIs and functional objectives, ultimately informing individual priorities. Such centralized planning is no longer sustainable and better suited to the entropic Stalinist 5 year planning cycle of the Soviet Union.

Clearly governments in the region are increasingly activist in terms of their policy – making in general, and with respect to labour market reform in particular. In many cases, with the scope and scale of labour market regulations expanding (along with the parallel introduction of corporate taxation and VAT in 2018) private sector employers and even many employees, would argue that what we need is less and not more regulation. Over the next decade more than 1 billion young people will enter the global labour market, and only 40% will be working in jobs that currently exist, estimates the World Bank. Some 90% of new jobs are created by the private sector. The best thing for job creation is economic growth, so policies that promote growth are particularly good for the young. Removing regulatory barriers can also boost job creation, although they can also create greater uncertainty for young job seekers, requiring better career guidance to promote more efficient labour markets and more investments in character development and positive education focused on developing Grit, Resilience, Growth Mindset, Self – Efficacy, etc.

There are many uncertainties in the economic future of the GCC, whether we consider the impact of environmental degradation, transition to a post – oil society or geo-political challenges for example, especially as our VUCA world accelerates still faster into a vortex of ongoing change. Achieving a successful transition towards more efficient, effective and sustainable labour markets is as urgent and important as any of the above challenges. Making the experience of work better – for societies, organisations and individuals during the rest of the century is critical for the GCC.

This is a regional issue, which must be put into context within the global context. During the century ahead, when the human population is predicted to peak at above 11 billion people, a successful transition to sustainable labour markets is only possible if work itself becomes more human. Promoting the creation of more positive and productive employment opportunities is key for the GCC if a demographic time bomb is to be avoided. Legislation which creates ever more segmented and sclerotic labour markets is of questionable value in preparation for the future of work. Focusing on the differential treatment of nationals and expatriates, men and women, elites and exploited are a distraction from our shared experience as human actors in the workplace and society in general, especially when we compare ourselves against the common challenges of artificial intelligence and automation to come. "Work" is a human social institution, shaped by all the stakeholders represented in this book, and if it is no longer fully functional, then it will need to be changed. This means creating jobs, educational experiences and organisations which are designed with people in mind, so that we can make the most of our demographic dividend and endowment of potential people productivity.

Dubai, April 2017

1

The Governance of the Labour Market: Labour Policies of the Gulf Cooperation Council

Sophie Olver-Ellis

Introduction

The labour market is an arena fundamentally constructed by social, political and economic forces and therefore, the structure of a country's labour market is determined by the national politico-economic framework, the workforce composition, the national development agendas and policies which are implemented to regulate and govern its national and global activity. It is within this arena where social, political and economic agendas are represented and during times of politico-economic instability, the governance of the labour market is often used as a mechanism to restore order amongst the ranks of society.

Against the backdrop of the rentier based political economies of the Arabian Gulf, over the last five decades, the region has been able to successfully advance by adopting an oil-led development model, which has enabled the region's governments to heavily invest revenue into the development of world-leading infrastructure, whilst offering the national citizenry exceptional welfare provisions such as free healthcare, education and critically, guaranteed public sector employment. In the present day, the Arabian Gulf continues to be a strategically vital area of the globalised world, because the region is host to some of the most economically rich countries and holds nearly half of the globe's confirmed and extractable oil and gas reserves[1].

However, despite the region's oil-led development model generally succeeding, unexpectedly in 2011, socio-political unrest swept throughout the Arab World, whereby the national citizenry took to the streets in opposition to the longstanding authoritarian based rule, the deep-rooted and pervasive corruption amongst the ranks of the political elite and the continued unequal distribution of oil wealth[2]. The greatest determinant underpinning the Arab Spring, however, was entrenched in daily welfare issues, whereby the national population were demanding greater employment opportunities within the national labour market, higher salaries and for the political regime to address the burgeoning unemployment rate, especially amongst the female and youth demographic groups[3]. The Arab Spring was a mass movement therefore, due to the national citizenry's longstanding socio-economic frustration[4]. Critically, these issues underpinning the eruption of the Arab Spring in 2011 were not new, or sudden.

Alongside the exceptional socio-economic prosperity and advancement the oil-led development model has facilitated over the last fifty years, the governments of the Arabian Gulf have had to contend with a burgeoning unemployment rate, especially amongst the female and youth population, the continued dependence on the migrant labour force and critically, an extremely segmented economic and social structure. Consequently, in the era of low oil prices, these inextricably linked issues are deemed crucial to address, because they constitute a demographic time bomb, but more so, will influence the future legitimacy of the ruling political elite and will significantly inform the post-rentier development agenda of the Arab States. Therefore, the labour market and its actors need to be regulated in a manner that reflects and is responsive to the requirements of the current national political economies.

To address these issues, as they are considered to be deeply rooted in the rentier constructed labour market, policy measures which seek to address the widespread employment practices, especially within the private sector, and reforming the role of both the national and migrant labour force across both the economic and socio-political arena is critical[5]. Therefore, throughout the GCC, nationalisation based policies and the Kafala system have been adopted in order to address the distortive legacy associated to the rentier. The GCC states have also begun to focus on their post-oil development agenda and in doing so, National Visions are continually being announced, of which, the governance of the labour market is a central component and will guide their transition into the post-oil era. The question central to this paper, therefore, is how are the governments of the GCC attempting to restructure their labour markets in order to transition away from their oil-based politico-economic structures? The main policies drawn upon will be through critically exploring the regionally adopted policies of the Kafala System and Nationalisation based programs, because through their concurrent application to the labour market, they seek to regulate the activity of private sector actors and the role of the national and migrant workforce. The GCC states of Saudi Arabia, Kuwait and Qatar have been selected for this policy focused article, because all three governments have and continue to actively pursue the implementation of the restrictive Kafala system and have adopted their own variations of the nationalisation policy. Warranting their analysis is also the fact that although each are adopting similar governance strategies to aid their diversification away from their oil led development model, their socio-political and economic landscapes differ alongside their future development agenda ambitions and so, the future characteristics of their labour markets will continue to differentiate. Consequently, through exploring their labour market governance strategies, this paper will attempt to identify the marked diversity within the regionally adopted policies and therefore, contribute to the literature surrounding the taxonomy of the governance of the labour markets in the Gulf Cooperation Council.

Methodological Approach

The critical comparative analysis of this policy-focused article is derived from a wider doctoral based study which explored and contributed to the taxonomy surrounding the emerging post-rentier structures of labour market governance in the Arabian Gulf, most notably in the case of Saudi Arabia, Kuwait and Qatar. Through exploring the governance of the labour markets by critically analysing policy documents which address the Kafala and Nationalisation based policies and by conducting elite semi-structured interviews with government officials, private sector actors, senior economic and legal advisors, this provided the primary data from which the analysis of this article is derived. Due to the socio-political sensitivity surrounding the topic, anonymity of the participants was and has continued to be adopted, in order to protect the identity of the participant. This enabled the participants' narrative to be presented and to critically contribute to the primary based literature and taxonomy surrounding the governance of the labour markets in the GCC.

The Policy Response: A Protectionist Approach to Reform

Throughout the twenty-first century, it is widely expected that the Arabian Gulf's political economies will transform towards a post-rentier governance structure and development model[6]. Underpinning this successful transformation will be rooted in how the region's governments effectively regulate the rentier constructed labour market. Reforming the capacity of private sector actors and the role of both the migrant and national labour force will also be critical, because through their productive participation, it should contribute to the region's political economies to sustainably diversify towards a post-rentier model of development.

Within the current policy response, the governance strategies adopted throughout the labour markets in Saudi Arabia, Kuwait and Qatar is predominantly protectionist in approach, whereby the regulatory approaches adopted seek to influence the supply and demand of both migrant and national manpower, especially within the private sector. However, as will be discussed, although the Kafala System, but more so the Nationalisation based policies, share the same core objectives, they differ in the implementation phase, in order to reflect the requirements of the politico-economic contexts of the individual GCC member state. Moreover, despite their longstanding implementation, questions continually arise as to whether the current policy response is feasible and whether the Kafala system and nationalisation based policies will successfully facilitate the labour market transformations required to contribute to sustainably diversify the national politico-economic structures of the region and adapt to the post-oil era.

The Governance of the Migrant Labour Force: The Incumbent Kafala System

The Kafala 'sponsorship' system is rooted in the region's Bedouin tradition of hospitality, whereby the national citizen, also formally referred to as a kafeel, was obligated to offer their transient guests food, shelter and protection. This ideological-based custom was then developed and adopted as a regulatory mechanism during the early 20th century, when the region became host to a large volume of migrant labour arriving en masse to participate in the region's expanding oil industry[7]. Within the context of the migration phenomenon, the traditional system was applied by making the Kafeel legally responsible for the socio-political and economic activity and general welfare of the migrant worker during their employment and residency within the GCC member state[8].

In the present day, the modernised Kafala system continues to be a central and mandatory governance mechanism which strictly regulates the migrant labour force across the GCC member states and has continually been developed and codified by national laws[9]. Due to its longstanding adoption, the system has also evolved into a fundamental regulatory framework ensuring that the labour migrant population's socio-economic activity is temporary and therefore, the system is applied to all non-national workers in both the private and public sector[10]. Within the current system, the Kafala acts as a socio-economic contract, whereby the labour migrant is formally invited to a GCC member state to participate within the national labour market, by being socio-economically tied to a national sponsor[11]. Therefore, despite the Kafala being centrally administrated throughout the region by each country's Ministry of the Interior, who are responsible for issuing the residency permits and employment visas, this system essentially delegates the governance of the migrant population to the national citizenry[12]. Identified in Fig.1, the stipulations of the Kafala across the GCC are comparable and have the same central attributes and reinforces the regionally shared goal of ensuring that the migrant labour population are transient and short- term contractual workers[13].

The Kafala System is an important governance mechanism throughout the GCC as regulating the migrant work force is not only a critical economic issue, but more so, a major socio-political concern[14]. This is particularly evident in the strictly applied stipulations, because a primary objective throughout the region is to inhibit the migrant labour force from integrating into the region's national political economies and therefore, restrict their access to acquiring the exceptional socio-economic provisions which are reserved as a right for being a national citizen[15]. Moreover, it is evident that the structure and function of this labour market governance system is the same throughout the Arabian Peninsula[16]. As a result of these similarities, this has also led to similar ramifications associated to the Kafala throughout the region, for example, assisting the abuse of the migrants labour based and human rights, whilst also facilitating private sector actors to participate in dubious employment practices such as adopting ghost workers and visa trading.

Table 1: Summary of The Kafala System in Saudi Arabia, Kuwait and Qatar[17]

Legal Requirement For Sponsorship	To be granted an entry visa and to participate in the labour market, the migrant requires the formal sponsorship of a national Kafeel, who is also their employer
Legal Requirement To Return Migrant's Passport	The Kafeel is legally required to return passport and travel documents to the migrant worker once visa and residency permit have been issued / renewed
The Transfer Of Sponsorship	**Saudi Arabia:** Legally referred to as 'transfer of services', a migrant worker may transfer sponsorship once they have worked for their current employer for a minimum of one year and hold a valid residence and work permit. **Kuwait:** Permission of the current employer must be given and one year of continuous residence is required. Worker recruited by government contracts require three years continuous labour residence and Domestic workers cannot transfer sponsorship. **Qatar:** Written agreement between the current and new employer is required which the Ministry of Labour must approve.
The Ban on Return	A worker found working for an employer who has not recruited them may result in a two-year ban.
Seconding Workers	**Saudi Arabia:** Employers are unable to recruit seconded workers unless legal rules and procedures are adhered. **Kuwait:** Employers may not employ workers who hold no work permit or hold a work permit for another employer. **Qatar:** Workers may be seconded if authorised by the relevant ministry, for a period of no more than six months. Foreign workers may be approved to work for another employer outside of the usual working hours of their employment if their sponsor approves.

The Governance of the National Labour Force: The Nationalisation Policies

Throughout the GCC member states, the governments are continually renewing their commitment to developing the nationalisation based policies, because it is widely considered to be of great strategic importance that the role of the national and migrant labour force are altered in a way which is conducive to the future sustainable development of the region's political economies in the post-oil era[18]. The current nationalisation policies are essentially a manpower replacement scheme, whereby the national labour force is encouraged to seek private sector employment, thus replacing the migrant work force who have come to dominate the sector, whilst the private sector companies are also encouraged to actively employ workers from the national labour pool[19]. Through adopting this policy approach, a central objective across the region is to reduce the extensive and deep-rooted dependence on the migrant labour force, so contributing to effectively restructuring and diversifying the labour market towards a more productive economic base, whereby the national workforce and private sector actors are key stakeholders.

The main objectives that have come to be central to the region's nationalisation efforts can be traced back to the 1980s, when state-owned businesses and the public sector's across the GCC focused on predominantly recruiting national manpower, in order to address and impede the burgeoning unemployment pressures the region faced[20]. In the present day however, the nationalisation efforts have shifted focus towards the private sector, whereby market based measures have been adopted in order to encourage and increase the productive participation of the national workforce. This development in the nationalisation policy was not only actively implemented in order to reduce the longstanding extreme dependency on the migrant labour force, but also because in the present day, the GCC governments are no longer able to act as the first and indefinite employer of the national citizenry[21]. Other justifications which underpin the nationalisation based policies is that by reducing the extreme dependency on the migrant labour force, the ruling political elite are able to maintain political independency, the socio-cultural milieu of the region will be preserved, whilst also being an advantageous move towards sustainably diversifying the economic base and development trajectory away from the Rentier mode of development[22]. However, although the central objectives and justifications that underpin the adoption of the nationalisation policy are the same throughout the region, there are variations within the national policy frameworks, especially in regards to the set goals and implementation mechanisms. As will be discussed, the variation in the nationalisation approach is due to the fact that the national political economies differ and therefore, the nationalisation policies need to reflect the requirements of the national development agenda and post-oil vision.

The Kingdom of Saudi Arabia: The Saudisation and Nitaqat Program

The Kingdom of Saudi Arabia has been referred to as being the region's laboratory for designing and implementing labour market reforms[23]. This perspective is evident, especially in the case of the Kingdom's quantitative focused manpower replacement program, because the goals and implementation mechanisms have continually evolved and been reformulated to meet the requirements of the national economy and development agenda. Originally, the nationalisation based initiative was supported by The Kingdom's Labour and Workman Law of 1969, which legally stipulated in Article 48 and 49 that employment was reserved for the Saudi workforce and only in certain circumstances, can the position be filled by a labour migrant (Labour and Workman Law of 1969).

Over the following decades, Saudisation continued to be on the national policy agenda, but had renewed focus in the sixth development plan (1995-2000), whereby it was announced that increasing the national participation rate in the private sector was an urgent priority for the sustainable future of the Kingdom. This was because during this time period, the Saudi government had to address the burgeoning national unemployment, increasing budget constraints and the recognition that the Kingdom needed to diversify their economic base away from the oil-led development model[24]. Consequently, within the sixth development plan, it identified that to effectively address the socio-economic and demographic challenges the Kingdom was facing, it was critical to create a relevantly educated and skilled national workforce, who could be active participants within the development of the socio-political and economic arena. Over the proceeding decades and development plans, as identified in Table 2, this theme continued and was a central component of the Saudisation targets, which were continually reformulated to meet the requirements of the labour market.

Table 2: The Evolution of Saudisation Based Goals[25]

First Development Plan (1970-1975)	• Saudi labour force should constitute 75 per cent of a private sector company's workforce • 51 per cent of the wage bill should be directed towards the national employees salary
Sixth Development Plan (1995-2000)	• Increase private sector national manpower employment by 466,000 and create 182,000 new jobs • Reduce migrant labour employment by 1.5 per cent • Nationalise approx. 319,500 jobs during development plan • Increase national workforce by 5 per cent in companies with 20 workers or more
Seventh Development Plan (2000-2005)	• 25 per cent of private sector employment opportunities to be filled and reserved for the national workforce • Create 800,000 new opportunities of employment throughout the economy
Eighth Development Plan (2005-2010)	• Retain targets from seventh development plan

Despite the Saudisation regulatory framework continually evolving into a comprehensive nationalisation policy, and persistent efforts by the government over the decades, it is widely recognised that the success of the policy in achieving its set goals have been minor. Consequently, in 2011, due to greater urgency in rebalancing the demographic profile, addressing the burgeoning unemployment and restructuring the labour market to contribute to the national diversification efforts, the government implemented a renewed Saudisation based initiative formally named the Nitaqat, which is considered to be a more sophisticated and applicable governance system[26]. The implementation of the Nitaqat seeks to assist the Saudi government in achieving their goal of creating at least 3.5 million new employment opportunities for the Saudi workforce in the private sector by 2025[27]. In achieving this goal, the Ministry of Labour consider that this will provide the much needed labour market reforms which are required to establish a more efficient and productive private sector and a more socio-economically productive national workforce.

Under the Nitaqat scheme, it builds upon the previous Saudisation policy in terms of similar objectives and implementation mechanisms, but is more applicable to the labour market structure and activity[28]. Within the current framework, private sector companies are classified into one of four colour-coded bands that represent their level of Saudisation[29]. However, in order for the company to be informed of the colour-coded band of which they are positioned, their Saudisation quota is firstly determined by their workforce size, industry sector and labour market based activity, as identified in Table 3.

Table 3: The Five Classifications of The Nitaqat Scheme

Micro Company (1 to 9 Employees)	Excluded from being required to impose the Nitaqat program
Small Sized Company (10 to 49 Employees)	Nitaqat Target of 5 to 24 per cent
Medium Sized Company (50 to 499 Employees)	Nitaqat Target of 6 to 27 per cent
Large Sized Company (500 to 2999 Employees)	Nitaqat Target of 7 to 30 per cent
Giant Sized Company (3000+ Employees)	Nitaqat Target of 8 to 30 per cent

Through classifying these companies as identified, the core objective is that 50 per cent of companies within each category are within the top two Nitaqat Bands of Platinum and Green[30]. Once the company has been classified and set their nationalisation ratio, they are to continually adhere to their quota and will either receive incentive or punitive based measures, depending on their band category as discussed in Table 4.

Evidently, Saudisation based programmes and the more recent Nitaqat have been an active and consistent governance strategy over the decades and will continue to develop in response to the socio-economic and labour market conditions of the Kingdom. However, the effectiveness of the policy continues to be questioned, especially surrounding its ability to substantially increase the real productive participation of national manpower, especially in the private sector. Critically, the government has recognised that restructuring the private sector labour market cannot be achieved by the application of quotas alone and therefore, needs to be part of a wider diversification process which addresses the national human capital capability and availability, employment practices and role of different actors, such as the private sector and labour force.

Table 4: Nitaqat Implementation Mechanisms[31]

Platinum & Green Nitaqat Band	Rewarded with incentive based measures • Companies are able to recruit manpower from both national and international labour market • Employers are able to recruit migrant workers from companies within the yellow and red Nitaqat band without obtaining consent from migrants employer • Migrant labour are able to fill occupations reserved for Saudi workforce
Yellow & Red Nitaqat Band	Face punitive measures • Restricted in recruitment of both migrant and national labour • Migrant labour issues short-term visas and prohibited to apply for new employment visas once their original one has expired • Companies are unable to transfer their employees sponsorship to another employer • Migrant worker is able to seek employment opportunities in the excellent and green bands and transfer sponsorship without obtaining approval of their current sponsor • As a consequence of companies restricted socio-economic mobility, they gradually lose their workforce and ability to economically expand in the Kingdom

The State of Kuwait: The Kuwaitisation Policy

In the late 1970s, Kuwait had a burgeoning youth population, whereby approximately half of the national citizenry were 15 years of age or under and consequently, the economic productivity of the country was the lowest throughout the region[32]. Due to these socio-economic dynamics, the Kuwaitisation policy was implemented in order to regulate the composition of the labour market, by restricting the expansion and socio-economic mobility of the migrant labour force, thus, replacing them with the rapidly expanding national workforce[33]. Over the decades, this regulatory approach has continued to be a prominent policy in the governance of the Kuwaiti labour market, but due to the country being a high rent country, like Qatar, as the national labour force is small enough to be absorbed into the private sector, this has informed the nature of the Kuwaitisation quotas and implementation mechanisms adopted. As will be evident, despite the policy being on the governance agenda for many decades, this labour market reform policy in Kuwait is considered to be less comprehensive in comparison to other GCC states[34].

The Kuwaitisation policy is widely regarded to be a manpower replacement strategy by decree and similar to other nationalisation policies in the region, holds the central objective of increasing the productive participation of the national manpower in the Kuwaiti economy through the enforcement of strict quotas[35]. The implementation of the quota system was part of the original policy framework, whereby it commenced with extremely rigid directives that the entrance of the migrant labour force was to be restricted and those permitted to enter the country for employment purposes were to be single-status migrants[36]. As a result, this was deemed to achieve the government's objective of creating a demographic balance between the migrant and national population and therefore, began the movement towards replacing the migrant workforce with national manpower whenever possible[37].

Over the succeeding decades, as the requirements of the labour market changed and the extreme segmentation across the social and economic structures became more entrenched, the policy evolved in order to reflect these developments within the national political economy and consequently, sector based quotas began to be implemented. The primary focal point of implementation was in 16 occupations throughout the administrative, secretarial and IT sector, whereby employment opportunities were required to be restricted and reserved for national citizens[38]. Over time, the quota system continually evolved and by 2008, it was expected that banks were to nationalise 60 per cent of their labour force, the real estate sector had to nationalise 15 per cent of its labour force and the manufacturing industry had to nationalise 2 per cent of its labour force[39]. Moreover, across the private sector, a blanket Kuwaitisation Quota was implemented, whereby companies had to adhere to a general quota of nationalising 25 per cent of their labour force[40]. Through the application of these quotas, it was deemed to be an effective governance mechanism which would effectively contribute to rebalancing the labour market and demographic profile, because if private sector actors failed to adhere to these set quotas, they would face punitive measures such as economic penalties and sanctions[41].

The implementation mechanisms adopted under the Kuwaitisation policy is considered worth observing, because they are the only GCC State who has adopted a wage subsidy program to assist in the nationalisation efforts[42]. As identified in Fig. 5, the mechanisms adopted are in line with those applied to the Kingdom of Saudi Arabia's labour market, but also differ from the regional approach, because Kuwait has identified that private sector wages are a major obstacle to the participation of the national labour force and therefore, have actively pursued a wage subsidy program as a central implementation mechanism under their Kuwaitisation policy. Within this strategy, the wage subsidy initiative focused on closing the gap between public and private sector wages. This welfare-based scheme was promulgated by Law 19 of 2000 da'm al-'amala, which stipulated that in both the private and public sector, national citizens should be remunerated equally for participating in similar occupations and is irrelevant of which sector it is based[43].

Table 5: Kuwaitisation Implementation Mechanisms[44 45]

Wage Gap Reduction / Unemployment Benefits For Job Seekers	• The national citizenry who are unemployed are offered exceptional welfare support from the government whilst they actively seek employment opportunities within the private sector The welfare provisions and social based allowances continue after they have begun to productively participate in a private sector company • Reduce the wage gap between the private and public sector for the national workforce
Economic Incentives & Punitive Measures For Private Sector Actors	• In companies who have a national manpower comprising 40 per cent of their labour force and accrue a minimum of 40 per cent of the wage bill, the company is offered current and future governmental contracts and investment / funding • If the company fails to adhere to their Kuwaitisation quota, they face economic sanctions and impeded mobility within the economy. They are also required to pay higher taxes and higher visa based expenses which are applied to the recruitment and employment of their migrant labour force
Skill Development & Training Workshops	• Governmental funded skill development and training workshops and industry based work experience are available to the national citizenry, in order to enhance the national human capital to be more reflective of the requirements of the private sector • In some instances, it is legally required that private sector companies invest and assist in the skill development and education of their national workforce and in response to their active participation in developing the national human capital, receive economic benefits and governmental subsidies

Through adopting these implementation mechanisms, the primary objective is to encourage the productive participation of the national citizenry in the private sector labour market and therefore, contribute to the national diversification efforts towards the post-oil development model. Through exploring the nationalisation policy of Kuwait, it is evident that the policy is less comprehensive in regards to both its quotas and implementation mechanisms. However, it is important to recognise that despite it being one of the least comprehensive nationalisation policies of the GCC, through the wage subsidy program and extensive financial incentives available to the national citizenry, this addresses the 'culture of oil' and public perspective of private sector employment, which has been constructed and maintained by the Rentier development model and therefore, should be considered more applicable and responsive to the politico-economic context of Kuwait.

The State of Qatar: The Qatarisation Policy

In order to develop a competent national workforce, the Qatarisation policy has been adopted and is particularly focused on increasing the economic productivity and participation of the national workforce in the private sector, through human capital advancement based mechanisms[46]. Due to Qatar having a small national working age population, migrant manpower has dominated both the public and private sector and therefore, Qatar's nationalisation approach has been more lenient in comparison to other GCC states[47]. However, with the implementation of Qatar's National Vision 2030, Qatarisation has evolved into a more formal regulatory framework and is focused on 'quality not quantity' based nationalisation. This approach is deemed more relevant to the Qatari economy and population structure and will be more conducive in Qatar fulfilling their ambition of transforming into a knowledge-based economy[48].

In the early 2000's, Qatarisation was part of the national policy agenda, but was focused more on being implemented within the oil and gas sector and public sector, whilst being implemented on an ad hoc basis into the private sector[49]. Within the original Qatarisation strategy, the central goal was for Qatari manpower to constitute at least fifty per cent of the oil and gas sector workforce[50]. This quota then evolved in order to be applicable to the private sector, whereby it was required that in private sector entities, a minimum of twenty percent was to be comprised of Qatari nationals[51].

In the last decade, Qatarisation has evolved into a prominent regulatory framework, because it is considered to contribute to creating a committed Qatari workforce and through advancing the national human capital, they will become key actors within the national diversification efforts[52]. Within the most recent Qatarisation framework, it is advocated that in all employment opportunities, the Qatari workforce are to be considered first and if the employer is unable to find a relevantly skilled national, they are able to recruit a migrant worker to fill the role, in the last instance (Article 18 of the Labour Law No. 14 of the Year 2004). Through the implementation of the National Vision 2030, there is an overarching goal across both the public and private sector that a minimum of 50 per cent of socio-economically productive employment opportunities are to be filled by the Qatari workforce[53]. The quota system was also adopted in order to advance the national human capital, whereby companies who have a workforce of fifty employees or more are required to provide training opportunities to at least 5 per cent of their national manpower (Art 12 & 27, Law No 14 of the Year 2004).

Within the current implementation framework, the Qatarisation policy sets out to increase the role of the national population, by encouraging participation in activities that enhance their skill set and offers socio-economic provisions that encourage their participation in the labour market[54]. This is evident within the current implementation mechanisms adopted, as shown in Fig.6, where it identifies that the current Qatarisation efforts surround wage gap reductions, economic incentives for both the national labour market and private sector entities and increased assistance in developing the national human capital[55].

Table 6: Qatarisation Implementation Mechanisms[56]

Economic Incentives & Wage Gap Reductions	Increased income levels applied to professional / management based roles in health, business, education
Public & Private Sector Funding	Increase Governmental funding to public and private sector entities to increase their skill development program which are available to the Qatari workforce
Training & Skill Development	Encourage the participation of Qatari population in labour market by offering greater vocational training and skill development
Increased Support For Qatari Female Workforce	Increase participation of female demographic in labour force through greater access to employment opportunities and vocational training
Re-Focused Recruitment and Selectivity of Migrant Manpower	Recruit and maintain a mixed and relevantly skilled migrant manpower and retain those who have provided excellent services during their employment and residency in the State

Although the Qatarisation policy was originally applied as a quota for the oil and gas sector, which has also been implemented on an ad hoc basis, through the new development agenda adopted within Qatar's Vision 2030, the policy has evolved into a critical regulatory framework which seeks to contribute to the construction of a strong and diversified knowledge based economy[57]. For example, to enhance the role of a competitive private sector and a national labour force who are both relevantly skilled and capable key agents in the national diversification efforts, these incentive and supportive based measures are considered to strengthen the labour market and role of different labour based actors. These are more conducive to achieving Qatar's post-oil development ambitions, in comparison to the strict punitive based measured adopted under other nationalisation based policies which have to date, have generally failed to produce significant reforms to the labour market[58]. Conversely, as these developments within the Qatarisation policy are only recent and in response to the newly adopted development agenda, it is recognised by the government that it will take decades for the policies to have any substantial impact on the structure of the labour market and wider diversification efforts and therefore, the Qatari government is encouraging a flexible implementation approach of the Qatarisation policy[59].

The Governance of the Labour Market: Barriers to Reform

The Arabian Gulf, a strategically vital region which has undergone important oil-led economic and socio-political transformations over the last century is once again at a critical juncture, whereby through the emergence of a new geo-political order, is shaking the deeply entrenched rentier structures of the region's political economies. Declarations are continuously being made from the GCC states as to what will characterise the development agenda of their post-oil era, whereby terms such as 'economic powerhouse', 'regional trading hub' and 'knowledge-based economy' underpin many of their post-oil ambitions. Central to fulfilling these new development visions is restructuring the labour market, whereby there is a greater role of the private sector and national labour force. This brings into question therefore, that to date, have the labour market policies discussed been successful in restructuring the labour market and will they contribute to transforming the political economies of Saudi Arabia, Kuwait and Qatar in the post-oil era?

In order to prepare for the impending post-oil era, it is widely considered that to successfully diversify the economic base, restructuring the labour market and ridding its rentier-constructed attributes is critical[60]. Therefore, the labour markets need to transform from its low-skill, low-productivity and public sector dominated formation and be exchanged with a highly skilled, high productivity and productive private sector driven economy[61]. The labour policies therefore, especially the nationalisation programs, which seek to encourage the productive participation of the national labour force in the private sector, is fundamental in the transformation of the region's labour markets and politico-economic structures towards the post-rentier[62]. Moreover, through shifting the labour market towards more productive and sustainable modes of employment and economic activity, this should gradually deconstruct the rentier formulated addiction of the government being the main driver of economic growth and more critically, the public sector being the first and last employer of the national citizenry[63].

Through exploring the labour market policies, despite their longstanding adoption and the government's resolute effort to continually develop the regulatory frameworks, it is widely considered that in Saudi Arabia, Kuwait and Qatar, the policies have largely failed in their attempt to restructure the national labour markets and instead, have further entrenched the rentier nature and labour-based challenges the policies seek to address[64]. It has been evident that the implementation mechanisms of the policies, especially in the case of the nationalisation based initiatives, differ. For example, Qatarisation focuses on quality based nationalisation and human capital advancement, whilst Kuwaitisation focuses on wage gap reduction between the public and private sector and the Saudisation and Nitaqat based policy focuses on applying strict quotas across the private sector. With these varying policy implementation mechanisms and quota based systems, this brings into question, why have they all generally failed? Therefore, what is impeding their effective implementation? As will be discussed, in Saudi Arabia, Kuwait and Qatar, a myriad of deep structural barriers exists and have impeded the effective governance of the national labour markets. In doing so, despite these states continually developing these labour market policies and adopting new development Visions, until the governments comprehensively address and effectively regulate the rentier constructed political economies and labour market distortions, the segmented socio-economic structure will continue. This final section will explore the policies in practice, with particular focus on the barriers to their implementation and thus, offering evidence based explanations as to why they have generally failed to significantly restructure the labour markets in the case of Saudi Arabia, Kuwait and Qatar. The themes identified are derived from the interviews conducted and will offer the narratives given by those who design and implement the policies.

Dubious Employment Practices: Phantom Employment & Visa Trading

A major barrier to restructuring the labour markets in the GCC surrounds the dubious labour based practices adopted by actors within the private sector. Across each case study country, interview participants identified that despite the governments becoming stricter in their regulation of the labour market, private sector actors navigate around the policy stipulations in order to maintain their economic productivity and continue their employment practices, such as the vast recruitment of migrant labour[65]. The primary means of navigating around the labour market policies, especially that of the nationalisation based quota system, is through the adoption of ghost workers and the practice of phantom employment[66]. According to private sector actors across each case study, they reported that companies adopt the practice of ghost workers and phantom employment, whereby a national worker is on their company's payroll and have office space, but do not attend and undertake any work for the company[67]. In adopting these practices, this ensures that the private sector company meets their nationalisation quota, whilst enabling them to recruit from the migrant labour pool, who are considered more economically productive and easily disposed of if needed[68]. These practices were especially prevalent in the case of Saudi Arabia and Kuwait, because it was identified that due to the stricter regulation of the labour market, random inspections from the Ministry of Labour are becoming more widespread and therefore, companies need to be able to show that they are 'adhering' to their nationalisation quotas.[69]

The extremely profitable practice of visa trading and the formation of fictitious companies was also identified to be a primary means for private sector actors to navigate around the labour market policies. Across each case study, the establishment of fictitious companies to recruit migrant workers was identified to be a mechanism which facilitated companies to evade their quotas, because employers are able to recruit migrants on fraudulent visas and under the guise of another company and in doing so, alleviates the employer from their socio-economic responsibility associated to the Kafala system stipulations.[70] These practices were deemed to be one of the greatest barriers to the effective implementation and restructuring of the labour market, because the informal migrant labour force is burgeoning and continue to supply the private sector with a transient and disposable workforce.[71]

The Education Mismatch & Continued Culture of Oil

Another prominent barrier to restructuring the labour markets is due to the severe dearth of a relevantly skilled national labour force and the continued culture of oil. These are major obstacles to any future diversification effort, because resulting from the national citizenry receiving an unearned income, this destroys the individual work-reward nexus as their income is derived from the government due to being a national citizen, instead of productively participating in the employment domain[72]. Due to the national citizenry being guaranteed public sector employment, high salaries and beneficial working conditions, such as favorable working hours, are received and in doing so, negative attitudes towards private sector employment and manual labour also prevail and thus, explains as to why rentier states have a low-participation and low-productivity based labour market[73].

Due to this erosion of the work-reward nexus, this facilitates another feature of the culture of oil, which is the mass importation and extreme dependency on the migrant labour force, who become the economically productive actors in the development process[74]. Due to their substantial role, they evolve into a dominant socio-economic force, because they provide the essential manpower required for the national development agenda and through their prolonged presence, facilitate the onset of fragmenting the national socio-economic structure, whereby there is extreme segmentation between the public and private sector and between the national and migrant population[75].

In regards to education, any labour market reform policy will continue to fail because the education system and core curriculum throughout the GCC states fail to offer a relevant and comprehensive education across all levels which prepares the national citizenry for the labour market, especially that of the private sector. This disconnection between the education system and requirements of the labour market was raised by participants in each case, whereby it was continually raised that the majority of national students who participate in higher education undertake theological and humanity based degrees and therefore, the skill base and human capital of the national citizenry is severely lacking.[76] Due to this dearth in a skilled national human capital, the national citizenry are widely considered to be unable to effectively contribute to the national diversification efforts and economic expansion of the private sector.[77] This issue surrounding the education mismatch was considered to be a detriment to the private sector companies, because in their perspective across each case study, they are having to recruit national workers who do not have a relevant education and skill attainment level and therefore, reinforces the justification behind practices such as phantom employment.[78]

This issue surrounding the dearth of relevantly skilled manpower should also be attributed to the continuation of the culture of oil. Due to the private sector generally having lesser pay, less job security and longer working hours, this often deters a large portion of the national citizenry to seek employment in the sector and due to the current social contract guaranteeing them public sector employment, they fail to undertake any relevant education and skill development programs which would enable them to become socio-economically productive actors within the national political economies.[79] In regards to the labour market policies, therefore, this indicates that the governments can implement economic incentives and wage gap reductions, but as the private sector continues to be dominated by migrant manpower and the public sector being the primary choice for the national citizenry, it should be regarded that it will take more than a salary replacement scheme to truly restructure the labour market. Moreover, in order for the government to effectively transform their political economies and labour markets towards the post-rentier, they need to address and overhaul the current education system to be more responsive and representative of the private sector and new development agendas.

The Rentier Reaction

A more recent barrier to restructuring the labour market is the rentier reaction which ensued in response to the 2011 Arab Spring. During the socio-political instability which swept throughout the region, the GCC governments responded by implementing emergency laws which focused on expanding their rent-distribution mechanisms, such as increasing their exceptional welfare packages and greater employment opportunities within the public sector[80]. This issue was particularly raised by participants in the case of Saudi Arabia, whereby it was noted that the Kingdom's political elite rapidly responded to the region's sudden socio-political instability by announcing emergency redistributive measures and employment based packages in an attempt to retain socio-political order.[81] Within these welfare based packages, the government ensured that there was a minimum wage of SR3,000 ($800) for the national workforce in the private sector, whilst increasing the salaries and employment opportunities in the public sector.[82] A jobseeker-based initiative referred to as the 'Hafiz' program was also created, which provides both male and female citizens who are looking for employment a monthly grant of SR2,000 ($533) for up to one year.[83]

In the perspective of the participants who raised this issue, it was considered to not only reinforce the rentier constructed distributive based social contract, but also indicates that the government can actively design and adopt policies such as the nationalisation initiatives which hold the objective of increasing the national workforce's participation in the private sector, but this development objective is readily overturned in order to maintain their national political stability.[84] Therefore, despite their resolute effort to restructure the labour market through these policies, maintaining the rule of the political elite is often deemed more important therefore, maintaining the rentier constructed political economies of the Arabian Gulf.

The Governance of the Labour Market: The Way Forward

It is widely considered that throughout the region, there lacks any coherent and focused strategy on how to address the labour market distortions and demographic imbalance and therefore, the policies discussed are inconsistent and incompatible to the politico-economic structures which they seek to regulate.[85] Consequently, in the present day, the rentier constructed politico-economic structures prevail and extreme segmentation across economic and social lines continue[86]. However, the labour market reforms are being implemented amongst a politico-economic landscape which is continually evolving and due to issues such as the demographic imbalance and burgeoning unemployment of the national citizenry, the governance of the labour markets continue to be at the forefront of the policy agenda throughout the GCC. Therefore, despite the limited success of the current labour market policies in restructuring the labour market, this brings into question what is the future of these policies? When exploring the way forward with the interview participants, in each case study country, there were two distinct themes, one of abolishment and the other of continuation.

Across Saudi Arabia, Kuwait and Qatar, it was identified that each country has experienced opposition from the international community regarding the Kafala system and is often demanded to be completely abolished due to the abuse and exploitative employment conditions the system facilitates[87]. In the case of Qatar, the country was considered to have received the greatest criticism and calls for abolishing the system due to hosting the 2022 soccer World Cup and therefore, the plight of the migrant workers and abuse the system facilitates is more widely recognised.[88] However, as identified, the Kafala system is predominantly structurally the same throughout the region and therefore, has the same ramifications in each state. As a result, it was widely considered that for these states to adhere to the international labour standards and conventions associated to labour and human based rights, participants consider that over the next decade the Kafala will be completely abolished or undergo significant reforms.[89] If the system is not abolished, the reforms made to the Kafala in each country was considered to surround the relocation of the system to be centrally administrated by the governments and therefore, in effect, the governments acquire the role of the Kafeel. Thus, private sector employers recruit migrant workers from the government and cease to take on the traditional role of the Kafeel and its associated socio-economic responsibility.[90] However, it was also recognised that abolishment and reformulating the Kafala system has been constantly on the agenda for a substantial period of time and thus, numerous participants across each case consider that no significant changes will occur to the system in the foreseeable future.[91]

The nationalisation based strategies were considered to be a central governance mechanism which will contribute to restructuring the labour markets and with the region looking towards economically diversifying toward the post-oil development model, the policy approach will continue to be a central labour market policy.[92] However, it was noted that as the demands of the economy, diversification efforts and development visions change, the stipulations of these policies will alter in order to reflect the politico-economic conditions of Saudi Arabia, Kuwait and Qatar.[93] This governance mechanism was also deemed to be a critical policy, because in the era of global oil price volatility, it is placing strain on the redistributive capacity of the government and undermining the rentier constructed social contract.[94] Therefore, creating a more robust employment system which restructures the labour market alters the role of private sector actors, the governments and the national and migrant workforce will be critical for the future advancement of these countries throughout the twenty-first century.

Conclusion

Through exploring the labour market governance strategies in the case of Saudi Arabia, Kuwait and Qatar, it is evident that they are all taking a protectionist approach to their labour market governance strategy and in doing so, they all seek to restructure their labour markets to fulfil their post-oil era ambitions. As discussed, the Kafala system, which is structurally the same across the GCC, seeks to regulate the socio-economic mobility and presence of the migrant labour force, whilst the nationalisation based policies seek to increase the productive participation of national manpower in the private sector. Through exploring these policies, it has been evident that although these selected case study countries differ in their nationalisation based programmes in regards to their quotas and implementation mechanisms, they have all primarily failed in their attempt to restructure the national labour market. This is due to the numerous barriers to reform, such as dubious labour practices, an irrelevant national human capital, human rights and labour based abuse and rentier reactions in response to socio-political instability undermining any real progress towards transforming the political economies and restructuring the labour market. Conversely, with the Arab Spring giving greater impetus behind addressing the labour based issues and socio-economic segmentation, as the post-oil era is on the horizon, the region's political economies and labour market of the GCC will gradually transition towards a post-rentier formation. However, this transition will be complex and produce many challenges for the ruling political elite and policy makers, because in order to adopt their new post-oil development agenda and fulfil their post-rentier ambitions, they will have to not only restructure the socio-economic landscape, but will also have to redraw their social contract with society, therefore, reformulating the foundation which has underpinned their political legitimacy over the oil-development decades. Critically, restructuring the private sector labour market cannot be achieved by the application of quotas alone and therefore, needs to be part of a wider diversification process which addresses the national human capital capability and availability, employment practices and role of different actors, such as the private sector and labour force.

References

Aissaoui, A. 2011. Economic Development, Diversification and the Role of the State, *Economic Commentary*, Vol. 9, No. 5, May 2014

Al Masah Capital Limited, 2011. *MENA: The Great Job Rush – The 'unemployment' ticking time bomb and how to fix it*

Al-Razzaz, *The Treacherous Path Towards a New Arab Social Contract*

Al-Saqabi, N. 2011. *Figures and Results Confirm Leading Position of Kuwait Banks*. Kuwait Banking Association

Alsheikh, H. M. 2015, Current Progress on the Nationalisation Programmes in Saudi Arabia, *Gulf Labour Markets and Migration*, No.2/2015

Babar, Z. 2013, Labour Migration in the State of Qatar Policy Making and Governance, *IFRI Center for Migrations and Citizenship*

Bajracharya, R & Sijapati, B, 2012, The Kafala System and its Implications for Nepali Domestic Workers, *Centre for the Study of Labour and Mobility*

Beaugrand, C. 2006. Nationality & Migrations Control in the Gulf Countries. *INAMO*. pp.10-14

Berrebi, C. Martorell, F. Tanner, J. Qatar's 2009. Labor Markets at a Crucial Crossroad. *Middle East Journal*. Vol, 63. No.3.

Brocard &Vallet. *The Rentier State in the Middle East*

Constant, S; Sayre, E; Abdelkader, N, 2015 *Implications of Qatarization: Qualitative Assessment and Possible Policy Responses* [ONLINE] Available through: http://www.syria.jadaliyya.com/pages/index/21008/implications-of-qatarization_qualitative-assessment

De Bel-Air, F. 2015. The Socio-Political Background and Stakes of 'Saudizing' the Workforce in Saudi Arabia: the Nitaqat Policy, *Gulf Labour Markets and Migration*, No.3/2015

Dito, M. 2008. *GCC Labour Migration Governance*. United Nations

Dorsey, J. 2015. *2022 World Cup Sparks Labour Reform, Just Not In Qatar*. Fankultur-Institute.

Elfakhani, S & Ghanem, A, 2011. Privatisation of Gulf industrial institutions: The Secret of Success, *Middle East Policy*, Vol. XVIII.

Esim, S & Smith, M. 2004, Gender and Migration in Arab States: The Case of Domestic Workers, *International Labour Organisation*

Forstenlechner & Rutledge, The GCC's "Demographic Imbalance"

Fasano, U. & Goyal, R. 2004. Emerging Strains in GCC Labor Markets. International Monetary Fund.

GSDP, *National Development Strategy: Goals and Benefits*, [ONLINE] Available through: http://www.gsdp.gov.qa/portal/page/portal/gsdp_en/nds/goals_benefits

Gulseven, O. 2015. Challenges to Employing Kuwaitis in the Private Sector, *Labor Market Dynamics in the GCC States*, Autumn 2015

Held, D & Coates-Ulrichsen, K .2013. The end of the American Century: from 9/11 to the Arab Spring. Cambridge, UK

Hertog, S. State and private sector in the GCC after the Arab uprisings

Hertog, S. 2011. Good, Bad, or Both? The Impact of Oil on the Saudi Political Economy, Center for International and Regional Studies: Georgetown University.

Hukoomi, 2016, [ONLINE] http://portal.www.gov.qa/wps/portal

Khan, A & Harroff-Tavel, H, 2011. Reforming the Kafala: Challenges and Opportunities in Moving Forward, *Asian and Pacific Migration Journal*, Vol. 20, Nos 3-4

Levins, The Rentier State and the Survival of Arab Absolute Monarchies

Looney, R. 2004. Can Saudi Arabia reform its economy in time to head off disaster? *Strategic Insights*, Vol. 3, No.1

Mirkin, B. 2010. *Population Levels, Trends and Policies in the Arab Region: Challenges and Opportunities*. Arab Human Development Report. United Nations.

Njoku, E. 2007. Employees' Attitude Towards The Privatisation Of Kuwait's State Owned Enterprises (SOEs). Maastrict University.

Okruhlik, G. 1999. Rentier Wealth, Unruly Law, and the Rise of Opposition: The Political Economy of Oil States. *Comparative Politics*. Vol, 31. No.2. Pp.295-315.

Qatar Foundation, *Qatarization* [ONLINE] Available through: http://www.qf.org.qa/content/about/jobs/qatarization

Qatar Ministry of Development Planning and Statistics [ONLINE] http://www.mdps.gov.qa/en/Pages/default.aspx

Randeree, K. 2012. Workforce Nationalization in the Gulf Cooperation Council states, *Center for International and Regional Studies*

Saudi Hollandi Capital, 2012

Shah, N. M. 2006. "Restrictive labor immigration policies in the oil rich gulf: effectiveness and Implications for sending Asian countries". United Nations Expert Group Meeting on International Migration and Development In The Arab Region.

Shah, N. 2008. *Recent Labour Immigration Policies in the Oil-Rich Gulf: How Effective are they Likely To Be?* International Labour Organization.

Shaham, D. 2009. Foreign Labour in the Arab Gulf: Challenges to Nationalization. *Al Nakhlah: The Fletcher School Online Journal for Southwest Asia and Islamic Civilization.*

Ulrichsen, K. 2011. Qatar and the Arab Spring: Policy Drivers and Regional Implications, *Carnegie Middle East Program*

Winckler, O. 1997. The Immigration Policy of the Gulf Cooperation Council States. Middle Eastern Studies. Vol. 33. No.3. pp.480-493

Zahra, M. 2015. 'The Legal Framework of the Sponsorship Systems of the Gulf Cooperation Council Countries: A Comparative Examination', *Gulf Labour Markets and Migration,* No 10/2015

Notes

1 Babar, Z. 2013, Labour Migration in the State of Qatar Policy Making and Governance, *IFRI Center for Migrations and Citizenship*

2 Al Masah Capital Limited, 2011. *MENA: The Great Job Rush – The 'unemployment' ticking time bomb and how to fix it*

3 Aissaoui, A. 2011. Economic Development, Diversification and the Role of the State, *Economic Commentary*, Vol. 9, No. 5, May 2014

4 Hertog, S. 2011. Good, Bad, or Both? The Impact of Oil on the Saudi Political Economy. Center for International and Regional Studies: Georgetown University.

5 Fasano, U. & Goyal, R. 2004. Emerging Strains in GCC Labor Markets. International Monetary Fund.

6 *Held, D & Coates-Ulrichsen, K .2013. The end of the American Century: from 9/11 to the Arab Spring. Cambridge, UK*

7 Bajracharya, R & Sijapati, B, 2012, The Kafala System and its Implications for Nepali Domestic Workers, *Centre for the Study of Labour and Mobility*

8 Khan, A & Harroff-Tavel, H, 2011. Reforming the Kafala: Challenges and Opportunities in Moving Forward, *Asian and Pacific Migration Journal*, Vol. 20, Nos 3-4

9 Beaugrand, C. 2006. Nationality & Migrations Control in the Gulf Countries. *INAMO*. pp.10-14

10 Khan, A & Harroff-Tavel, H, Reforming the Kafala

11 Bajracharya, R & Sijapati, B, The Kafala System and its Implications for Nepali Domestic Workers

12 Beaugrand, C, Nationality & Migrations Control in the Gulf Countries.

13 Esim, S & Smith, M. 2004, Gender and Migration in Arab States: The Case of Domestic Workers, *International Labour Organisation*

14 Shaham, D. 2009. Foreign Labour in the Arab Gulf: Challenges to Nationalization. *Al Nakhlah: The Fletcher School Online Journal for Southwest Asia and Islamic Civilization.*

15 Beaugrand, C, Nationality & Migrations Control in the Gulf Countries.

16 Zahra, M, The Legal Framework of the Sponsorship Systems of the Gulf Cooperation Council Countries
17 Zahra, M. 2015. 'The Legal Framework of the Sponsorship Systems of the Gulf Cooperation Council Countries: A Comparative Examination', *Gulf Labour Markets and Migration,* No 10/2015
18 Shah, N. M. 2006. "Restrictive labor immigration policies in the oil rich gulf: effectiveness and Implications for sending Asian countries". United Nations Expert Group Meeting on International Migration and Development In The Arab Region.
19 Mirkin, B. 2010. *Population Levels, Trends and Policies in the Arab Region: Challenges and Opportunities.* Arab Human Development Report. United Nations.
20 Shaham, D. Foreign Labour in the Arab Gulf
21 Forstenlechner & Rutledge, The GCC's "Demographic Imbalance"
22 Elfakhani, S & Ghanem, A, 2011. Privatisation of Gulf industrial institutions: The Secret of Success, *Middle East Policy,* Vol. XVIII.
23 Hertog, S. State and private sector in the GCC after the Arab uprisings
24 *Ibid.*
25 Looney, R. 2004. Can Saudi Arabia reform its economy in time to head off disaster? *Strategic Insights,* Vol. 3, No.1
26 Saudi Hollandi Capital, 2012
27 *Ibid.*
28 *Ibid.*
29 Randeree, K. 2012. Workforce Nationalization in the Gulf Cooperation Council states, *Center for International and Regional Studies*
30 Saudi Hollandi Capital, 2012
31 *Ibid.*
32 Randeree, Workforce Nationalization in the Gulf Cooperation Council states
33 Shah, N. 2008. *Recent Labour Immigration Policies in the Oil-Rich Gulf: How Effective are they Likely To Be?* International Labour Organization.
34 Hertog, S. State and private sector in the GCC after the Arab uprisings
35 *Ibid.*
36 Randeree, Workforce Nationalization in the Gulf Cooperation Council states
37 Winckler, O. 1997. The Immigration Policy of the Gulf Cooperation Council States. Middle Eastern Studies. Vol. 33. No.3. pp.480-493
38 Dito, M. 2008. *GCC Labour Migration Governance.* United Nations.
39 Randeree, Workforce Nationalization in the Gulf Cooperation Council states
40 Shah, N, *Recent Labour Immigration Policies in the Oil-Rich Gulf*
41 Al-Saqabi, N. 2011. *Figures and Results Confirm Leading Position of Kuwait Banks.* Kuwait Banking Association
42 Hertog, S. State and private sector in the GCC after the Arab uprisings
43 Gulseven, O. 2015. Challenges to Employing Kuwaitis in the Private Sector, *Labor Market Dynamics in the GCC States,* Autumn 2015
44 Njoku, F. 2007. Employees' Attitude Towards The Privatisation Of Kuwait's State Owned Enterprises (SOEs). Maastrict University.
45 Shah, N, *Recent Labour Immigration Policies in the Oil-Rich Gulf*
46 Hukoomi, 2016, [ONLINE] http://portal.www.gov.qa/wps/portal
47 Constant, S; Sayre, E; Abdelkader, N, 2015 *Implications of Qatarization: Qualitative Assessment and Possible Policy Responses* [ONLINE] Available through. http://www.syria.jadaliyya.com/pages/index/21008/implications-of-qatarization_qualitative-assessmen
48 *Ibid.*
49 Fasano, U. & Goyal, R, Emerging Strains in GCC Labor Markets. International Monetary Fund.
50 Constant, S; Sayre, E; Abdelkader, N, *Implications of Qatarization*
51 *Ibid.*

52 Hukoomi, 2016
53 Qatar Foundation, *Qatarization* [ONLINE] Available through: http://www.qf.org.qa/content/about/jobs/qatarization
54 GSDP, *National Development Strategy: Goals and Benefits,* [ONLINE] Available through: http://www.gsdp.gov.qa/portal/page/portal/gsdp_en/nds/goals_benefits
55 *Ibid.*
56 Qatar Ministry of Development Planning and Statistics [ONLINE] http://www.mdps.gov.qa/en/Pages/default.aspx
57 GSDP, *National Development Strategy: Goals and Benefits*
58 *Ibid.*
59 *Ibid.*
60 Dorsey, J. 2015. *2022 World Cup Sparks Labour Reform, Just Not In Qatar.* Fankultur-Institute.
61 GSDP, *National Development Strategy: Goals and Benefits*
62 Berrebi, C. Martorell, F. Tanner, J. Qatar's 2009. Labor Markets at a Crucial Crossroad. *Middle East Journal.* Vol, 63. No.3.
63 Forstenlechner & Rutledge, The GCC's "Demographic Imbalance"
64 Alsheikh, H. M. 2015, Current Progress on the Nationalisation Programmes in Saudi Arabia, *Gulf Labour Markets and Migration,* No.2/2015
65 Personal interviews, Kuwait, Qatar, Saudi Arabia, 2014
66 *Ibid.*
67 *Ibid.*
68 *Ibid.*
69 *Ibid.*
70 *Ibid.*
71 *Ibid.*
72 Al-Razzaz, *The Treacherous Path Towards a New Arab Social Contract*
73 Brocard &Vallet. *The Rentier State in the Middle East*
74 Okruhlik, G. 1999. Rentier Wealth, Unruly Law, and the Rise of Opposition: The Political Economy of Oil States. *Comparative Politics.* Vol, 31. No.2. Pp.295-315.
75 Levins, The Rentier State and the Survival of Arab Absolute Monarchies
76 Personal Interviews, Kuwait, Qatar, Saudi Arabia, 2014
77 *Ibid.*
78 *Ibid.*
79 *Ibid.*
80 De Bel-Air, F. 2015. The Socio-Political Background and Stakes of 'Saudizing' the Workforce in Saudi Arabia: the Nitaqat Policy, *Gulf Labour Markets and Migration*, No.3/2015
81 Personal Interviews, Saudi Arabia, 2014
82 De Bel-Air, 2015
83 Hertog, 2014
84 Personal Interviews, Kuwait, Qatar, Saudi Arabia, 2014
85 *Ibid.*
86 De Bel-Air, The Socio-Political Background and Stakes of 'Saudizing' the Workforce in Saudi Arabia
87 Personal Interviews, Kuwait, Qatar, Saudi Arabia, 2014
88 *Ibid.*
89 *Ibid.*
90 *Ibid.*
91 *Ibid.*
92 *Ibid.*
93 *Ibid.*
94 *Ibid.*

2

Reevaluating the Saudi 'Social Contract': The Perspective of Saudi Male Graduates

Mark C. Thompson

Introduction

Following the 1970s oil boom, the Saudi state was able to gather income from oil production and distribute it throughout the economy and society. As Champion argues this was compatible with traditional Arabia values and allowed the ruling family to enhance its:

... unique blend of religious and political ruling legitimacy with a comprehensive system of largesse known as the 'Saudi social contract'. This 'unwritten' contract committed the state to taking charge of the welfare of its population in return for acceptance of the established political order.[1]

Nowadays, in Saudi Arabia a new generation of leaders led by Deputy Crown Prince Mohammed bin Salman is transforming the traditional state-society relationship, specifically with the launch of Saudi Vision 2030. In turn, this has resulted in the Kingdom's predominantly youthful, and often well-educated, population reexamining the existing social contract at a time of significant socio-economic change.[2] This is because the economics of the social contract have come under increasing strain as a result of low oil prices thereby impacting on Saudi Arabia's economy; in particular the related issues of employment and housing. Moreover, due to the low oil price, the Saudi government has started to impose fiscal restraint and this presents a significant challenge since its citizens are accustomed to government largesse.[3] Indeed, the participants at a 2016 Chatham House workshop on "The Social Contract in the Gulf Cooperation Council (GCC)" agreed that as GCC governments respond to the challenges of falling revenues and the need to diversify their economies away from hydrocarbons, the impact of contemporary socio-economic realities on the existing social contract will require "new strategies of consulting and communicating with the various domestic stakeholders and managing public expectation".[4] Indeed, as Hertog notes, each economic crisis in Saudi Arabia creates pressure for 'radical' reform and/or a redefinition of the Saudi 'distributional' system or 'social contract'.[5]

However, the usage of the term 'social contract' is often criticized as being euro-centric – as well as not being understood in the same way when translated to Arabic – and thus, does not explain adequately the relationship between the governing and governed in the Kingdom.[6]In addition, in the Saudi context, the English language usage often has negative connotations as it suggests 'cooptation' of diverse societal constituencies by the Saudi government. Hence, according to Saudi academic, in the domestic context the idea of a social contract is best understood as "mutual benefits" between authorities and citizens. That is the government benefits from this contract as the citizen pledges loyalty to the political system and in return the government provides welfare and, for example, a job for life.[7] Thus, as Belbagi argues, the force holding the social contract together is "the good citizen".[8] Nonetheless, how do young male Saudis interpret this 'mutual bond' between the government and citizens? Furthermore, does their interpretation of these mutual benefits match that of the authorities? Because if a 'mismatch' exists then this would require a revision of the role of the state in the economy or in fact a shift in the government's economic relationship with society.

Moreover, quite clearly a social contract does not simply entail socio-economic factors, but also includes non-economic elements. These non-economic elements can include values, justice, socio-political participation and/or inclusion in decision-making processes. Hence, to what extent do these young Saudis consider these non-economic elements to be an integral part of a social contract? How are they linked to an individual's perception of his role in society, his place in the labour market as well as his willingness and desire to contribute to national development? Indeed, a comprehension of how young male Saudis perceive the changing nature of the social contract is not only applicable in the overall Saudi national context, but also in multiple Saudi domestic contexts, in light of oil-market developments, economic policy and their impact on socio-economic and political transformation.

Methodology

This paper is part of an ongoing larger research project looking at Saudi socio-political, socio-economic and socio-cultural issues from the perspective of young Saudi men aged approximately 19-25.[9] The project discusses the impact of issues related to rapid societal transformation in the Kingdom, including reimagining the social contract, and the challenge this poses to young Saudi men. This paper is based on primary research including, interviews, focus group discussions, online surveys (both written and multiple-choice responses)[10] as well as student projects conducted with Saudi male graduates across the Kingdom as well as with approximately 400 undergraduate students at King Fahd University of Petroleum and Minerals (KFUPM) and their extended networks.[11] Relevant findings from these surveys are presented in tables throughout the text in order to support some of the discussed themes.

The author has respected the wishes of the interviewees, focus group members and online respondents who, unless named in this study, asked to remain anonymous. The paper is also informed by the author's participation at a Chatham House workshop "The Social Contract in the GCC" convened in London, UK, 11-12 January, 2016.[12]

Background

In order to understand the changing nature of the Saudi social contract amongst young male Saudis, it is necessary to provide context including perceptions of societal transformation and the impact of social media usage on societal norms.[13]

Societal Transformation

To what extent do young Saudis who comprise the majority of the population see society as changing?[14] In terms of the overall picture, the majority of respondents believe that considerable changes are occurring in Saudi Arabia with 61 per cent saying Saudi society is changing quickly whilst in contrast only 28 per cent see little change.[15] Nevertheless, there is consensus that the biggest changes have occurred in socio-cultural areas although there is considerable debate about whether this is a positive or negative development.[16] Respondents also point out that Saudi society has undergone many transformational phases since the *Sahwa* movement.[17] Nowadays, for many respondents Saudi society is seen as "more open-minded" because societal change is mainly positive as "people become more civilized".[18] Even so, many respondents make the very important point that societal transformation in Saudi Arabia is not uniform across the Kingdom. It varies according to province, age, education, tribal status and gender although there is consensus that youth desires greater change than the older generations.[19]

Looking to the future, nearly two thirds of these young people believe that in the next decade Saudi Arabia will change considerably. Thus, some astute respondents argue that it is necessary to start establishing a post-oil mentality in Saudi society. Furthermore, when these young men think about their futures, they identify employment (60.7 per cent), education (40.5 per cent), cost of living (38.1 per cent) and affordable housing (31 per cent), in that order, as the most important and potentially problematic issues they will face – particularly if the oil price stays low.[20]

An Online Generation

Saudis, in particular youth, are now connected to each other in ways that would have been unthinkable only a few years ago; they have become the 'online generation' with awareness that they are more connected to the outside world than would have been possible a decade ago.

Table 1: To what extent do you feel you are connected to the world?[21]

	No. of respondents	%
Very much	76	14.5
To a great extent	210	40.1
To some extent	172	32.8
Not very much	47	9.0
Very little	14	2.7
I do not feel I am connected to the world	3	0.6
I do not know	2	0.4

As Sukarieh and Tannok write, young people's (netizens) social media usage is characterized by being autonomous, global, open and participatory and notable in the Saudi context, spread horizontally rather than being vertically organized.[22] In addition, young Saudis are also more knowledgeable about life in general and, as Murphy notes, more outspoken as the Internet offers them a degree of protection through its anonymity.[23]

Table 2: If you feel you're connected, why is that?[24]

	No. of respondents	%
Because of social media	486	93.6
Because of education	239	46.1
Because of travelling	161	31.0
Because of communicating with foreigners	125	24.1
Because of traditional media	52	10.0
Because of e-government	10	1.9
Because of government policy	20	3.9
Because I make the effort	137	26.4

Table 3: In your opinion, does being 'connected' change the way you look at your society?[25]

	No. of respondents	%
Yes, Very much	150	28.7
Yes, to a great extent	183	35.1
Yes, to some extent	130	24.9
No, not very much	37	7.1
No, never	9	1.7
I don't know	13	2.5

Since 2010 there has been a huge increase in online participation on social networks and instant-messaging applications such as WhatsApp, Facebook and Twitter. For example, the 2010 Twitter usage increased by 440 per cent in the Kingdom in comparison to a 95 per cent increase worldwide.[26] A 2013 study found that Twitter's penetration growth rate increased by 3,000 per cent from 2011 to 2012 with the majority of users aged 18-34.[27] In addition, according to the *Social Clinic* in Jeddah, 96 per cent of Saudi Internet users watch videos on YouTube and at least 7 million users have uploaded videos once in their lifetime.[28]

Table 4: Which social media / communication applications do you use?[29]

	No. of respondents	%
Twitter	2172	59.8
Instagram	2425	66.8
Snapchat	1916	52.8
Path	478	13.2
Facebook	799	22.0
Other	557	15.3

In the opinion of some respondents a positive development has been that ordinary Saudis now have a degree of influence over the Saudi leadership's decision-making process by highlighting issues such as the need for economic reforms on social media. As a young Saudi business graduate says "social media makes it very easy for us to share our opinions and to communicate with the state". Thus, in his opinion, the public's views are beginning to play a role in state decision-making to the extent that "Nowadays, the government has started to take our opinions very seriously".[30] In fact, Kinninmont argues that Twitter is part of "a wider distribution of power over information away from governments and towards individuals" especially youth.[31]

Certainly, there is an argument about whether the 'online generation' has any real political influence, but what is probably significant is the perception amongst some young people that a space has become available where they can voice their opinions and be heard. As one young Saudi engineer contends "Youth is starting to understand the world much better so hiding the truth and/or audience manipulation is harder in this era. The government is being careful because every move is noticed by its youthful public".[33] Nevertheless, during 2015 there was a crackdown by the government on freedom of online expression, principally on Twitter. In consequence, although many individuals ceased commenting online, those Saudis who had sufficient influence and *wastah* continued to criticize government policies, but simultaneously toned down that criticism.

Table 5: When you think of social media, which of these statements do you agree with?[32]

	No. of respondents	%
Nowadays in Saudi Arabia we have an online civil society	88	36.9
Social media has brought the government closer to the people	77	32.3
Social media has increased socio-political awareness	117	49.1
Social media has created socio-political problems	81	34.0
Social media could be dangerous for Saudi Arabia	58	24.4
Social media is damaging Saudi norms	65	27.3
Social media is threatening Saudi identity	50	21.0
Social media is creating links between different societal groupings	83	34.9
Social media has helped increase tolerance and understanding	71	29.8
Social media has helped increase intolerance and extremism	59	24.8
People talk a lot of rubbish on social media	134	56.3
People should think carefully before tweeting	129	54.2
Social media can be both positive and negative so you need to be careful how you use it	155	65.1

Defining the Saudi Social Contract

Evolving State-Society Communication

To what extent has widespread access to social media in Saudi society changed the ways by which citizens negotiate their 'social contracts' with the government? The increase in social media usage is the main factor for pushing the government to speed up its socio-economic reforms[34] as it has played a profound role in changing communication between the government and citizens.[35] Significantly, societal concerns now reach the authorities without any of the usual 'wastah' due to social media usage.[36] Thus, social media, one individual argues, has helped link the government and the citizen in a way that strengthens the voice of the citizen whilst ensuring that government bodies abide by their responsibilities.[37] Thus, there is consensus amongst respondents that social media usage has contributed to a significant transformation in "free and open political discussion" as well as demands for greater socio-political involvement and participation.[38] Conversely, societal demands regarding the nature of reform have not really changed, but social media has highlighted reform demands by making the issues more accessible and open to discussion.[39] Indeed, citizens have a voice – and a political space – where they express their opinions. In fact, this space has increased as in the last few years a newer online version of civil society has emerged via the increased use of social media that they recognize has become a Saudi 'norm'. In fact, as a 2014 study "What Matters Most to Saudi Arabia's Youth" notes, digital communication has been integrated into the traditional lifestyle.[40] Nonetheless, the real question is whether the government is listening and taking citizen input seriously. Or, according to one viewpoint, the government's response might be purely cosmetic; deceiving citizens by making them believe that their points of view are relevant because they are "allowed to be expressed" on the Internet.[41]

Table 6: To what extent have channels of communication through which citizens negotiate their 'social contracts' with the government changed?[42]

	No. of respondents	%
Changed completely due to technology	24	11.4
Changed a great deal due to technology	65	31.0
Changed to some extent due to technology	37	17.6
Changed a little due to technology	29	13.8
Not changed at all	15	7.1
I don't know / not sure	40	19.0

That said social media and 'electronic gateways' are being used by some ministries and their departments to support communication with wider Saudi society. In fact, nowadays most government officials have a Twitter accounts (or similar) so that they can respond to people's complaints and suggestions quickly.[43] Nevertheless, some individuals maintain that this is an issue of providing services rather than listening to societal opinions. In fact, unless the government is fully transparent and accountable it will be unable to establish a viable social contract because transparency and accountability must be the cornerstones of the state.[44]

Table 7: To what extent are the ways in which the Saudi government seeks to create bonds with citizens changing due to current socio-economic conditions?[45]

	No. of respondents	%
Changing completely	11	5.2
Changing a great deal	53	25.2
Changing to some extent	64	30.5
Changing a little	34	16.2
Not changing at all	24	11.4
I don't know / not sure	24	11.4

However, since the fall in the oil price, socio-economic realities have impacted negatively on ordinary Saudis.[46] For some individuals the deterioration in the standard of living[47] is a step toward the worst case scenario.[48] As one engineering graduate explains:

> Things are changing within the government, but still our connections with the government are not clear. We see so many important issues being affected negatively: housing problems, unemployment, private sector jobs and even government jobs. The problem is that I do not know how to give back to my country so that my country can give back to me. Should I relay on my education? It is not clear. Nowadays, most engineering graduates rely on banks for money. Additionally, his house and car are rented and his wedding can cost up to SAR 200K. How I can get this money for a house, furniture and car? And we have not even started discussing the honeymoon.[49]

In fact, as the impact of the low oil price impacts on the individual Saudi's pocket, some maintain that the citizens are more aware than before about the rising cost of living and the need to not spend on luxury items.[50] Though, in the opinion of some individuals a major headache for the government is that society is not ready to accept changes to, for example, power and water subsidies. Thus, in order for the government to be able to cut subsidies effectively society will need to be educated to accept these changes.[51]

Table 8: To what extent could the low oil price destabilize the mutual bond or social contract?[52]

	No. of respondents	%
A great deal	85	40.1
To some extent	62	29.2
It would have an effect	24	11.3
Not that much	17	8.0
I don't know / not sure	24	11.3

Awareness of a Social Contract

Graduates were asked about the extent that they are aware of a 'social contact' between themselves (their families) and the government. In addition, they were asked to say what they believe a social contact includes and whether this is important.[53]

Table 9: To what extent do you feel it is the government's responsibility to provide you with employment and welfare benefits such as housing loans?[54]

	No. of respondents	%
It is the government's responsibility and duty to provide all the assistance it can	106	50.5
The government should help as much as it can, but it is also my responsibility	88	41.9
The government is not fully responsible, in fact, the responsibility should be mainly with individual citizens	4	1.9
It should be the responsibility of citizens alone to look after their families	5	2.4
I don't know / not sure	7	3.3

For many respondents the social contract incorporates necessary "life services" provided by the government such as education, health, and social security, but they argue strongly that any social contract can only be effective if the government is able to provide these essential life services.[55] However, simultaneously they believe a "good social contract does not humiliate the citizen in return for security and benefits".[56]

For some individuals the social contract comprises a collection of rules and regulations between the government and the people that help people organize their daily lives because without a social contract *fitna* (anarchy and discord) would dominate.[57] For those individuals who see the social contract in a positive light, it is also about the individual fulfilling his civic duties to the government and vice-versa:

> I am very aware of the Saudi social contract and I think it is about obeying the king, maintaining social unity and the individual's contribution in developing the Kingdom through knowledge, economy, security and religion. In turn, I benefit from government services and land resources. I think that this social contract is very important because it explains the relationships and corresponding responsibilities between all Saudis.[58]

However, other respondents explained that they did not understand the term until they read the description provided although were still unclear about whether a social contract exists in Saudi Arabia or not.[59] However, even with the explanation some respondents were unclear about the meaning saying for example "I know it is important, but I do not know about the details".[60] Another viewpoint is that the social contract is important as it assists both the government and society to organize daily life.[61] Others state that they were not aware of a social contract and its importance, but if "it means providing living necessities such as water and electricity for extra payment then it becomes complicated".[62]

Table 10: Read the following statements about the social contract between citizens and the government and tick all you agree with:[63]

	No. of respondents	%
A social contract exists and it is a positive thing	59	27.7
A social contract exists, but it is a negative thing	5	2.4
It has never occurred to me that there is a social contract	89	42.0
The idea of a social contract is important	100	47.2
The idea of a social contract is not important	3	1.4
The idea of a social contract is understood by society	11	5.2
The idea of a social contract is not understood by society	115	54.2
I do not understand what a social contract means	53	25.0

Nonetheless, some respondents state that an effective social contact could increase productivity and contribute in developing the Kingdom.[64] In addition, a viable social contract can help improve society by increasing knowledge, cultural awareness, and economic growth.[65]

Respondents who understand and/or have an awareness of a social contract state that it describes a mutual relationship between the citizens and the government;[66] that is "symbiotic interests" between the government and its citizens in order to maintain the Kingdom's security and the stability whilst both sides profit from the contract.[67] Nevertheless, even if the government provides these services for society, there is sometimes confusion regarding an individual's corresponding civil duties. One respondent says he want to participate, but does not know a) how he can participate, and b) what is acceptable to the government (or not).[68]

However, another respondent maintains that any transformation in the current social contract is only partial as the government continues to provide services for citizens in every aspect of life including education, health and employment opportunities—and at the same time does not tax citizens.[69] However, taxation is a contentious issue as most Saudi families are not wealthy and for that reason usually have two or more parallel incomes.[70] Therefore, the idea that ordinary Saudis might have to pay income tax in the future is completely rejected. It is thought that rather than introducing income tax, the government should concentrate on implementing policies that discourage over-consumption.

According to one individual, the most important element of the Saudi social contract is that it "protects the citizen and his freedoms" through legal and just government rules as long as the citizen follows these rules". This is because the Saudi social contract is understood to represent the "foundation of citizenship" that is the citizen has both rights and duties.[72] Certainly, a social contract is seen as important, but what is more significant is for the citizen to understand his contractual obligations in terms of "the rights and responsibilities of both sides". For example, if the government is seen to be doing its best to provide jobs, houses and security then the average Saudi citizen will contribute to the contact by utilizing his knowledge and respecting his duties.[73]

Table 11: To what extent are you aware of a 'social contact' (mutual bond) between you or your family and the government?[71]

	No. of respondents	%
In my opinion, a social contract definitely exists	22	10.5
I believe there is some sort of social contact	46	21.9
There is a social contact in certain areas	33	15.7
I don't this this is an important issue	3	1.4
There is no social contract	28	13.3
I don't understand what is meant by a social contract	30	14.3
I don't know / not sure	48	22.9

According to one individual, the most important element of the Saudi social contract is that it "protects the citizen and his freedoms" through legal and just government rules as long as the citizen follows these rules". This is because the Saudi social contract is understood to represent the "foundation of citizenship" that is the citizen has both rights and duties.[72] Certainly, a social contract is seen as important, but what is more significant is for the citizen to understand his contractual obligations in terms of "the rights and responsibilities of both sides". For example, if the government is seen to be doing its best to provide jobs, houses and security then the average Saudi citizen will contribute to the contact by utilizing his knowledge and respecting his duties.[73]

Different Social Contracts?

Society in Saudi Arabia is not homogenous.[74] In fact, even within seeming single geographic area such as the metropolitan conurbation of al-Khobar-Dhahran-Dammam[75] there are multiple societal constituencies both Saudi and expatriate.[76] Therefore, do these young Saudi men think that there are different contracts for diverse Saudi constituencies? Given the current socio-economic climate, if graduates believe that different social contracts exist, then who benefits and who loses?

However, some individuals do not see a disparity between different constituencies; they stress that main issue is that all the Saudi citizens are involved in a fair social contract.[77] According to some respondents, the educated elites are conscious of public opinion so in turn, the general public has become more politically aware because of their connections with these elites.[78] However, one individual points out that difference contracts are visible between different societal groups; for example the social contract between the government and a religious establishment has religious dimensions and the social contract between the government and business has economic dimensions.[79]

Table 12: To what extent do you believe that there are different social contracts with different Saudi constituencies? Tick all you agree with:[80]

	No. of respondents	%
There is definitely only one social contract and everyone is treated the same way	7	3.3
In general, there is only one social contract and everyone is treated the same way	15	7.1
There are variations of the social contract based on region	38	18.1
There are variations of the social contract based on tribal affiliation	41	19.5
There are variations of the social contract based on economic background/class/professional status	69	32.9
There are variations of the social contract based on sectarian issues	23	11
There are variations of the social contract based on generational differences	38	18.1
I have no opinion / do not know	105	50

Other respondents disagree strongly and stress that there are constituencies with power that impose their influence inside the government, thereby weakening and marginalizing other societal groupings.[81] These respondents identify this constituency as the Salafists and for this reason "the winner will always be the government and those close to it".[82] However, ultimately, the losers are both the government and its people because the former "fails to occupy the same space as the people".[83] However, the danger is that there are many societal constituencies, e.g. tribal, urbanized/modernized, or those with religious and/or philosophical ideologies who would seize the opportunity to promote their own interests should the government lose control and/or strengthen their own interests and ideologies with a fragmented government. If this should transpire, then sadly, the losers in the absence of a social contract would be ordinary citizens who would be forced to support one of these powerful constituencies so as to maintain their social benefits as part of a reconfigured social contract.[84] Nonetheless, some respondents argue that the government is the only winners even though the services it provides are not proportionate to its income (at least in comparison to neighboring Gulf states) so citizens can only "win" when the cost of living is acceptable, the price of goods low, and there are no taxes.[85]

However, there is a degree of cynicism regarding income inequality as the government "represents a bank and Saudis are the borrowers" – so definitely the government is the winner with some small benefits for Saudi society;[86] after all, it is always the wealthy that benefit most.[87] But, regardless of whether the government or citizens "win" with the current social contract, in the current economic climate for many it is difficult to ascertain winners and losers particularly as the Saudi government is attempting to overhaul its economic policy. Nonetheless, others take a longer view, believing that ultimately, in the long-term the loser will probably be the government because inequality will undermine the emergence of any nascent Saudi nationalism.[88]

Jobs for Life?

Until summer 2014, it was a given for KFUPM graduates to receive four to five good job offers either in the public or private sectors from companies such as Saudi Aramco, Haliburton and Schlumberger. As Saudi Arabia's 'best and brightest' in the fields of petrochemicals, engineering and commerce, these young men are selected and educated to take their place as leaders within their respective fields, and by extension contribute to the creation of a twenty-first century knowledge-based Saudi economy and society. However, since the drop in the oil price, significant economic transformations and realities have impacted dramatically on the Saudi labour market. For example, in summer 2015, KFUPM graduates received at best two to three job offers and by January 2016 graduates were lucky to receive one. Indeed, one astute student points out that if KFUPM is affected, then the employment prospects for other young Saudi male graduates further down the academic scale are likely to be much worse. In fact, although KFUPM graduates maintain that it is far easier for them to find employment than their peers from other Saudi universities, many respondents are under no illusions that the 'dream job' may not materialize – particularly given the current economic climate. Therefore, there is a growing realization that they might have to compromise. Indeed, Professor Mohamed Ramady, an expert on the Saudi economy, notes that "due to social values, many young Saudis do not want, although some unemployed Saudis are beginning to accept seemingly social 'demeaning' jobs" such as supermarket cashiers and gym receptionists.[89] Indeed, as a result of the contracting Saudi labour market, many respondents comprehend that after graduating a first position might not be a perfect fit and the threat of unemployment may force some graduates to take up positions they do not really want.

Nevertheless, some individuals contend that it is the responsibility of the government to encourage young Saudis to enter the private sector. Hence, regarding private sector employment opportunities, a clearer political will is required from the government especially as public sector salaries, for example in education and the military, are stagnating. In consequence, it is probably not surprising that respondents feel varying degrees of anxiety about entering the workplace. Nevertheless, respondents believe that one way to increase the numbers of young Saudis entering the workforce and simultaneously enhance job satisfaction is greater government encouragement for entrepreneurship. In spite of this, they note that there are many barriers to the development of entrepreneurship in particular technology start-ups. One KFUPM student project cites market entry regulations, shortage of funds and lack of market experience as three of the principal problems facing young entrepreneurs.[90] In addition, the complexity of laws and regulations and not knowing who to talk to pose real challenges to young people with innovative ideas.

Table 13: To what extent do you expect a 'job for life' (particularly in the public sector)?[91]

	No. of respondents	%
100%	30	14.3
90%	29	13.8
75%	35	16.7
50%	30	14.3
25%	28	13.3
There is no such thing as a job for life these days	37	17.6
I don't know / not sure	21	10.0

According to one focus group, "most graduates" are looking for a job for life: a position in the public sector or with a major corporation whereby the individual is guaranteed a lifelong salary plus accompanying benefits such as health care for both himself and his family.[92] However, the group recognizes that the impact of the low oil price is reducing these opportunities.[93] The group also points out that many Saudis want public sector jobs and/or a job with a company such as Aramco as everyone knows that "Saudis are never fired from Aramco. Foreign companies fire Saudis, but Saudi companies do not".[94] Yet, one group member believes that a job for life is a personal choice and in fact, more ambitious individuals who are actively seeking a challenge will change jobs in order to gain valuable experience[95] In fact, individuals understand that in the current economic climate they might have to move from job to job.[96] Still, there is consensus amongst all respondents that in Saudi Arabia a job for life is important for a young man's marriage prospects as it provides a stable future. For example, an individual might get a first job in the private sector but he will then try to move to a company such as Saudi Aramco as this will increase his chances of a good marriage.[97] Indeed, the importance of being able to make a good marriage cannot be underestimated, highlighting as it does the importance of understanding the Saudi socio-cultural context.

One engineering graduate maintains that the narrative of "oil running out and going back to the desert" is discussed in wider Saudi society. He says that "My grandmother always says to me "I told you about the poverty we used to live in, but I am worried that you will tell your grandchildren about the wealth you used to live in".[98] Regarding attitudes to money, although some survey respondents claim that Saudi understanding of the value of money is changing,[99] members of this focus group disagree strongly.[100] They point out that young Saudi males continue to spend too much money on smartphones and cars — usually by borrowing money from a bank, thereby increasing their personal debt. They say that

Saudi banks keep giving loans without "asking too many questions" so that young men are even taking out loans pay off other loans. Many young men also take out loans to pay accumulated traffic fines, but if an individual continues to borrow money he will eventually "lose his freedom", thus storing up huge problems for the future.[101]

Saudi Vision 2030 (National Transformation Plan)

Saudi Vision 2030 (National Transformation Plan), which promises a better future and better governance, is raising hopes and expectations amongst ordinary Saudis. Therefore, it is important that the Saudi government includes the majority of its youthful population because any society that deprives half its population from nation-building is doomed to failure.[102]

Table 14: To what extent do you feel you should contribute to national development? Tick all you agree with:[103]

	No. of respondents	%
It is my responsibility and duty to contribute to national development	164	77.7
It is not my responsibility and duty to contribute to national development because it is the responsibility of the government	7	3.3
Saudis should be encouraged by the government to contribute to national development	114	54.0
National means that everyone should be involved	119	56.4
Contributing to national development is important due to the new economic realities	63	29.9
I would like to contribute to national development, but do not know how I can do this	42	19.9
I would like to contribute to national development, but is this possible?	45	21.3
I do not know / not sure	10	4.7

Graduates were asked whether they considered Saudi Vision 2030 important and to a greater degree, it appears that Saudi Vision 2030 has been welcomed, albeit tentatively, as a positive step forward.[104] However, a major complaint amongst respondents is that in its initial stages they had to learn about Saudi Vision 2030 from foreign media such as Bloomberg[105] which "indicated a continuing lack of transparency at that time",[106] but nowadays around 30 per cent of respondents say that this is an initiative "they know well and are optimistic".[107] One individual states that he follows news about the project closely as he believes it is significant since it could "change the country's history forever".[108] In fact, this youthful optimism was evident on social media following the Vision's unveiling:

> Following the announcement of the government's Vision 2030 plan, tens of thousands of young Saudis took to social media to debate plans to reform the kingdom's oil-reliant economy marking a shift in how Saudi Arabia's rulers interact with their citizens. The announcement strategy used Twitter alongside traditional media to build anticipation and introduce hashtags.[109]

However, even if some individuals admit to not knowing a much about the Vision, they state that it could be important in the long-term as the Vision could demonstrate the extent that the rulers are interested in developing Saudi Arabia with input from its (young) citizens.[110]

Table 15: How much do you know about the Saudi Vision 2030?[111]

	No. of respondents	%
I know a lot about it	65	30.7
I know something about it	71	33.5
I have heard of it, but I do not have detailed knowledge	41	19.3
I have heard the name, but that is all	13	6.1
I know nothing about it, but would like to know about it	6	2.8
I have never heard of it	9	4.2
I don't know / not sure	7	3.3

For some, real knowledge about the subject is scarce because so far "it has only been headlines"[112] and there is concern that the details of the Vision are vague.[113] Furthermore, many individuals point out that the implementation of the Vision will be more important that its unveiling.[114] Indeed, many young Saudis (who watched Prince Mohammed bin Salman's interview on al-Arabiya when he introduced the Vision) are asking whether the Vision can or indeed, will be implemented.[115] Moreover, they stress that it needs to be implemented correctly as this is an opportunity to prevent future economic crises and maintain, or even raise, living standards in the Kingdom.[116] These individuals argue that the Kingdom must attempt to diversify its economy sooner rather than later as the country will need alternative sources of income due to low oil prices. They see first-hand the ramifications of the low oil price on the citizens' side of the social contract.[117]

Nevertheless, from what some respondents understand "the Vision is just a proposal linked to economic issues without a clear outline"; one that depends mainly on privatizing areas such as education and health, raising taxes as well as improving quality and performance indicators within government ministries and departments.[118] For this reason, one individual laments that the Vision disregards ordinary Saudis because its goal is to increase the government's treasury rather than the "suffering citizens" who have no input into the Vision.[119]

However, in the opinion of one graduate one of the most interesting things about Saudi Vision 2030 is how it reflects importance of Saudi public opinion, or indeed the impact of the Kingdom's new online version of civil society. For example, following a public outcry, the government was forced to admit that the strategy behind the increase in water bills (spring 2016) had been an abject failure as quite clearly "it was not thought through properly".[120] Indeed, the government was fully aware that Saudi society was furious as the new billing often did not make any sense, e.g. "charging people the incorrect amounts or sending households the wrong bills. For that reason, the government was forced to reverse the price increase and have the minister in charge sacked.[121] What is interesting about the water bills affair is that it demonstrates how far the government can go (at this point) in terms of taxing wider Saudi society. Clearly, there are certain areas that are "off-limits" to Saudi society and others such as the "sin taxes" that society accepts. The government is obviously cognizant of this fact and therefore, any proposed income tax is not on the table—this is something that Saudi society totally rejects.[122] In fact, Saudi Vision 2030 cannot succeed unless the government has Saudi society 'on-side'.

According to a Saudi political-scientist another extremely important issue relates to the fact that:

> The government has so far failed to produce policies and plans that target specific Saudi societal constituencies. You cannot treat the citizens of Al Qassim in the same way as the citizens of Jeddah or for example, the Shia community in Qatif. These are very different groupings with very different requirements and aspirations.[123]

Nevertheless, for others Saudi Vision 2030 is being interpreted by many as a blueprint for more inclusivity and societal participation, i.e. a renegotiated Saudi social contract. Nonetheless, fortunately for the government it seems that the majority of well-educated young Saudis understand that the principles behind the Vision 2030 project are necessary because the Kingdom has entered a new era that requires adopting a completely new mentality. However, although Prince Mohammed bin Salman has the backing of society (for the moment), his actual National Transformation Plan has to deliver on the details because if the plan fails to meet these societal expectations then societal disappointment could potentially destabilize the existing social contract.[124] For the time being it seems that Saudi society is giving Prince Mohammed bin Salman the benefit of the doubt and/or a "honeymoon period" for his Saudi Vision 2030 – as long as there is no mention of income tax.

Conclusion

The Saudi government is selling the much discussed Saudi Vision 2030 as a socio-economic project. However, in contemporary Saudi Arabia economic issues are linked to socio-politics and vice-versa. Whatever economic plans are put forward by the Vision will have political consequences:

> The problem is that the government and most ministers simply do not appear to understand this. In my opinion, there seems to be a complete disconnect between the government and society. And that of course could be potentially dangerous. If you try and point this out to government ministers (or criticize government ministers) you just get blindsided with endless statistics and data that "prove" the government is listening to societal concerns.[125]

Hence, there is a danger that those in very senior positions, both Al Saud and non-royal, operate in a bubble that is completely removed from the general public.[126] As one respondent contends a decade ago this would not have been much of a problem, but today it is different because the Kingdom's predominantly young population is much better educated and connected due to widespread Internet access.[127] Many young Saudis understand socio-political and are skeptical of what the government tells them to believe, but the problem is that government ministers are often unaware that this is the new reality'.[128]

Certainly, Saudi Vision 2030 is a welcome initiative, but it cannot disguise the fact that current socio-economic realties have exacerbated internal divisions and social problems within the Kingdom. In fact, as a Saudi political-economist argues "Saudi Arabia is a state, but it is not a nation". In addition, internal divisions, whether regional, tribal, economic and class have always been very pronounced, but the economic downturn, and the government's preference for promoting Najdis at the expense of other constituencies is placing great strain on social harmony. Nevertheless, for the time-being many Saudis have given Saudi Vision 2030 – and by extension Prince Mohammed bin Salman – the benefit of the doubt. However, two critical issues, employment and lack of affordable housing are causing major concern throughout society, particularly amongst the 25 and under age bracket. Unfortunately for the government this demographic is also the most vociferous and internally well connected through social media usage.[129] This is potentially dangerous as the combination of lack of jobs and affordable housing coupled with rising living costs is pushing a great many young Saudis to the margins of society. This must be addressed otherwise it will undermine any efforts to implement Saudi Vision 2030. Indeed, government failure to tackle major societal problems – particularly amongst males under 25 – will create larger problems in the future. As one respondent argues "It is one thing to use a lot of fine words to describe Saudi Vision 2030, but quite another to deal effectively with serious internal issues such as unemployment".[130]

What does the future hold for Saudi youth who are on average around twenty years old? Many young Saudis surveyed for this paper are certain that their parents' generation experienced the 'good times' and that their own lives will be much more difficult in both economic and political terms. Indeed, the under 25 demographic is key to understanding the future of Saudi Arabia. In fact, Ramady points out that states with a large "youth bulge" can "experience a high level of political violence and civil strife" if exacerbated by a lack of meaningful employment opportunities.[131] Ulrichsen also highlights the urgency of addressing unemployment in a region where youth constitutes such a high proportion of the population[132] and Jones and Punshi point out that "our collective choices and actions" will be determined whether the government "can reap this demographic dividend or decelerate towards a demographic disaster".[133]

In addition, we must also recognize that the educational process is raising the hopes and aspirations of young Saudis and this in turn but this poses the question of how young Saudis are going to be gainfully employed as well as the degree to which they will be able to participate in decision-making processes. Because in conclusion, Saudi Arabia's greatest resource is not oil; rather it is many of the Kingdom's educated and ambitious young people. Critically, many young Saudis do not simply want jobs; they want rewarding careers that they enable them to contribute to individual, corporate and national development. For this reason, it is imperative that we understand not only their aspirations and concerns, but also how they see their futures in the contemporary Kingdom. Because these young Saudis understand that current socio-economic changes have long-term consequences for their relationship with the state. A reconfigured Saudi social contract can only be viable and effective if the Kingdom's youthful population is given a say in expanding the economy as well as being allowed to participate in national decision-making processes.

References

Almaeena, K., "No Turning Back", in *Trends: The international Magazine on Arab Affairs*, No. 210, February, 2016, pp. 21-22.

Al Qassemi, S., "The Gulf's New Social Contract", 8 February, 2016, *Middle East Institute*. Available at: www.mei.edu/content/article/gulfs-new-social-contract

Al Shihabi, A., *The Saudi Kingdom: Between the Jihadi Hammer and the Iranian Anvil*, Princeton, Markus Wiener Publishers, 2016

Anon, "Water tariff to rise 50% next month", 2 November, 2015, *Arab News*. Available at: http://www.arabnews.com/saudi-arabia/news/829286

Anon, "The State of Social Media in Saudi Arabia, Vol. 3", 23 September, 2016, *The Social Clinic*. Available at: www.thesocialclinic.com/the-state-of-social-media-in-saudi-arabia-vol-3/

Anon, "The Social Contact in the GCC: Workshop Summary", January 2016, *Chatham House*, London, UK. Available at: www.chathamhouse.org/event/social-contract-in-gcc

Atwood, E., "Twitter usage rockets in conservative Saudi Arabia", 5 January, 2011, *Arabian Business*. Available at: www.arabianbusiness.com/twitter-usage-rockets-in-conservative-saudi-arabia-371485.html

Belbagi, Z., "Renegotiating the Social Contract in the GCC: Lessons from the Rousseau Playbook", in Labour Markets Dynamics in the GCC States, Etheridge, J. (ed.) *Gulf Affairs*, Autumn 2015, pp. 2-5.

Calabro, P., "Saudi Arabia's post-oil plan enters slippery slope", 27 May, 2016, *Al-Monitor*. Available at: http://tinyurl.com/ydhkldcv

Champion, D., *The Paradoxical Kingdom: Saudi Arabia and the Momentum for Reform*, New York, Columbia University Press, 2003.

Economist Briefing Saudi Arabia, "Young prince in a hurry", 9 January, 2016, *The Economist*. Available at: http://tinyurl.com/hdvzoux

Friedman, T., "Letter from Saudi Arabia", 25 November, 2015, *New York Times*. Available at: http://tinyurl.com/ydc8tonz

Gause, F.G. and Crystal, J., "The Arab Gulf: Will Autocracy Define the Social Contract in 2015? Identifying Change in Saudi Arabia", in *The Middle East in 2015: The Impact of Regional Trends on US Strategic Planning*, Yaphe, J. (ed.) Institute for National Strategic Studies, 2002, pp. 164–176.

Hertog, S. 'Segmented Clientelism: The Political Economy of Saudi Economic Reform Efforts', in P. Aarts and G. Nonneman (eds), *Saudi Arabia in the Balance: Political Economy, Society, Foreign Affairs*, London, C. Hurst and Co., 2005, pp. 111-143.

Hildebrandt, J. et al, "What Matters Most to Saudi Arabia's Youth?: Helping Policy Makers Address the National Challenges", June 2014, *The Boston Consulting Group*. Available at: http://tinyurl.com/yb27j33z

Jones, D. and Punshi, R., *Unlocking the Paradox of Plenty: A Review of the Talent Landscape in the Arab World and Your Role in Shaping the Future*, Dubai, Motivate Publishing, 2013.

Kinninmont, J., "Future Trends in the Gulf", *Chatham House*, London, UK, 2015. Available at: http://tinyurl.com/jnpsnfu

Kinninmont, J., "To What Extent Is Twitter Changing Gulf Societies?" February 2013, *Chatham House*. Available at: www.chathamhouse.org/publications/papers/view/189413

Lacroix, S., *Awakening Islam: The Politics of Religious Dissent in Contemporary Saudi Arabia*, Harvard University Press, USA, 2011.

Muhammad, F., "Twitter usage in KSA grows '10 times' the world average", 6 January, 2013, *Saudi Gazette*. Available at: http://tinyurl.com/acu5z7y

Murphy, C., "Will the house of Saud adapt enough to survive ... again?" 9 February, 2011, *The Star*. Available at: http://tinyurl.com/yd2str3p

Nereim, V. and Abu-Nasr, D., "How Much Longer Can Saudi Arabia's Economy Hold Out Against Cheap Oil?", 21 August, *Bloomberg Business*. Available at: http://tinyurl.com/y7mpngnb

Ramady, M., 'Gulf unemployment and government policies: prospects for the Saudi labour quota or Nitaqat system', *International Journal Economics and Business Research*, Vol. X. No. Y. 2013, pp. 476-498.

Sukarieh, M. and Tannok, S., *Youth Rising: The Politics of Youth in the Global Economy*, Abingdon, Routledge, 2015.

SUSTG team, "Internet Penetration in Saudi Arabia at 93%, Daily TV Viewership Down 16%", 27 May, 2016, *Saudi-US Trade Group*. Available at: http://tinyurl.com/ych4s96j

Thompson, M., "Youth Issues and Societal Frustration" in *Saudi Arabia and the Path to Political Change: National Dialogue and Civil Society*, London, I.B. Tauris, 2014.

Thompson, M., "Saudi Youth: Challenges for the Future", *Orient IV*, 2012.

Ulrichsen, K., 'The Challenge of Transition: Gulf security in the twenty-first century', in Held, D. and Ulrichsen, K. (eds.) *The Transformation of the Gulf: Politics, economics and the global order*, Abingdon: Routledge, 2012.

Notes

1 Champion, D., *The Paradoxical Kingdom: Saudi Arabia and the Momentum for Reform*, New York, Columbia University Press, 2003, pp. 309-10.

2 King Salman's preferred son Deputy Crown Prince Mohammed bin Salman who is 31 years old has initiated a Saudi Vision 2030 (National Transformation Plan) in order to diversify the Kingdom's economy away from oil and petrochemicals. Tagged "Young prince in a hurry" by the Economist, the prince's policies are ambitious, but controversial. See: 9 January, 2016, *The Economist*. Available at: http://tinyurl.com/hdvzoux

3 These issues were discussed at a Chatham House workshop where the author was a participant. See, www.chathamhouse.org/sites/files/chathamhouse/events/110416-GCC-Social-Contract-Workshop-Summary.pdf/ www.chathamhouse.org/event/social-contract-in-gcc www.chathamhouse.org/about/structure/mena-programme/future-trends-gcc-project

4 Ibid., p. 2.

5 Hertog, S. 'Segmented Clientelism: The Political Economy of Saudi Economic Reform Efforts', in P. Aarts and G. Nonneman (eds), *Saudi Arabia in the Balance: Political Economy, Society, Foreign Affairs*, London, C. Hurst and Co., 2005, p. 111.

6 In order to counter this problem, the two online surveys conducted for this paper both provide an explanation of the term 'social contract'. English: A Social Contract is an implicit/understood agreement between citizens and the government whereby the citizens are provided with services and benefits by the government in return for citizens fulfilling their civic duties that contribute to the nation. Arabic: العقد الإجتماعي هو اتفاق ضمنيّ بين المواطن والحكومة بحيث يتلقى المواطن الخدمات والفوائد مقابل أدائه لواجباته المدنية التي تساهم في إعمار الوطن

7 Interview with Dr. Abdulrahman Al Lily, al-Khobar, April 2016.

8 Belbagi, Z., "Renegotiating the Social Contract in the GCC: Lessons from the Rousseau Playbook", in Labour Markets Dynamics in the GCC States, Etheridge, J. (ed.) *Gulf Affairs*, Autumn 2015, p. 3.

9 The completed project will be published by Cambridge University Press as a book titled *Being Young, Male and Saudi: Identity and Politics in a Globalized Kingdom.* My current interest in this area stems from my work at KFUPM, where I am immersed in discussion of these issues as I engage daily with young Saudi men from all parts of the Kingdom and all walks of life. Furthermore, my experience is not limited to my current employment at KFUPM as since early 2001 I have also worked with young Saudis at other institutions in various parts of the Kingdom such as Prince Sultan University and the Saudi Arabian National Guard.

10 One written survey and one multi-choice survey:العقود الإجتماعية في المملكة العربية السعودية

11 KFUPM is the highest ranked university in the Arab world (QS 2016: 189) with an enrolment of approximately 10,000 students.

12 See: www.chathamhouse.org/event/social-contract-in-gcc; www.chathamhouse.org/about/structure/mena-programme/future-trends-gcc-project

13 For more detailed information, see, "Youth Issues and Societal Frustration" in Thompson, M., *Saudi Arabia and the Path to Political Change: National Dialogue and Civil Society*, London, I.B. Tauris, 2014; Thompson, M., "Saudi Youth: Challenges for the Future", *Orient IV*, 2012.

14 The population is divided among different age groups. The 0-14 age group contains the median amount of the population, comprising 32.4 per cent of the total. The middle age group of 15-64 makes up the greatest share of the total population, about 64.8 per cent. The 65+ age group comprises 2.8 per cent of the total population. See: http://worldpopulationreview.com/countries/saudi-arabia-population/

15 Online survey "التحول الإجتماعي و الرأي العام"

16 Nevertheless, some individuals state that the situation is difficult to assess because, in reality, social media usage conceals people's real opinions about societal transformation.

17 Al Sahwa Al Islamiyya (Islamic Awakening) is a faction of Saudi Salafism and has been involved in peaceful political reform. Dr. Salman Alodah is its best-known advocate. Dr. Alodah is very active on social media and has earned some support amongst more educated youth (including KFUPM students). On Twitter, see, @Salman_Al_Odah. See also, Lacroix, S., *Awakening Islam: The Politics of Religious Dissent in Contemporary Saudi Arabia*, Harvard University Press, 2011.

18 Ibid.

19 Ibid.

20 In 2014, when graduates were asked about the future nearly 60 per cent said that in the future, life in Saudi Arabia would probably be much more difficult than today, whilst simultaneously over 50 per cent of respondents were optimistic about their own individual futures. However, in 2016 that optimism is fading.

21 Online survey "التحول الإجتماعي و الرأي العام" (Societal Transformation and Public Opinion) with 530 respondents

22 Sukarich, M. and Tannok, S., *Youth Rising: The Politics of Youth in the Global Economy*, Abingdon, Routledge, 2015, p. 104.

23 Murphy, C., "Will the house of Saud adapt enough to survive ... again?" 9 February, 2011, *The Star*. Available at: http://tinyurl.com/yd2str3p

24 Ibid.

25 Ibid.

26 Atwood, E., "Twitter usage rockets in conservative Saudi Arabia", 5 January, 2011, *Arabian Business*. Available at: http://tinyurl.com/2e4e2p2

27 Muhammad, F., "Twitter usage in KSA grows '10 times' the world average", 6 January, 2013, *Saudi Gazette*. Available at: http://tinyurl.com/acu5z7y

28 See: The State of Social Media in Saudi Arabia, Vol. 3, 23 September, 2016, *The Social Clinic*. Available at: www.thesocialclinic.com/the-state-of-social-media-in-saudi-arabia-vol-3/

29 Online survey "تأثير الشبكات الإجتماعية على خصوصية المجتمع السعودي" (Privacy and Social Media Usage in Saudi Arabia) with 3630 respondents

30 7th written survey response

31 Kinninmont, J., "To What Extent Is Twitter Changing Gulf Societies?" February 2013, *Chatham House*. Available at: www.chathamhouse.org/publications/papers/view/189413

32 Online survey "مسح وسائل الاعلام الاجتماعية السعودي" (Saudi Social Media Survey) with 238 respondents.

33 Interview with Saudi engineer

34 9th written survey response

35 16th written survey response

36 According to some respondents "Saudis are able to influence and/or demonstrate their political opinions to the king via hashtags on Twitter when they wish to see senior officials removed from the government".

37 14th written survey response

38 However, other respondents say that even though the public is asking for reform, everything has changed because state-society commination channels have been cut. This is considered to be extremely problematic particularly if the voice of the ordinary citizen cannot reach the authorities in a "peaceful" way.

39 7th written survey response

40 Hildebrandt, J. et al, "What Matters Most to Saudi Arabia's Youth? Helping Policy Makers Address the National Challenges", June 2014, *The Boston Consulting Group*. pp. 5–6. Available at: www.bcglondon.com/expertise_impact/Industries/Public_Sector/PublicationDetails.aspx?id=tcm:86-

41 19th written survey response

42 Online survey: العقود الإجتماعية في المملكة العربية السعودية

43 24th written survey response

44 10th written survey response

45 Ibid.

46 6th written survey response

47 12th written survey response

48 10th written survey response

49 Electrical engineering graduate

50 16th written survey response

51 See for example, "Water tariff to rise 50% next month", 02 November, 2015, *Arab News*. Available at: http://www.arabnews.com/saudi-arabia/news/829286

52 Ibid.

53 See: footnote 4.

54 Online survey: العقود الإجتماعية في المملكة العربية السعودية

55 7th written survey response

56 21st written survey response

57 22nd written survey response

58 20th written survey response

59 24th written survey response

60 3rd written survey response

61 15th written survey response

62 8th written survey response
63 Ibid.
64 5th written survey response
65 22nd written survey response
66 10th written survey response
67 1st written survey response
68 19th written survey response
69 20th written survey response
70 Focus group, Eastern Province
71 Ibid.
72 14th written survey response
73 13th written survey response
74 For an explanation of regional and sectarian divisions in Saudi Arabia, see, Al Shihabi, A., *The Saudi Kingdom: Between the Jihadi Hammer and the Iranian Anvil*, Princeton, Markus Wiener Publishers, 2016, pp. 90-91.
75 Nowadays, Shia Qatif is a suburb of Dammam
76 This paper targets one particular demographic, however a comprehension of how expatriates in the Kingdom understand their contract with the government and/or authorities is also of critical importance.
77 25th written survey response
78 22nd written survey response: "In addition, there is more freedom and transparency in expressing opinions".
79 20th written survey response
80 Ibid.
81 10th written survey response
82 9th written survey response
83 12th written survey response
84 13th written survey response
85 19th written survey response
86 21st written survey response
87 18th written survey response
88 16th written survey response
89 Ramady, M., 'Gulf unemployment and government policies: prospects for the Saudi labour quota or Nitaqat system', *International Journal Economics and Business Research*, Vol. X. No. Y. 2013, pp. 476-498.
90 KFUPM: GS 447 Globalization course, student project, 2015
91 Ibid.
92 Focus group, Eastern Province.
93 Ibid. Even the number of available work internships is being affected.
94 Ibid.
95 Ibid.
96 Ibid: "Everyone is talking about the current economic and political situation. In fact, even kids talk about political issues such as the oil price and Syria these days".
97 Ibid.
98 Older Saudis who lived through the second Gulf war have already experienced this and so are not as worried as the younger generation.
99 Focus group, Eastern Province.
100 Ibid.
101 Ibid: "Al Inma Bank actually calls all graduating senior KFUPM students offering them loans (but at 10% interest)".
102 Almaeena, K., "No Turning Back", in *Trends: The international Magazine on Arab Affairs*, No. 210, February, 2016, pp. 21-22.
103 Ibid.

104 In Saudi Arabia it is often the case that highly publicized government initiatives and/or projects go unnoticed by large part of the population. The question is why the government's and/or institution's message fails to connect with the general public.

105 Focus group, Eastern Province.

106 12th written survey response

107 9th written survey response

108 24th written survey response

109 SUSTG team, "Internet Penetration in Saudi Arabia at 93%, Daily TV Viewership Down 16%", 27 May, 2016, *Saudi-US Trade Group*. Available at: http://sustg.com/internet-penetration-in-saudi-arabia-at-93-daily-tv-viewership-down-16/

110 23rd written survey response

111 Ibid.

112 19th written survey response

113 7th written survey response

114 18th written survey response: "it a high risk since it is a transformation plan".

115 25th written survey response

116 22nd written survey response

117 8th written survey response

118 10th written survey response

119 13th written survey response

120 Focus group, Eastern Province

121 25th written survey response: "Frankly, the deputy crown prince had no other choice as the water bills fiasco coincided with the launch of his Vision 2030"

122 Al Qassemi writes that "Taxation in exchange for ensuring the security of citizens in an increasingly dangerous neighborhood might be the new accepted social contract, but Gulf states should tread carefully nonetheless. While security remains the foremost shared interest for both citizen and ruler today, there is no certainty that demands and expectations of Gulf citizens will not change in the future". See, Al Qassemi, S., "The Gulf's New Social Contract", 8 February, 2016, *Middle East Institute*. Available at: www.mei.edu/content/article/gulfs-new-social-contract

123 Interview with Saudi political-economist in Jeddah

124 See, for example, Calabro, P., "Saudi Arabia's post-oil plan enters slippery slope", 27 May, 2016, *Al-Monitor*. Available at: http://tinyurl.com/ydhkldcv

125 Interview with Saudi academic and think-tank director

126 However, Prince Mohammed bin Salman declared ""Seventy per cent of Saudis are under age 30, and their perspective is different from the other 30 per cent. I am working to create for them the country they want to be living in in the future." See, Friedman, T., "Letter from Saudi Arabia", *New York Times*, 25 November, 2015. Available at: http://tinyurl.com/ydc8tonz

127 26th written survey response

128 Interview with Saudi political-economist in Riyadh

129 Ibid: "Do not forget that what we read on social media is only the tip of the iceberg. Plenty of other things are being discussed Kingdom wide at the personal level".

130 10th written survey response

131 Ramady, M., 'Gulf unemployment and government policies: prospects for the Saudi labour quota or Nitaqat system', *International Journal Economics and Business Research*, Vol. X. No. Y. 2013, p. 3.

132 Ulrichsen, K., 'The Challenge of Transition: Gulf security in the twenty-first century', in Held, D. and Ulrichsen, K. (eds.) *The Transformation of the Gulf: Politics, economics and the global order*, Abingdon: Routledge, 2012, p. 283.

133 Jones, D. and Punshi, R., *Unlocking the Paradox of Plenty: A Review of the Talent Landscape in the Arab World and Your Role in Shaping the Future*, Dubai: Motivate Publishing, 2013, p. 19.

3

Omanisation, Youth Employment and SME Firms in Oman

Iram Ansari and Jacqueline McGlade

Introduction

As reported by Oman's National Centre for Information and Statistics (NCIS) as of 2014-2015, only 14% of Omanis worked in private companies compared to a rate of 84.5% in government employment. In a NCIS April 2016 study, "The Youth in Lines," numbers in the 15-29 age group – the prime group for first time and/or professional workers, now constitute 30% of the total Omani population. With young males outpacing females at 51% to 49%, the total Omani population as of spring 2016 sat at 2.4 million representing a 3.73% increase largely due to the expanding youth group (NCIS, March 2016). However, the employment prospects for young Omanis, especially males, in both the government as well as private job sectors, remains a troubling one.

In a 2014 report on the Omani labor market, Crystal A. Ennis and Ra'id Z. al-Jamali also note that based a 3.9 per cent annual population growth rate, Oman had climbed into the top five countries globally in terms of population increase by 2012 (Ennis and al-Jamali, Chatham House, 2014). Along with sizable annual indigenous population growth, expat levels also rose at the astonishing rate of 17.7 percent in 2012 alone, placing Oman at the top of the World Bank's ranking of imported labor markets. The drive for oil extraction and exports, which climbed since 2000 to 80% of Oman's GDP, certainly facilitated a rapid expansion of corporate-based job. However, foreign workers occupy almost 60% of such employment vs. only a third of Omanis. Also, Omani unemployment rates overall has persisted at around 15 per cent with youth unemployment at above 30 per cent (Buckley, Graeme and Rynhart, Gary, 2011). As a result, the negative nature of the Omani indigenous labor market demonstrates that "the livelihood of a majority of nationals is intricately tied to the state, notwithstanding the welfare benefits that extend to the total national population" (Ennis and al-Jamali, Chatham House, 2014).

This evidence also counters the assertion by Steffan Hertog in his 2012 work, "A Comparative assessment of labor market nationalization policies in the GCC" that Oman's "use of market-based incentives make national employment more attractive," when compared with its GCC neighbors (Hertog, 2012). However, the NCIS 2015-2016 figures reveal that the large imbalance between public and private employment opportunity has not significantly been reduced despite such policies and efforts by Oman's Sultanate government. At the heart of a market-base strategy sits two initiatives -100% "Omanization" of the workforce employed in the nation's private sector and deliberate diversification of Oman's corporate sector beyond oil and gas production. Presumably, these two inter-twined initiatives should favor greater opportunity and absorption of young Omanis into an expanded, innovative private business-driven economy.

As of 2016, however, this has not been the case with signs that, even the government sector especially in light of the recent world oil prices crisis, no longer rests as a "safe haven" for Omani employment. Overall, the languishing, low wage private employment base and disappearing government jobs presents a depressingly daunting landscape for Omani youth employment at all educational levels and training backgrounds. In terms of public jobs, members of the youth group from 18-29 years of age constitute only one quarter of the total workers in the Oman government sector, which encompasses almost 85% of all national employment. As the male-female ratio of young workers sat equally at 50%, males whose numbers are 2% higher than females in the same age group, suffer further disadvantages in terms of government employment. The percentage of young people working in the private sector reached about 43% only out of the total Omanis with youth unemployment rates hovering overall at 25.6% (NCIS March 2016).

In light of the continued imbalance in favor of expats over Omanis in national employment rates, especially in better-paying, higher skilled/education level jobs, the overall employment picture remains stubbornly segmented in the composition of national workers to the disadvantage of Omani youth. While the majority of expats still occupy manual/low skilled labor positions unattractive to Omani nationals, nevertheless, trends for the private employment of higher educated young Omanis remains out of balance with employer preferences for imported foreign professionals. (NCIS March 2016).

This study then probes the serious constraints involved with Omani youth employment, especially the clear preference of both Omani as well as foreign owned companies to hire and retain expats over Omani workers. This study will also examine the persistence of employment prejudice revolving around perennial employer arguments that Omanis lack the "soft" as well as hard job skills necessary for companies to function and compete. The authors will note that employers may have been justified in the 1990s through the early 2000s to make such arguments in terms of hiring practices as the Sultanate had just started the originations of national universities, colleges, and training centres (both public and private). As a result, Oman at that time lacked a "critical mass" of higher-educated/trained

Omani nationals to occupy the highly-technical and skilled jobs demanded by the country's emerging oil and gas business sector.

This is no longer the case, however, as post-secondary national graduation rates reaching into the thousands and over 250 colleges and universities operate all throughout the Sultanate's largest population areas. In examining the continued preference of imported professionals over young Omanis college graduates, the authors will explore the use on the part of Oman companies, whether owned by nationals or foreign sources, of a deliberate application of labor arbitrage strategies common to modern corporations in hiring operations worldwide. In this way, the authors consider that, unlike the past where a lack of national education and training centres constrained the preparation of an indigenous professional workforce, labor arbitrage, not an inherent deficiency in the capacity of Omani youth to master and employ useful higher-level jobs skills, may be in play here as a further justification for continued large numbers of expat hiring.

Overall then, this study seeks to provide an in-depth update on the actual landscape and future challenges facing Omani youth employment taking into account both job trends and activities in both the government and private employment sectors. As part of this study, the authors will share their efforts to begin a research study in cooperation with the Muscat Securities Market of 197 publically-listed Oman/foreign companies, which represent a small but potentially important sector for the acceleration of national employment expansion. The list constitutes the basis for an ongoing research project that a) analyzes the potential of medium-sized Oman/foreign firms for jobs growth expansion and b) provides detailed business case studies on the level of corporate modernization in line with international/regional competition standards and management imperatives.

When taken together, the two aspects of research and analysis hopefully will reveal firms positioned for market share advantages that, through development efforts, could lead to real jobs creation and employment expansion for young Omanis. As this is a long-term project, the authors for the purpose of this study, will attempt to offer preliminary analysis of this corporate group as a way to provide a clearer view of the realities of the actual and potential private employment position for young Omanis in the nation's non -oil and gas business sectors.

However, this study will also note that the viability of the private hiring landscape seems to be taking a negative turn in light of the world drop in oil prices, resulting in sizable market constrains for new employment growth and opportunities for Omani college graduates. Also, this study probes the double negative effect on the Omani youth employment picture related to the tendency of private firms, whether local or foreign owned, to employ the global corporate trend of labor arbitrage. As a general worldwide managerial strategy to hold down labor costs, labor arbitrage in the context of Oman has resulted in the corporate favoring of short-term costs and benefit commitments attached to expat hires over long-term, higher benefit commitments involved with a largely indigenous workforce. When taken together, the dual impact of a stagnating/receding corporate growth environment tied to falling oil prices plus the long-time application of labor arbitrage strategies further challenges the success, let alone the future feasibility, of Omanisation and other forms of government policy pressures to convert the national private employment base away from expat in favor of indigenous professionals and workers.

Rising Omani Youth Unemployment despite Omanization and Higher Educational Attainment

Since its inception by Royal Decree 95/97 in 1988, the Omanization program has been intended to replace foreign workers and expatriates with trained Omani citizens. While the number of Omanis in government services exceeded the set target of 72% by 1999, Omanisation has lagged far behind in private business with current workforce composition rates at 47.4 per cent Omani against 52.6 per cent expatriates (Muscat Daily, April 8, 2015). While targets were also set for six industries: transport, storage and communications at 60%, finance; insurance and real estate at 45%; industry at 35%; hotels and restaurants at 30%; wholesale or retail trading at 20% and contracting at 15%, only Omani established and Islamic banks have reached such sectoral targets (OmanInfo.com). A mismatch between Omani youth educational skills training and development in line with employer expectations and needs, often emanating from foreign-managed companies has been targeted as a central problem in the achievement of Omanization labor policies and goals.

With unemployment reaching a peak in April 2015 at 11.75%, the youth un/under employment picture despite Omanization policies remains troubling, especially in light of Oman levels sitting among the highest in the GCC region. As reported by the National Centre for Statistics and Information (NCSI), overall unemployment rates in age categories rest at young adults (15-29) year-old at 30 per cent with 60 per cent between 15 and 64 in age. However, when broken further by age ranges and education, Omani job seekers in the 25-34 in age range have increased year on year since 2010 with the largest rise among those with postsecondary education rising to 58.9 per cent (Times of Oman, February 9, 2016). This rise of the highly educated un/under employed young Omanis poses new disturbing trends that seem to match trends across the MENA region.

In a 2010 report, the World Bank noted that higher education in the MENA region had increased by 20 to 30 percent from 2000 to 2008, with women comprising 62 percent of total college enrollments in GCC countries. Oman currently sits below this high average for female college students though just-released 2014-2015 admission figures by the Ministry of Higher Education placed women students at 57.7 per cent vs. men at 42.4 per cent out of 131,760 enrollees (Muscat Daily, May 18, 2016, p. 5). Nevertheless, the overall rising female and falling male higher education numbers pose new challenges for Oman as well as many countries in the MENA region in terms of traditional gender separation and family employment roles. Again, the 2010 World Bank report underscores the socio-cultural shifts looming connected to gender and work roles, especially in traditional Muslim societies, as gross higher education enrollment rates climb from 25.8 percent in 2010 to an expected 40 percent by 2030 based on the regional expansion of secondary education capabilities and current MENA population trends. The rising condition of unemployment among higher educated MENA youth also matches Oman's experience with the World Bank reporting that 2010 MENA youth unemployment rates, with the Middle East at 21% and North Africa at 25%, sat as the highest of any world region and that college graduates comprised "nearly 30 percent of unemployed in MENA" (World Bank, 2010).

While the International Labor Organization (ILO) reported in October 2015 that global youth unemployment rate had "stabilized at 13 per cent" after a rise from 11.7% in 2007 to over 20% by 2010, the Middle East and North Africa still sat with the highest youth unemployment rates at 28.2 and 30.5 per cent, respectively. The ILO also noted that, despite an overall decrease of 1.4% since its peak in 2009 of youth unemployment in Developed Countries, Developing Countries, especially in the MENA region, experienced increases in the youth unemployment rate between 2012 and 2014. As part of its new "school-to-work transition surveys (SWTS)" project, the ILO further noted that the transition period "attain a stable job" for most work-age youth (18-24 years of age) sat at an average of 19 months, with college graduates holding a edge at "one-third of the time needed for a youth with primary education." While Oman's higher education graduate job attainment profile belies the ILO SWTS data that "in most cases the transition takes longer for young women than men," the Omani college graduates mirror overall the overall ILO findings that, "more young people in developed economies are now finding work but the quality of jobs is below their expectations. And still too many remain stuck in long-term unemployment." (ILO Youth Report, Oct 8 2015).

The New Unemployment Challenge: Under/Un-employed Higher Education Graduates

This rise of the highly educated under as well as un employed youth across the MENA region clearly reflects the experience of Omanis college graduates. Imbedded in these trends (which match the overall world experience of college educated youth in Developed Countries though at much higher rates) are disturbing trends that call into serious question the ultimate effectiveness of Omanization as well as higher education expansion as dual remedies pushed by the government to indigenize Oman's employment environment. The rise of a new sector of (potentially long-term) highly educated un/under employed young Omanis carry many disturbing challenges to traditional forms of Oman socio-cultural stability. Beyond general disappointment/dissatisfaction related to after-graduation job expectations, a prolonged under/unemployment struggle by Omani college graduates also damages their expectation of improved livelihoods as many have already come from or justifiably aspire to the attainment of middle and upper class living standards.

Such negative attitudinal responses are readily becoming apparent in the job seeking activities and efforts of the Omani higher educated youth sector. While college graduates only composed 9.3 per cent of all job seekers in 2015, a February 9, 2016 survey by the NCSI revealed that Omani college graduates now wait on average 3.5 years to find a job that matches their educational training and professional interests (NCIS, March 2016). In large part, this lag has been attributed to the long-held expectation and hold-out rates for Omani college graduates to enter public service jobs over employment in private enterprises. This sense of entitlement of a publically-funded job, in line with the experience of their families since the ascension of the Sultanate, now seems an elusive, if not unrealistic goal for many young Omanis in light of Oman's current revenue crisis.

This negative public sector job environment, however, is particularly pronounced when applied to Omani college graduates, who while seemingly well-academically prepared, also struggle to displace expat competitors in the Oman private labor markets. In order to dig deeper into college graduate unemployment picture, the Ministry of Higher Education, conducted a new survey in fall 2015, which attempted to match the employment status of graduates with work qualifications and skills as outlined by employers' hiring expectations and job needs. The survey involved 12,551 graduates of public and private higher education institutions and graduates of external scholarships for the years of 2009/2010 and 2012/2013. The results were profoundly disappointing, with only 47.7% of participants reporting active employment (Ministry of Higher Education, 2015 Graduates Survey).

Among the factors examined, the employed graduates' time duration to first job emerged, according to the NCIS, as important "indication of the extent to which the labor market needs certain graduates in specific specializations." While nearly half of the employed graduates received their first job opportunity in the first six months out of completing their degrees, the average time to securing a first job was 4 to 6 months. In a further breakdown, 32.1% of employed graduates were hired during the first three months after graduation, with 18.9% hired between 4 to 6 months, and 26.1% of the graduates waiting over a year to get job in their field of study. Hiring duration, however, shortened for graduates in 2012-2013 when compared with their peers who graduated in 2009/2010. 54.2% of 2012-2013 graduates secured their first job in the first six months after graduation compared to 47.2% of 2009-2010 graduates. Also, graduate numbers waiting more than a year also dropped from 33.8 % in 2009-2010 graduates to 19.6 % for 2012-2013 graduates. Among both graduate pools, the graduates who experienced the shortest employment time of three months or less rested in the fields of Health Studies, Education, then Engineering respectively and graduates in the fields of Creative Arts and Religion and Philosophy took as long as 10-12 months to secure a job (Ministry of Higher Education 2015 Graduates Survey).

While a potential mismatch of Omani graduates' degree choices with real labor market demands may underpin the unemployment of Oman's higher educated youth, traditional socio-cultural dynamics are also imposing countervailing effects. According to the fall 2015 NCIS survey, 16.5 % of the total number of unemployed graduates have rejected a job offer with males demonstrating a slightly higher percentage of refusals at 17.5% to females at 16.4 %. Gender differences for refusing work also emerged among single and married men and women. Married female graduates tended to reject more job offers than single female graduates did but men rejected jobs regardless of marital status. Male graduates' reasons for rejecting jobs also differed from female graduates with "unsuitable salary" topping male reasons while "unsuitable field of specialization" was cited by females (Ministry of Higher Education 2015 Graduates Survey). In remaining unemployed longer, Omani male higher education graduates risk then occupying later (and in some cases at all) the important social status as the central "bread winner" in his family with females moving increasingly, even if underemployed, into this primary role.

While the NCIS study then reflects the World Bank and ILO conclusions that MENA, and by extension, Oman higher education graduates sit out longer in attaining postgraduate jobs and are generally under-employed in relation to their academic training and salary needs when hired. While Oman also reflects generally the GCC/MENA problem of lower male employment rates, it also provides a contrasting picture of MENA female un/under employment with Omani women increasingly achieving gender parity (or beyond) in overall graduation rates, higher-salaried employment opportunities and managerial job status. In the female lower employment portrait offered by labor economist Paole Verme, women in the MENA region tend to leave the workforce by 25 due to marriage, pregnancy and/or family care obligations. He also notes a lagging of services-based over manufacturing jobs, the former which tends to favor and absorb greater female employment (Verme, 2015, p. 19 and International Monetary Fund, 2013, p. 7). However, it must be noted that beyond higher college enrollments, Omani women may be gaining on men in labor markets, not solely based on educational training and job hiring parity, but due to an overall decline in male employment participation rates at home and across the MENA region.

Oman and Global Labor Arbitrage

Based on growing numbers of college graduates, presumably the older justification of employers for hiring expats, especially in well-paying jobs in Oman and other MENA due to a lack of available, scalable numbers of higher education trained nationals should be receding. Such upward educational trends should result in more Omanis advancing into positions of higher pay and managerial responsibility but recent NCIS data shows the continued stubborn preference for the hiring of foreign over indigenous professionals. While Oman's Minister of Manpower set a target in 2013 to reduce expat worker numbers in the private sector to 33 percent by 2015, as of April 2016 the expat ratio still sat to at 38 percent of the total national population (NCIS, April 2016; Times of Oman, April 20, 2016).

Beyond the fact that over three-quarters of Oman's expat workers occupy undesirable low paying, manual labor jobs, Middle East scholar Crystal A. Ennis cites the fact that private job creation remains constrained to "the largest Omani enterprises, comprising

10 per cent of the total, that are responsible for hiring almost 80 per cent of wage-earning nationals in the private sector." She also notes that while Oman's "largest companies contribute most to national employment" the "least capitalized ones ... hire the highest percentage of expatriates. According to Ennis, often expat hiring preferences emanate, not only from multinational/foreign-owned firms, but also from "large family enterprises" which "wish to be seen as contributing to national employment and economic goals," but nevertheless "benefit more from access to competitive foreign labour and large state contracts, and therefore have a vested interest in preserving the status quo" in expat hiring conditions (Ennis, 2013).

In this way, foreign and indigenous companies alike in Oman reflect the increasingly global presence and application of labor arbitrage strategies at all employee experience and education levels in corporate management. Since the 2008 Recession, subsequent waves of corporate downsizing and government spending cutbacks have generated grave public concerns and protests over the instability and declining position of employment markets and worker wage levels worldwide. According to the International Trade Union Organization Confederation (ITUC), the dramatic fragility of stable employment for workers has occurred due, in part to the "Americanization" of world labor relations – a model in workplace labor conditions and standards are "strongly tilted in favour of capital" posing "an extremely hostile environment" for independent worker organizational activities not driven by managerial prerogatives. (ITUC, April 2013).

As an illustration of growing managerial preference for labor arbitrage, noted economists Matthew Slaughter and Laura Tyson studied global dispersion of the jobs market relative to U.S. multinational companies since the early 2000s. According to Slaughter and Tyson, domestic employment in U.S. multinational firms, which experienced a 2 to 1 rise over the employment of foreign nationals from 1991-2005, has now reversed with a almost 2% loss in the hiring numbers American employees over overseas employees. (Slaughter (2004); Slaughter and Tyson, 2013). While workforce management strategies aimed containing costs has always been present in companies, global labor arbitrage or the replacement of homeworkers for equally qualified workers at the lowest wage population globally, has indeed accelerated in practice, especially in large and multinational firms.

Furthermore, the ITUC contends that the shift toward American-style managerial prerogatives over recognition of a universal set of labor rights, standards and protections has now been fully globalized in foreign as well as U.S. firms as "the asymmetry in power between capital and labour has been magnified in recent decades by open economies, financial market deregulation, tax competition, the erosion of the State and the growth of the service sector" (ITUC, April 2013). As part of the ITUC's 2013 Frontlines report, economist Joseph Stiglitz also echoed the ITUC's concern that "Globalisation, and the unbalanced way it has been pursued, has shifted bargaining power away from workers: firms can threaten to move elsewhere, especially when tax laws treat such overseas investments so favourably" (ITUC April 2013). As described by labor economists Raúl Delgado Wise and David Martin, labor arbitrage also remains an essential part of the general corporate "shift towards global production chains" which accounts for close to 60% of [the] total assets and employment" of the world's top 100 companies. According to Wise and Marin, the globalization of labor arbitrage tied to tighter supply chains has led to a new labor "nomadism" with locational decisions determined largely by where labor is cheapest" (Wise and Martin, 2015).

Labor and Business economists are increasingly pointing then to the accelerating ascendency of corporate aims as embodied by labor arbitrage as an unassailable assault on the protection of worker rights and collective employment standards.

Along with the decline of labor bargaining power, economists also point to a growing lack of resolve on the part of governments to reverse these alarming trends related to worsening position of workers. In some cases, this signals a historic shift in governmental alliances, especially in developed countries, away from workers towards companies as occurring in Germany, previously committed to strong, mediated corporate-labor partnerships and collaborative planning as the basis for national economic organization and progress (European Industrial Relations Observatory (EIRO), 2009).

In many ways, the case of Oman illustrates both trends in globalized labor arbitrage in which government first encouraged liberal private hiring practices to accelerate job growth but resulted in a grave imbalance of expat over indigenous workers (Beblawi, H., 1987). Now at the point in which the Oman government needs to re-orient its rentier relationship with private firms in favor of more costly indigenous over lower cost expat employment, eroding economic conditions are rapidly driving greater dependencies in favor of managerial over government labor controls.

Also, Oman's long-standing expat over indigenous labor hires constitutes a form of worker "nomadism" in the extremist form where government policy enabled, if not encouraged, Omani locally-owned as well as foreign firms to engage in labor arbitrage practices. While this show of labor arbitrage is most noticeable at the lowest wage, manual jobs level, it also has gone on for decades in the most highly educated, higher paid senior ranks of employment. Driven mainly by Oman's need to import foreign "knowledge workers" due to the lack of indigenous college graduates to meet job demands, the entrenchment of expat employment dependencies are particularly profound in the natural resources extractive and processing industries, university teaching, healthcare, advanced manufacturing, and information technology sectors. The issue to date then is whether the Oman government can quickly reverse and re-balance the labor arbitrage situation related to excessive knowledge worker importation in favor of indigenous college graduates fast enough and in large enough job opportunities numbers to staunch the negative flow of un/underemployed higher education Omani youth.

Re-Aligning Omanization with Knowledge Worker Segments

On May 18, 2016, Oman's Majlis Shura issued a report that expanded the Omanization targets to cover "senior posts" in corporate managerial ranks. Citing Ministry of Manpower figures that only 21 percent of Omanis hold managerial or "decision-making positions" in private companies vs. 79 percent expats, the Shura called upon firms to show a five percent increase in Omani managerial hires each year to reach a forty percent threshold by 2020. As the Shura's Head of the Youth and Human Resource Committee, Mohammad bin Salim Al Busaidi insisted that annual corporate hiring and training plans submitted each year for government approval demonstrate the five percent increase as "in the next two years most of the Omanis will be graduating ... from universities and colleges...and every year there are about 44,000 Omani job seekers" (Times of Oman, May 18, 2016).

Such upward educational trends should result in more Omanis advancing into positions of higher pay and managerial responsibility but recent NCIS data shows the continued stubborn preference for the hiring of foreign over indigenous managerial professionals. In the April 2016 hiring bulletin, the NCIS reported "a marginal rise" of 0.2 percent in Omanis employed in the private sector at 210,074 with women only constituting less than a quarter of the total workers. Wage figures though showed an even gloomier picture for Omani workers with 62,577 out of 210,074 earning only 325-400 OMR per month – equivalent to 577.676 -710.981 GBP or 844.156 -1,038.96 USD (May 24, 2016 retrieved at: http://www.xe.com/currencyconverter). In the 400-500 OMR segment, Omanis though experienced the highest rise in numbers at 1.4 percent or 48,767 with the 900-1000 OMR and over 2000 OMR segments reaching 0.7 (5,422) and 0.6 percent (7, 812) increases respectively (Muscat Daily. May 22, 2016). With the majority of Omanis entering the private workforce at OMR wage levels comparable to minimum wage levels in the United Kingdom and the United States, 62% of Omani professionals surveyed by Bayt.com in 2016 stated that their salaries were not covering rises in living costs (54 percent in rent, 64 percent in food, and 58 percent in utilities) stimulated by price rises, the ending of government subsidies and general inflationary pressures (Muscat Daily. May 18, 2016.).

On May 18, 2016, Oman's Majlis Shura issued a report that expanded the Omanization targets to cover "senior posts" in corporate managerial ranks. Citing Ministry of Manpower figures that only 21 percent of Omanis hold managerial or "decision-making positions" in private companies vs. 79 percent expats, the Shura called upon firms to show a five percent increase in Omani managerial hires each year to reach a forty percent threshold by 2020. As the Shura's Head of the Youth and Human Resource Committee, Mohammad bin Salim Al Busaidi insisted that annual corporate hiring and training plans submitted each year for government approval demonstrate the five percent increase as "in the next two years most of the Omanis will be graduating ... from universities and colleges...and every year there are about 44,000 Omani job seekers" (Times of Oman. May 18, 2016).

Beyond the primary urgency of employing Omanis, especially in the young college graduate segment, several other economic pressures will continue to drive more draconian government policies aimed at reversing expat hires. As reported in the 2016 World Bank Migration and Remittances fact book, Oman sits fourth among world countries in terms of the highest rates for expat salary remittances at 12.6% of GDP (Times of Oman. May 12, 2016). At 27 billion in expat wage outflows, reversing remittance presents a large challenge as well as opportunity for the government in light of the dramatic loss of oil revenues. While remittance outflow in the past was "good for the country" in repressing local inflation, Omani officials, now recognized the necessity to capture the local buying and investing power of expat wages into national GDP goods and services percentage formulations to compensate for and re-balance corresponding deficits in oil-related revenues and business generation. As remittance outflows countermeasures, some Majlis Al Shura representatives have started to encourage the State Council to liberalize and relax expat labor laws in order to encourage greater residential benefits such as buying real estate, saving and investing locally, allowing full family visas, etc. (Times of Oman, May 12, 2016).

However, a shift in government policy towards greater visa/residency liberalization for expat workers to encourage a reverse flow internally of remittances runs counter to the equally urgent need to replace foreign labor with Omanis. At this point, expanding jobs creation through hyper-acceleration of the growth and diversification of private business in Oman poses the most viable strategy for the Oman government to balance any continuing needs for expat labor while significantly alleviating indigenous youth unemployment conditions. Also, the remittance GDP outflows problem should be alleviated by higher paid Omanis gaining private employment, who would spend more at home per capita than typically a low-paid migrant expat worker whose salary is constrained to purchasing power parity at a subsistence, not aspirational living standards level.

Oman SMEs: Current and Comparative Contexts

Worrying youth employment figures then, especially related to higher educated Omanis, have shaped recent government debates and initiates in the areas of jobs creation, manpower capacities, educational training, and business development. By 2009, there were more than 100,000 registered job-seekers that led to the 2011 unemployment protests posing the greatest socio-political crisis that Oman had faced since the dynastic change in the 1970s (Chatham House 2014). The 2011 crisis, along with growing number of unemployed higher education graduates, has pushed government efforts, particularly since 2013, in the direction of accelerating the growth of the small and medium size enterprise (SME) sector.

In the past few months, the Sultanate's focus on SME development tied to youth-centered entrepreneurship and employment has further intensified in light of current negative national revenue/budget situations that will limit public service jobs creation, if not retention, in the long as well as short-term. Reflecting an intensified drive to boost private over public jobs creation, Khalifa Al Abri, chief executive officer of the Public Authority for SME Development announced on January 26, 2016, new classification levels for micro, small and medium enterprises intended to broaden the scope and opportunities for SME growth and private financing in Oman. (Times of Oman, January 25, 2016). This action is part of a long term strategy first set in 1996 by the Sultanate to intensify SME development to boost private business ownership and local jobs creation. (OmanInfo.com).

While strong government promotional efforts are evident, particularly since 2008, current data on the composition, growth rate, and overall state of Oman's SME sector remains sketchy. Based on statistics offered by HSBC in the Oman Economic Review 2008, 15,000-20,000 SMEs were operating in Oman but employed less than 20% of the national workforce. (R. Ashrafi and M. Murtaza, 2011, p. 359). A 2012 study by P. Brinda Kalyani and L. Al Yahyaee pegged the number of "active enterprises" in Oman at 118,386 in 2009, of which "117,914 enterprises were SMEs" accounting for "more than 95% of the economic activity" (Kalyani and Al Yahyaee, pp. 163-170). In a July 27, 2015 online Oman Economic Review (OER) article, "All Round Effort," reported that "around 121,000 SMEs constituting more than 90 per cent of the economic activity and around 20 per cent of the country's gross domestic product (GDP)" in Oman. In terms of size and employment base, the OER also noted, however, that "a vast majority" of Oman's SMEs "are micro enterprises employing five or less persons" (Oman Economic Review, July 27, 2015).

In the past few months in 2016, the Ministries of Commerce and Industry (MOIC) and of Manpower (MOM), along with the Public Authority for SMR Development (Riyada), have announced more initiatives to drive SME growth. Along with offering preferential rates for telecom and IT services, the Riyada has coordinated with MOIC and MOM agencies to organize job fairs for Omanis aimed at private job markets, by abolishing previous high levels of capitalization needed to start firms in Oman, and launching a new online "Cloud Smart Learning" platform intended to deliver low-cost certifications and vocational training modules aligned with growing business and job markets for young Omani entrepreneurs and job seekers (Times of Oman, May 23, 2016).

Comparatively then, Oman reflect overall trends in terms of SME composition and governmental development efforts in the GCC region, which according to the World Bank International Finance Corporation (IFC) 2015 figures, sits at 60% micro firms followed by 28% of small firms and 12% medium-size firms. At 20-25%, Oman's portion of SME in the overall composition of and contribution to national business is line with the overall GCC SME sector average of 22% and 90% of all firms registered. However, Oman's SME sector is dominated by micro firms (5 employees or less) at 90% and Oman SMEs overall employ only 20% of the national workforce vs. the GCC average of 40%. (Mahate, 2015; Blossom, Neelufer, and Al Said, 2014.)

When compared with U.S. and European SME rates of 55-70% in terms of business composition, GDP contributions, and 80-90% workforce participation, Oman lags far behind both GCC and world SME performance benchmarks (Saleem, 2012; Hertog, 2012; Amico,

2004). In general, international economic agencies including the International Finance Corporation of the World Bank, the International Monetary Fund, and the Organization of European Economic Development (OECD) have all targeted then SME development, especially in the GCC and MENA regions, as essential platforms for economic growth, business diversification, and employment expansion beyond the structural confines of oil-driven national business and wealth creation arrangements.

Important Growth Drivers-Oman Medium-Size Firms

However, can SME development realistically and quickly reverse the Omani unemployment crisis, which youth constitute 30% many of whom are higher educated graduates? As outlined by predominant Oman political commentator Saleh Shaibany, 2015 already stands as "the worst year for job creation in recent times" in which "the private sector created only 9,500 new jobs, compared to more than 33,000 registered job seekers" – a marked contrast to 2014 in which "over 14,000 new jobs were created for the unemployed pool of about 42,000." Shaibany also warns that 2016 may top the dismal 2015 rates as "currently, more than 55,000 are unemployed and the figure is set to rise by more than 20 per cent when new graduates are awarded their certificates this summer" (Shaibany, 2016).

Just as disturbing are Shaibany's figures in relation to new business development in Oman, which fell in terms of total numbers by 28% from 2011 to 2015 with less than 300 new businesses started each year. As Shaibany asserts, "new businesses, depending on the size, create an average 34 positions each within 12 months of their establishment," so "2,000 new businesses [need to be]are created every year ....[to] absorb a significant number of new job seekers." He also warns that business development needs to rapidly go beyond Muscat where 80% of all new jobs enter the national employment pool each year. "If the policy is to pull young people out from the streets, the number of new businesses needs to rise, not plunge south" and the creation of new businesses needs to happen "in different cities and towns [which] would help youngsters find employment in their own home towns" (Shaibany, May 21, 2016).

Despite Oman governmental enthusiastic support for jobs creation tied to SME development, the current position of SMEs as potential drivers of greater Omani youth employment are not known. Certainly Shaibany's figures point to a reversal, not an acceleration of SME or any other real gains in terms of private business growth. While still under-developed, Oman's SME sector, however, does possess encouraging signs that medium-size firms can be/are positioned to drive greater national business growth in terms of economic/sectors diversification, jobs creation, and larger output levels.

In all size categories, the annual growth rate of Oman SMEs has been small but steady at 1.5 per cent per annum since 2002. However, the importance of medium-size companies, especially in the area of industrial enterprise, in Oman's economic activity and growth increases substantially when comparing values contributed by micro, small and large firms.

As reported by the Ministry of Commerce and Industry, out of 833 industrial units with a capital investment of RO 5,000 or more, 48% of Oman firms are considered small, with the medium comprising 43% of the industrial units, and only 9% considered as large (250 employees and over). While a large companies dominate in Oman business sectors at 59% of the employment generation activities and 63% of the value added, medium-size firms account for 35% of the employment and value added in Oman's industrial economy. With small firms only contributing to about 6% of national employment and 2% of value added industrial activity, medium-size firms are clearly positioned to rise closer to the industrial performance levels of large firms, both in terms of employment, value creation, and output (Blossom, Neelufer, and Al Said, 2014).

However, these outdated figures need serious revision to reflect the current state and contributions of Oman medium-size firms in relation to the composition of national economic activity, business diversification, industrial development, employment and growth. In order to examine the state and potential of Oman's medium-size business sector in detail, the authors, in partnership with the Director's Office of the Muscat Securities Market (MSM), have secured first of a kind data reports that profile key operational and financial characteristics of the sector including: industry of operation; major product/service; listing status; size in terms of sales, total assets and no. of employees; date of establishment; ownership details; founder information (at least the name); and other statistics available for 197 companies. Based on this list, the authors will conduct a broad survey and target specific companies in order to produce formal business case studies as well as sectoral and operational analyses of the participating firms for academic publication and public dissemination.

The project overall will use the data and information procured to consider the kinds of problems/challenges/difficulties Oman medium-sized companies face as state sources of investment/funding lessen and regional competition tighten. In particular, the authors will analyze the types of management development and/or re-structuring internal management organization/practices that have occurred or need to occur in order to achieve greater overall efficiencies and increased employment capacities. The project also examines which types of companies included in the study would be the most open and/or vulnerable to potential new volatilities in public/private financing, external competition (whether Omani or foreign-based), and other business pressures, e.g. profitable pricing, commodities sourcing, new markets access, etc. in light of their position as first generation and/or family-owned firms with little accumulated long-term wealth/capital reserves.

In all, these factors and others will be critical in determining the viability of Omani medium-size firms to attract and secure private investment, meet existing and future competitive pressures, and create job placements/absorb young Omani professionals and workers either constrained or unable to secure employment in traditional government and/or large-cap business enterprises. In this way, the research project will also offer important insights that can be useful for Sultanate policymakers, investors and business leaders as well as academic audiences.

Conclusion

The overall inability of macro government policy approaches (e.g. five year economic plans, Omanization, liberal/restrictive swings in expat employment laws, state support for SME development, etc.) to increase indigenous (and especially youth) employment in Oman can be seen as both possible state misdirection and also increasing corporate preferences for global labor arbitrage strategies and practices. In light of the globalization of labor arbitrage, the question arises as to whether the Oman government needs to insist on and then enforce stricter "hire nationally" commitments, especially in the case of large local companies along with SMEs, and also as part of existing and future rentier arrangements with foreign firms and employers. Tackling labor arbitrage in locally-owned firms will be difficult, however, based on mounting anecdotal evidence that Omani-nationals as business owners also prefer to hire expat over indigenous workers at all education levels. The advance of several generations of Omanis as college graduates, however, substantially weaken older employer arguments that Omanis lacked modern forms of work knowledge, skills and training necessary to assume and advance in corporate jobs. Again, the stubborn preference for expat hiring raises the issue that levering lowest labor costs through expat importation, not the lack of qualified indigenous professionals, has become a common business strategy held by Omani company owners and managers regardless of national or non-national affiliation.

If so, this reliance on labor arbitrage as a reflection of global macro trends in corporate hiring strategies, trends and patterns may pose a problem well beyond the current reach of Oman government authority solely. Indeed, ending labor arbitrage may be a viable platform for GCC unified policmaking. However, with the economies of UAE and Qatar thriving off of expat labor while also weathering any economic downturns related to the 2014 and forward oil prices crisis, achieving uniformity in labor laws across the GCC that restrict companies to high percentages of indigenous hires may not be achievable. Indeed the GCC as a region may have lost in times of high oil prices, especially since the 2000s, the economic well-being along with highly educated population base to force companies to hire large numbers of indigenous over expats workers. The collapse of oil prices now and in the foreseeable future is now increasing dramatically a new kind of dependence of GCC countries on accommodating corporate preferences in hiring practices, which still tend to favor highly fluid and shorter-term costing expats over long-term national hires.

As a result, corporate global labor arbitrage strategies and practices along with drastically diminished oil revenue flows may greatly hinder Oman and other GCC/MENA countries to re-shape national labor markets largely in favor of indigenous employment in high-skilled, better wage jobs. Only economic diversification into home-bound companies with potential for reaching and dominating home consumer markets along with some export capabilities may be the sector that Oman and other GCC countries need to target for expansion. Instead of broad strategies for sectoral expansions (e.g. tourism, logistics, mining, etc.) that lead to only further dependencies on large multi-nationals/regional/local firms engaged in labor arbitrage, Oman should look to targeting medium-size local companies positioned for employment growth. Also, the Oman government needs to actively move large local firms to shedding expat employees in favor of hiring higher educated indigenous professionals, especially in the recent college graduates category. Finally, Oman government promotion of SME development also needs to align with encouraging businesses that support the greater employment of indigenous knowledge workers particularly college graduates. However, to do so the government must look to drastically limiting imports that could be offset by local start-up businesses and production, especially in the areas of consumer durables, perishable and non- food stuffs and agricultural products, and light manufacturing markets. These sectors, as opposed to tourism, mining and other natural resources extractive industries, hold the most promise for sustainable, higher paying jobs for young, higher educated Omanis as well as aiding Oman overall in greater national economic and business self-sufficiency.

References

Ashrafi, R. and Murtaza, M. 2011. "ICT Adoption in SME in an Arab Country: Oman," 2011, in E-Strategies for Resource Management Systems: Planning and Implementation, Hershey, PA: IGI Global.

Beblawi, H. "The Rentier State in the Arab World." Arab Studies Quarterly. Vol. 9. No. 4 (Fall 1987), pp. 383-398.

Blossom, C., Neelufer, A. and Al Said, A. 2014. "Challenges and Barriers Encountered by the SMEs Owners in Muscat." International Journal of Small Business and Entrepreneurship Research.

Buckley, G. and Rynhart, G. 2011. 'The Sultanate of Oman – The Enabling Environment for Sustainable Enterprises: An "EESE" Assessment', Employment Report, Employment Sector," International Labour Organization. Retrieved at: http://tinyurl.com/yabgtc7a

Carroll, W.K. 2004. Corporate Power in a Globalizing World. Oxford: U.K.: Oxford University Press.

Cooperation Council for the Arab States of the Gulf. March 2014. Secretariat General. GCC: A Statistical Glance, 2014', pp. 63–64. Retrieved at: http://tinyurl.com/yb6xvbme

Ennis, C. A. 2013. 'Rentier 2.0: Entrepreneurship Promotion and the (Re)Imagination of Political Economy in the Gulf Cooperation Council Countries', dissertation submitted to the University of Waterloo, Canada.

Ennis, C.A. and al-Jamali, R.Z. September 2014. Research Paper, Middle East and North Africa, Elusive Employment Development Planning and Labour Market Trends in Oman, Chatham House, London, UK.

European Industrial Relations Observatory (EIRO). "Decline in trade union membership lowest in recent years." Retrieved from: http://www.eurofound.europa.eu/eiro/2009/04/articles/de0904029i.htm

Hertog, S. 2012. "A comparative assessment of labor market nationalization policies in the GCC." in Hertog, S., (ed). National employment, migration and education in the GCC. The Gulf Region: economic development and diversification. Gerlach Press, Berlin, Germany.

International Labour Organization. Various Webpages Retrieved from: Global Employment Trends for Youth 2015: Scaling up investments in decent jobs for youth ILO Youth Oct 8 2015) http://tinyurl.com/y8odsr2p and http://tinyurl.com/p88uoll

- http://tinyurl.com/y8uadxke
- http://tinyurl.com/o6lfmtf
- http://tinyurl.com/m5xy94p
- http://tinyurl.com/y8kae2va

- http://tinyurl.com/yd5zv9b8
- http://tinyurl.com/kteznh7

International Monetary Fund. 2013. "Women, Work, and the Economy – IMF." Retrieved at: http://tinyurl.com/ycwro52p

International Trade Union Confederation. April 2013. "ITUC Frontlines Report Summary." Retrieved from: http://www.ituc.csi.org/IMG/pdf/ituc_frontlines_summary_report_april_2013_web.pdf

International Workers of the World. History webpage. Retrieved from: http://www.iww.org/en/history/chronology

Kalyani, P.B. and Al Yahyaee, L. 2012, "Factors influencing Entrepreneurship in the Rusayl Industrial Estate," Oman, International Conference on Technology and Business Management, 163-170.

Mahate, A.A. March 26, 2015. "SME Competitiveness: A Development Perspective of GCC Countries." United Nations International Trade Centre. United Nations Publications.

Muscat Daily.

- April 8, 2015. "Unemployment Rate in the Sultanate Touches 11.75%", p. 1. Retrieved at: http://tinyurl.com/yaxz3xt3
- May 18, 2016, "Female students outnumber males in higher education institutions," p. 5.
- May 22, 2016."0.2% rise in number of Omanis in private sector." p. 3.

Oman Economic Review. July 27, 2015. "All Round Effort." Retrieved at: http://oeronline.com/special-reports/progress-oman/all-round-effort.html.

OmanInfo.com. "Omanisation programme and Policy." Retrieved at: http://tinyurl.com/yc536h9b

Oman Ministry of Higher Education.

- 2015 Graduates Survey. Retrieved at: http://tinyurl.com/ycfy7klj
- 2014-2015 Admissions Report. http://tinyurl.com/yc8cveg2

Oman National Centre of Statistics and Information

- "Monthly Statistical Bulletin 2013", October 2013, p. 4, http://tinyurl.com/y9cpx4cy
- "Monthly Statistical Bulletin 2013, December 2013, http://tinyurl.com/y9vbkpt2
- Statistical Year Book 2013 http://tinyurl.com/y9cpx4cy
- "Monthly Statistical Bulletin 2015", March 2016, http://tinyurl.com/y7asfl68

Roberts, P.C. 2004. "Global Labor Arbitrage" Dismantling America." Retrieved from http://tinyurl.com/ya7f8bwc

Saleem, Q. 2012. "Overcoming Constraints to SME Development in MENA Countries and Enhancing Access to Finance." IFC Advisory Services in the Middle East and North Africa Report, International Finance Corporation, World Bank Publications.

Shaibany, S. May 21, 2016. "Address the slack in new business creation to boost job generation in Oman." Times of Oman. Retrieved at: http://tinyurl.com/yb5j7qp2

Slaughter. M.J. March 26, 2004. "Globalization and Employment by U.S. Multinationals: A Framework and Facts." Daily Report for Executives. Washington, D.C.: Bureau of National Affairs Publications.

Slaughter, M.J. and Tyson, L. March 2012. "A Warning Sign from Global Companies," Harvard Business Review. Cambridge, M.A.: Harvard University.

Times of Oman.

- January 25, 2016." "New classification to benefit more small and medium enterprises." Retrieved at: http://tinyurl.com/y78auayt
- February 9, 2016. "3.5 year wait for job for young Omanis." Retrieved at: http://tinyurl.com/y8vclyd9
- April 20, 2016. "Expat worker numbers hold steady in Oman," p. 1.
- May 12, 2016. "Remittance from Sultanate among highest in world," p. 1
- May 12, 2016. Visa Rules be Relaxed?" p. 1
- May 18, 2016. "Reserve 40% private sector's senior posts for locals: Shura."
- May 23, 2016. "First online e-platform for vocational training unveiled." p. 82.

United Nations. Research Institute for Social Development (UNRISD). May 6-8, 2013. "Potential and Limits of Social and Solidarity Economy (SSE)" Meeting. Geneva, Switzerland. Retrieved from: http://tinyurl.com/awbcmqm

Verme, P., January 29, 2015. "Economic development and female labor participation in the Middle East and North Africa: a test of the U-shape hypothesis." IZA Journal of Labor & Development, 20154:3, Springer.

Wise, R.D. and Martin, D. October-December 2015. 'The Political Economy of Global Labor Arbitrage." (UNAM) Problemas del Desarrollo Revista LatinoAmericano de Economiá, Volume 47, Number 185, Instituto de Investigaciones Económicas, Circuito Mario de la Cueva, Universidad Nacional Autónoma de México, Ciudad Universitaria, Coyoacán, CP 04510, México, D.F. Retrieved at: http://tinyurl.com/ybkustre

World Bank. 2010.

- Fact sheet, "Breaking even or breaking through: reaching financial sustainability while providing high quality standards in Higher Education in the Middle East and North Africa." Retrieved at: http://tinyurl.com/yakxgb42
- World Bank population growth (annual %). Retrieved at: http://data.worldbank.org/indicator/SP.POP.GROW.

World Economic Forum. "The Global Competitiveness Report 2011-2012." Retrieved from: http://www.weforum.org/reports/global-competitiveness-report-2011-2012

XE Currency Converter. May 24, 2016 Omani Rial ↔ British Pound 1 OMR = 1.77746 GBP; 1 GBP = 1.562599 OMR/Omani Rial ↔ US Dollar 1 OMR = 2.59740 USD 1 USD = 0.385000 OMR. Retrieved at: http://www.xe.com/currencyconverter.

4

Labour Market Challenges in Bahrain and the Path to Sustainability

Elinor Bajraktari and Ali Salman

Abstract

Full employment and maximization of the productivity of the labour force are Bahrain's two key labour market objectives. However, some of the policies it has undertaken might represent serious challenges in the way to achieving these objectives. Current labour market policies have facilitated the creation of a large public sector which employs a large number of Bahraini nationals and pays them wages which are considerably above private sector levels. This has created a high reservation wage for Bahraini nationals and has weakened their incentives to work in the private sector. At the same time, Bahrain has opened its labour market to foreigners and has encouraged the private sector to hire the cheapest labour it can find, rather than invest in the development of the national labour force. The main result of this policy has been the segmentation of the labour market in two distinct parts – the public sector dominated by nationals and the private sector dominated by foreign workers. While in the short run these imbalances have had a number of positive economic, social and political effects, in the long run they represent a significant risk for Bahrain because a considerable share of the labour force is not engaged in employment and uncompetitive, and therefore largely dependent on the state. This has had a detrimental effect on labour productivity, making Bahrain one of the countries with the lowest productivity scores. Until it addresses its labour market imbalances, Bahrain will struggle to build a competitive and diversified economy.

Bahrain's labour market model has been largely enabled by considerable oil revenues which have allowed the government to maintain a large public sector wage bill. However, in the long run this model is not sustainable. This is becoming obvious now that the effects of the lower oil prices which started in the second half of 2014 have begun to put considerable downward pressure on government expenditure. Although the sustainability risks of the existing labour market model have been recognized by the government for over a decade now and a number of reform initiatives have been undertaken, the situation remains precarious. The main reason for the lack of significant change in the last decade is the fact that the root cause of the imbalances – the large and generous public sector – has not been sufficiently addressed. With the current fiscal constraints forcing the authorities to limit the size of the government and the public sector wage bill, there is now an opportunity for Bahrain to reassess its labour market reform agenda and develop a package of measures that have the capacity to further transform the labour market.

Characteristics of Bahrain's Labour Market

In the 45 years of its existence as an independent state, Bahrain has made significant progress in the area of economic development. Riding on decades of admirable rates of economic growth, the country has managed to acquire the status of a high-income country, improve its ranking on all human development indicators[1] and build well-functioning state institutions. In this process of profound transformation, the labour market has played a key role by supplying the rapidly expanding economy with a steady reservoir of manpower.

One of the most particular features of Bahrain's labour market in these decades of strong expansion has been its high dependency on large-scale imports of foreign labour. The phenomenon of massive employment immigration has reached such out-of-ordinary proportions in the last decade that the size of the foreign population resident in the country has markedly outnumbered the local population. By 2014, the number of expatriates living in Bahrain was about 10% higher than the number of Bahraini nationals.[2]

In addition to its dependency on expatriate workers, Bahrain's labour market is characterized by two other interrelated features (which are also largely shared by the other Gulf Cooperation Council economies).

First, there is a remarkably low rate of participation of Bahraini nationals in the labour force. This phenomenon applies to both men and women, but is particularly stark for women. A vital part of the working-age Bahraini population does not work, which not only represents a significant loss of economic potential, but also has far-reaching social and political implications whose exploration falls outside the scope of this paper.

Second, the labour market is segmented in two distinct sections which to some degree operate in isolation from each other. One section corresponds to the public sector which employs mainly Bahraini nationals and has traditionally provided secure jobs and a steady source of income for most Bahraini families. The other section corresponds to the private sector which is largely dominated by expatriates, the majority of whom are low-skilled and low-paid workers living in the country on a temporary basis and under the sponsorship of their employers.

Low rates of participation of Bahraini nationals in employment and the segmentation of the labour market are characteristics which are neither new, nor unique to Bahrain. They are key features of a particular model of economic development that all GCC countries have adopted decades ago. This model has consisted of three core elements – i) the use of oil and gas revenues to rapidly build up infrastructure, services and key economic activities; ii) the use of large-scale foreign labour to support the expansion of economic activity; and, iii) the creation of an overstaffed public administration offering generous terms of employment, benefits, subsidies and other perks to the national population. This model has helped Bahrain (and the other GCC countries) achieve important results in the economic and social spheres. In particular, the large-scale importation of cheap foreign labour has fuelled the rapidly growing sectors (especially infrastructure, construction and services), while contributing to price stability by keeping down the cost of non-tradeables. This strategy has enabled Bahrainis to have access to higher incomes and affordable services and has ultimately contributed to the rise of their living standards.

The question, now, is not whether this model has served Bahrain (and the GCC region) well or not, but how effective and sustainable it is in the medium and long term, especially in light of the significant changes that have recently taken place in the regional and global context. The rest of this section will explore in more detail the peculiarities of Bahrain's labour market and will outline some of the challenges that they represent for its economy today (and in particular the government's priorities of economic diversification and competitiveness).

Low Labour Force Participation

As has already been mentioned, a remarkable characteristic of Bahrain's labour market is that a significant number of working-age[3] Bahraini nationals do not work. Table 1 shows that only 47% of working-age Bahrainis were working in 2013, a rate which stands in stark contrast with the 90% employment rate of working-age expatriates. In OECD countries, the average employment rate in 2014 was about 66%[4]. The low rate of employment of Bahraini nationals is reflected in the composition of the labour force. Although Bahraini nationals made up about 40% of the overall working-age population, they represented only 25% of the people who had a job in 2013[5].

Table 1: Working Age Population and Employed in Bahrain (2013)

Description		Nationals	Expatriates
Working Age Population (15 to 65)	Both sexes	392,479	587,999
	Females	192,537	138,592
	Males	199,942	449,407
Working Age Population Employed (15 to 65)	Both sexes	183,622	526,251
	Females	59,339	89,840
	Males	124,283	436,411
Share of Working Age Employed to Population	Both sexes	47%	89%
	Females	31%	65%
	Males	62%	97%

Source: Bahrain Open Data Portal (accessed on 15/5/2016): http://www.data.gov.bh/en/ResourceCenter

Also, differences in participation rates between Bahraini males and females are quite stark - 62% of working-age men were employed in 2013, compared to 31% of women. While such low female participation rates are the norm in all GCC countries, in the rest of the world they are quite unusual. In OECD countries, for example, the participation rate for women was 58% in 2014. For Bahraini expatriate females, the same rate was 65% in 2013. Given that female Bahraini nationals have on average higher educational achievements than males, they would be expected to have better labour participation rates than men. But skills and education are not closely correlated with employment in Bahrain's labour market.

Moreover, unemployment seems to be significant, especially for young people. This is happening at a time when the expatriate population, resident in the country as a result of demand for their labour, has become larger than the Bahraini population itself. The vast majority of the expatriates are employed in the private sector and allowed to stay in the country through a sponsorship scheme which enables business owners to recruit foreign workers for positions they cannot fill with local employees. Obviously, the low rate of employment of Bahraini nationals cannot be because of a lack of jobs – far from it, the Bahraini economy produces a lot more jobs than the Bahraini population can fill.

Segmentation of the Labour Market

Bahrain's labour market is segmented in two distinct parts which operate in some degree of isolation from one another. One section is represented by the government sector which employs predominantly Bahraini nationals and pays on average much higher wages. The other section consists of the private sector which is dominated by expatriate workers and pays on average lower wages. This duality in the labour market gives the semblance of two parallel labour markets which have little interaction with each other. The two sections of the labour market – the "***government sector – Bahraini nationals***" and "***private sector – expatriates***" – can be described as follows.

"Government Sector – Bahraini Nationals"

- The government sector employs primarily Bahraini nationals. At the end of 2015, about 85% of employees in the government sector were Bahrainis (see chart 2[6]).
- A significant number of working-age Bahraini nationals are employed in the government sector (see chart 1). At the end of 2015, about 40%[7] of Bahraini nationals active in the labour force were employed in the government sector.[8] This is a significant proportion by international standards. For example, in OECD countries, the average ratio of the labour force employed in the public sector is about 15%.[9]
- The government sector employs a significantly higher proportion of women than the private sector. At the end of 2015, 48% of Bahraini employees in the government sector were female, compared to only 30% in the private sector (see chart 3).

"Private Sector – Expatriates"

- The private sector employs predominantly expatriate workers. At the end of 2015, expatriates represented about 85% of total private sector employment (see chart 2).
- The number of expatriates employed in the public sector is extremely low in comparison to the number of those working in the private sector (see chart 1).
- Expatriates are mainly employed in labour-intensive sectors such as manufacturing, retail trade, construction and domestic work which typically employ low-cost, low-skilled and low-productivity workers (De Bel-Air 2015, 10; EDB 2013, 14). These are the sectors that have seen the fastest growth in the last of decade and have fuelled the rapidly-growing importation of foreign labour (EDB 2013, 14).
- The expatriate population is predominantly in the working age category, male and low-skilled, which shows a preference of the labour market for male, low-skilled and low-paid foreign workers.
- Bahrain does have a small number of highly-paid expatriate workers with high-end expertise. They are employed mainly in very specialized positions in the financial sector or the oil industry.
- The small number of Bahraini nationals working in the private sector are mainly employed in managerial positions in key sectors such as oil and finance.
- While the proportions of women and men are more balanced in the public sector, the private sector is largely dominated by male workers. Women constitute only about 30% of Bahraini nationals working in the private sector.

Chart 1: Employment of Nationals and Expatriates in the Public and Private Sectors at the End of 2015

(Source: Labour Market Regulatory Authority)

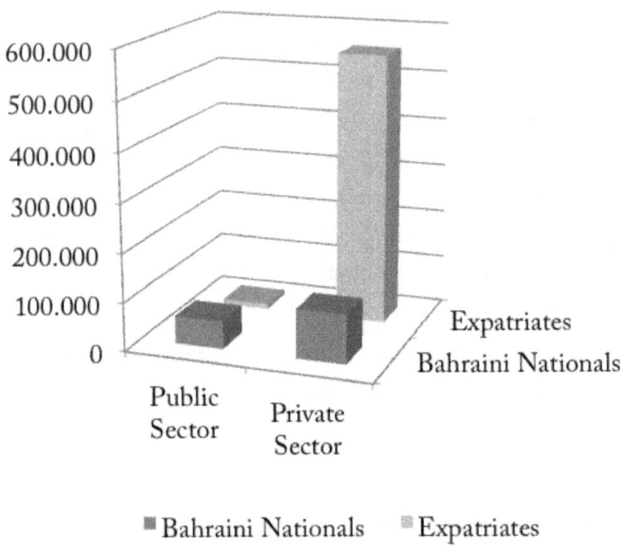

Chart 2: Shares of Employment of Bahraini Nationals and Expatriates in the Public and Private Sector in the 4th Quarter of 2015

(Source: LMRA data website)

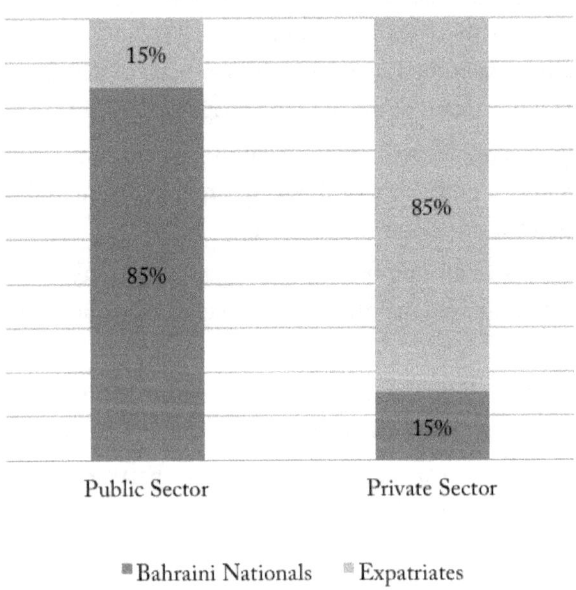

Chart 3: Shares of Male and Femal Bahraini Workers in the Public and Private Sector in the 4th Quarter of 2015

(Source: LMRA data website)

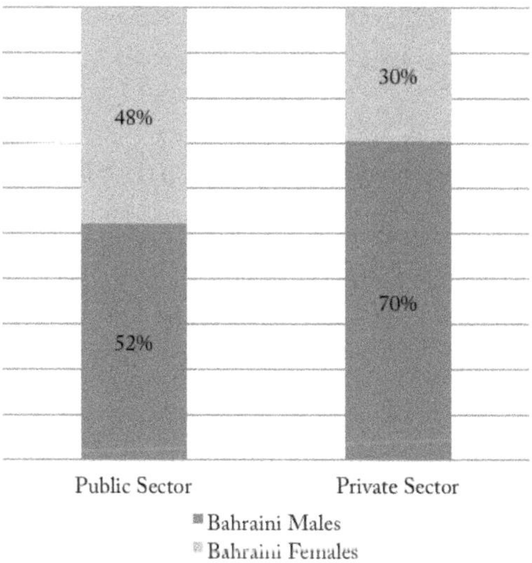

Another key feature of the labour market duality is the significant wage difference between the public and private sector and between Bahraini nationals and expatriates within each sector.

- Public sector wages in Bahrain are significantly higher than wages in the private sector. For example, in the last quarter of 2015, the median wage of Bahraini nationals in the private sector was BD[10] 386 – about half the median wage of Bahraini nationals in the public sector (which for the same period was BD 673).[11] Such large differentials between public and private sectors can be found only in the GCC region. Even when controlling for the level of education, average wages in the public sector remain significantly higher than in the private sector.
- The wage differential is even starker between Bahraini nationals and expatriates. For the same level of skills and effort and the same type of job, a Bahraini national is paid more than twice as much as an expatriate in the labour intensive sectors. For example, in the construction, trade, hotels and restaurants and small-scale manufacturing sectors (which are typically sectors where the bulk of expatriate workers are employed), the average wage is BD 525 for Bahraini nationals and BD 228 for expatriates.[12] Even when controlling for the level of education and productivity, wages for expatriates are much lower than for Bahraini nationals (except for highly skilled individuals). The main reason for this large wage differential is that the bulk of expatriate workers in Bahrain are wage takers. Given that Bahraini employers have access to an unlimited supply of expatriate labour in countries with an abundant labour force in South Asia and Southeast Asia,

expatriate workers have no real bargaining power over their wage which is effectively set relative to the wage level in their country of origin. Thanks to sponsorship rules and the absence of a minimum wage for foreign workers, Bahraini employers have a lot of leverage over expatriate workers which helps them keep expatriate wages at a very low level. Employers derive significant cost advantages from the employment of expatriate labour. Chart 4 (below) shows the significant difference in labour cost between Bahraini nationals and expatriates.

Chart 4: Labour Cost Gap (in BD)

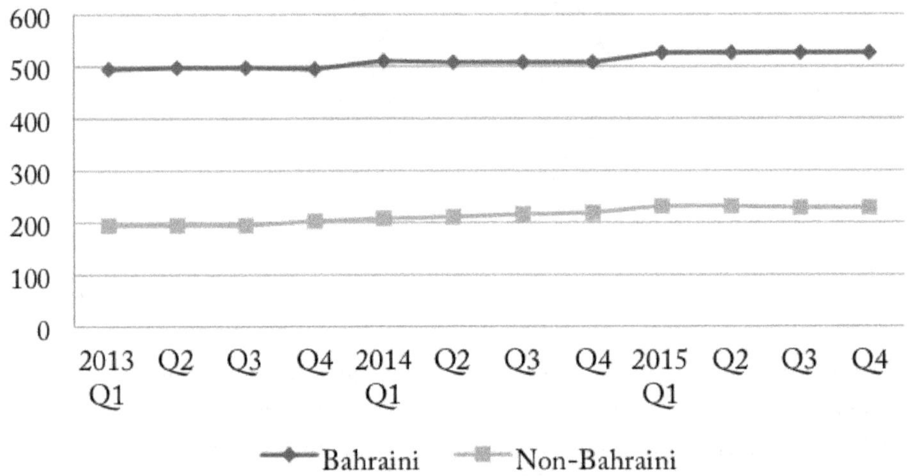

Source LMRA data website

Moreover, an overstaffed state sector, combined with high public sector wages and benefits, has made Bahrain's public sector wage bill significantly higher as a proportion of GDP than that of most other countries at a similar level of development. For example, the IMF (2013) reported that Bahrain's wage bill in 2012 was close to 12% of GDP (an increase of 3 percentage points from year 2000). Such a high wage bill ratio puts Bahrain on top of all GCC countries, including Kuwait and Saudi Arabia which are known for their bloated and well-paid public sector (in both countries the reported ratio of the wage bill to GDP was about 10% in 2012). By contrast, for the same year the average wage bill for all oil exporting countries was 5% of GDP (IMF 2013; 13). Between 2000 and 2012, Bahrain's wage bill has more than tripled, reaching a high of about 50% of government spending in 2012. [13]

Chart 5: Government Wage Bill, 2012 (Percent of GDP)

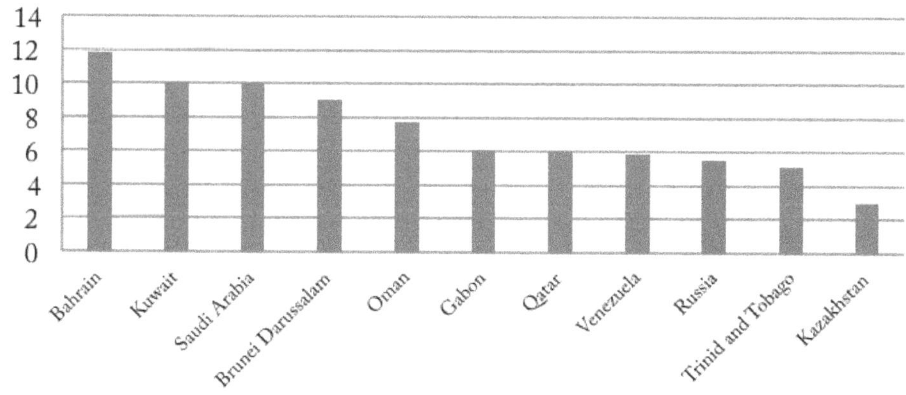

Source: IMF (2013)

Bahrain's generous public sector wage bill has been largely financed by revenues from the oil and gas exports. Given the absence of conventional forms of taxation such as consumption or income taxes, oil revenues have made up most of government revenue. For example, at the end of 2013 (shortly before the oil price crash of 2014), the share of oil and gas in government revenues had reached a high of 88% (EBD 2013). There is a direct link between how Bahrain raises its public revenue and the type of labour policy regime that it has adopted. It is inconceivable that Bahrain would have been able to afford its generous public sector employment policy, had it not had access to such large oil revenues.

Effects of Labour Market Policies

Bahrain's current labour market model is not the product of an evolutionary process in which the interplay of genuine market forces has gradually led to a balanced and optimal outcome for the economy. It is rather the result of deliberate policy choices made by the authorities on the basis of primarily political imperatives. Both the creation of a significant number of well-paid government jobs for Bahraini nationals (in addition to the various subsidies provided by the state) and the opening of the labour market to foreign workers are elements of a policy regime which has played an important role in the redistribution of the rapidly-accumulating oil wealth among the citizens, while enabling the economy to expand at a fast clip. Similar labour market policies in the GCC region are widely perceived as active mechanisms for the redistribution of the oil rent. Seen from this perspective, labour market policy is an integral part of the social contract between citizens and authorities whereby the state provides generous benefits and citizens reciprocate by accepting its authority and legitimacy.[14] This arrangement has provided authorities with significant political benefits and has contributed to the country's stability and security. Therefore, any assessment of Bahrain's labour market policies should go beyond the economic realm and take into consideration this political dimension as well.

The labour market policies that Bahrain has adopted have produced a number of effects which are briefly summarized below:

- ***Private sector increasingly oriented, and dependent, on cheap and low-skilled foreign labour*** – In large part as a result of the economic development model that Bahrain has adopted, centered on low intensity activities with low added value per worker, expatriate workers have been central to the profitability of Bahraini businesses. They are preferred by employers not only because of their lower wage expectations and better work ethics, but also because of their lower bargaining power and limited mobility which result from their dependency on the employer for their working visa sponsorship.
- ***Strong attachment of Bahraini nationals to the state*** – High public sector wages and benefits relative to the private sector have created strong incentives for nationals, especially low skilled ones, to prefer jobs in the public sector. This makes the state the employer of first choice for most Bahrainis. Government jobs not only pay higher wages, but also provide more job security, higher allowances, more perks, shorter working hours and less effort. The oversized public sector thus represents a sort of a safe haven and is highly preferred for employment by Bahraini nationals. As a result, a disproportionate number of Bahraini nationals are employed in the public sector. As noted above, with 40% of its labour force employed in the public sector, Bahrain has a much higher ratio of public sector employment than most other countries (the typical ratio for countries at Bahrain's level of income per capita is 15 – 20% - see above). Some Bahrainis are even willing to stay unemployed and wait for a government job to materialize (making the state the employer of first and last choice). Not only unskilled private sector jobs, but also skilled private sector jobs are unattractive to Bahraini nationals because of the still higher public sector benefits. Only certain specific and niche private sector jobs (i.e. high paying activities in the oil and financial sector) are sufficiently attractive to them.
- ***Bahraini nationals "priced out" of the private sector*** – High public sector wages have increased Bahrainis' reservation wage (the wage at which a person is willing to work), which has made them unattractive to the private sector. Even those nationals who are willing to work in the private sector often find themselves "priced out" because employers have access to a virtually unlimited supply of foreign workers with better skills and lower wage expectations whom they can sponsor into the country. The abundant supply of cheap expatriate labour has made Bahraini nationals, especially low-skilled ones, uncompetitive in the private sector. This further reinforces their dependency on the state.

The low participation of Bahraini nationals in the labour market and their lack of strong engagement with the private sector has negative implications for long-term economic activity and growth. First, Bahrain's human resources are allocated inefficiently. A significant section of the country's manpower is left untapped, which is a missed opportunity for increased economic output and wealth creation. Second, the overstaffed public sector represents an ineffective use of the skills and qualifications of a dynamic part of the population that could have been more productively deployed in the private sector. Third, the loss of potential is particularly high for Bahraini women, who typically have higher educational achievement, but extremely low participation rates in the labour market. This potential is not capitalized and represents a waste of educational resources. Fourth, the imbalances in the labour market have created an increasing dependency of a section of the population on family members who derive their income from employment in the public sector. Such dependency exposes Bahraini families to high economic vulnerabilities and social risks.

The negative consequences of labour market imbalances also extend to the educational sector and the development of human capital. High public sector wages have made many Bahraini nationals lack strong motivation to invest in the type of skills and qualifications that are prized in the private sector. Because the labour market does not provide clear signals about the needs of the market, Bahrain's tertiary and vocational training institutions do not supply skills that are needed by the private sector but are more aligned with the requirements of the public sector. A large proportion of Bahraini students graduate in humanities, rather than sciences and engineering (Hertog 2014b). This mismatch of skills between the demands of the economy and the supply of the educational system represents a waste of educational resources and a lost opportunity to further develop the national human capital.

Besides crowding out the employment of Bahraini nationals in the private sector, the labour market imbalances have also a direct negative effect on investment, productivity, and consequently on economic diversification and innovation – the stated priorities of government policy. First of all, funds spent on wages and subsidies could have been invested more effectively in productive activities which would have generated higher returns. Also, the disproportionate allocation of the human resource to the public sector, the extensive use of low-skilled labour in the private sector and Bahraini's lack of incentives to invest in skills and education which are relevant to the private sector have a direct negative effect on labor productivity. Moreover, the availability of abundant cheap labour has undermined incentives in the private sector for investments in productivity increases. Business owners have no motivation to invest in technology, innovation and entrepreneurship – all key factors of productivity. There is also a concern that bulking up the state bureaucracy with redundant employment has a negative effect on the productivity and efficiency of government organizations. Bahrain needs not only a dynamic private sector, but also an efficient and productive public sector.

As shown in table 2 below, Bahrain has had the lowest labour productivity in the GCC region in the last five years. Also, chart 6[15] below shows that labour productivity over the period 2000-20012 has decreased by about 2%, which represents a serious challenge for the competitiveness of the economy. As can be seen in the chart, Bahrain's performance in this area has been the weakest in the GCC region and below that of other countries that are heavy importers of foreign labour. The economic growth that Bahrain has achieved in the last couple of decades has not been derived from improvements in productivity, but from an expansion of production based on large-scale imports of foreign labour from countries with considerably lower wage levels. Bahrain's economic development strategy has been oriented on abundant cheap labour and labour-intensive industries, instead of high-productivity activities coupled with high technology and high-skilled labour (IMF 2003).

Table 2: Labor Productivity Per Person Employed in 2015 US$ (converted to 2015 price level with updated 2011 PPPs)

Country	2010	2011	2012	2013	2014	2015
Bahrain	81,837	82,323	84,007	87,274	89,693	90,410
Kuwait	130,292	143,925	151,200	148,343	144,484	142,632
Oman	113,061	109,926	108,349	106,090	103,267	102,503
Qatar	181,476	194,051	196,705	196,273	198,075	199,268
Saudi Arabia	150,065	159,073	161,035	160,100	162,910	164,599
United Arab Emirates	152,350	154,463	160,867	163,569	166,691	168,836

Source: Total Economy Database website (accessed on 28 May 2016

Chart 6: Labour Productivity, 2000-12 (Average annual change in percent)

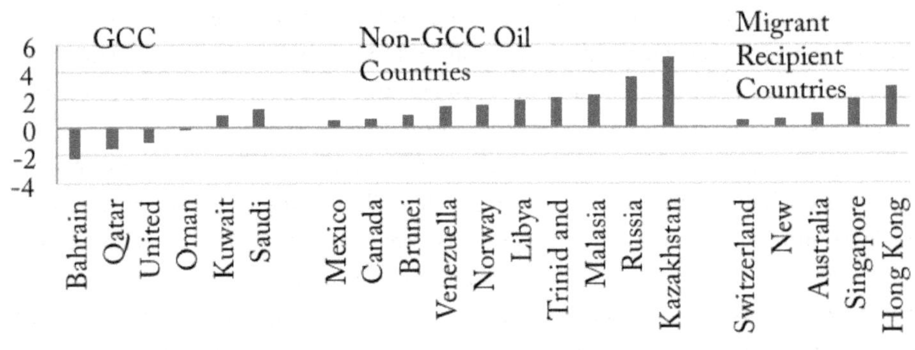

Source: IMF (2013)

Labour market imbalances have also hampered the creation of new businesses and the diversification of the economy by compartmentalizing the work force in two sections which are ruled by completely different, and largely contradictory, logics. On the one hand, expatriates who constitute 85% of workers in the private sector lack the freedom, mobility and necessary support to establish new businesses, invest and innovate. Therefore, a large majority of people involved in the private sector are shut out of opportunities to invest and open new business activities, leaving only 15% of the private sector labour force able to contribute their creativity, initiative and efforts towards start-ups and innovation. On the other hand, the majority of Bahraini nationals, who possess the mobility and means to create new businesses and innovate, are stuck in the public sector and lack any incentives to take risks and invest their skills and funds in the creation of new businesses. This contradiction represents an enormous challenge for the efforts of the government to steer the economy away from a heavy reliance on a handful of sectors – primarily oil and gas. If Bahrain's top economic priority is to promote innovations and diversify its economic activities, where are these new activities going to come from? Who is going to undertake these innovations and create the new businesses? How will Bahrain be able to tap into the creative juices of its people, and especially its youth bulge? No state has ever created a dynamic and innovative economy by relying entirely on the government to undertake all the necessary investments and economic activities. Although the role of the government is crucial, risk-taking and innovating private entrepreneurs are crucial for the diversification that Bahrain seeks to achieve.

Sustainability of Bahrain's Labour Market Model

As outlined in the previous sections, Bahrain's overstaffed public sector and generous public sector wages, coupled with the massive inflow of expatriate labour, have been key features of a labour market strategy that has helped Bahrain achieve a number of political and economic objectives. This strategy has contributed to political stability and social cohesion and has enabled Bahrain to build its infrastructure and services, while keeping the price of non-tradeables down. It has ultimately generated significant benefits for Bahraini citizens and contributed to the improvement of their living standards.

However, for all its advantages, this model has not been without its shortcomings. Amongst other things, it has diverted considerable resources away from investment, has kept productivity down and has reinforced the dependency of the economy on the oil and gas sector. The irony of this model is that it has generated advantages in the present, while building up challenges for the future. The key question facing Bahrain now is: - How sustainable is this model? Can Bahrain maintain it indefinitely and use it to its benefit? If not, what then needs to change and what are the implications of the change process?

The answer to these questions depends on a key factor which has largely shaped Bahrain's labour market strategy and economic development model over the last few decades – the availability of fiscal resources derived from oil revenues. These resources have enabled Bahrain to maintain and benefit from the existing labour market strategy. Without them the Bahraini government would not have been able to sustain the large number of jobs in the public sector, the generous public sector benefits and the outsize public sector wage bill. While it will be tempting for the authorities to continue to reap the political benefits of the current labour market model, its ability to do so will depend largely on the availability of fiscal means.

Concerns about the sustainability of oil revenues have been raised and widely discussed since the early 2000's. Realizing that Bahrain's oil and gas reserves were being exhausted and that a gradual reduction of production and revenues was inevitable, the government started looking into alternative paths out of the oil dependency. In the intervening years, however, fears of an impending drop in oil revenues did not materialize. Oil deals with Saudi Arabia[16] and high oil prices in the late 2000's and early 2010's helped Bahrain maintain the same level of oil production and revenues.

However, the status quo has come under immense pressure since the second half of 2014. Oil prices have taken a serious hit and are not expected to reach their pre-2014 levels in the near future. Some of the effects of this significant shift in the oil sector are already visible in the economy. Low oil prices have begun to bite on government revenues. According to data from the Economic Development Board (2016), the fiscal deficit deteriorated from 3.6% of the GDP in 2014 to an unprecedented 12% in 2015. In 2016 and 2017 the deficit is forecast to be 10% and 7% respectively.

If oil revenues do not recover soon, the consequences for Bahrain's public finances will be severe. The fiscal squeeze is going to put significant pressure on government spending. According to calculations by the Economist Intelligence Unit (2015:6), Bahrain has the highest fiscal break even oil price in the GCC region (estimated at US$130/b in 2014). It also has the smallest sovereign wealth fund in the region (Mumtalakat had around US$7bn of assets in 2015). With oil prices around $50 or $60 per barrel, the government will be unable to sustain the same level of expenditure for too long, especially given that Bahrain lacks any forms of conventional taxation. A restructuring of public expenditure will, among other things, have a significant impact on Bahrain's labour market because its labour market model requires an ever-increasing price of oil in order to balance the government budget.

The government has already reacted to this situation by taking a number of measures to rationalize spending and diversify the sources of revenue. A number of capital projects have been cancelled in the government budget. A major overhaul of the pervasive subsidy system is underway, with many crucial social subsidies being phased out[17] (EDB 2015: 27). Measures are being put in place to restructure recurrent expenditure and streamline and increase the efficiency and productivity of the public sector[18] (EDB 2015: 27). The introduction of a value-added tax has become part of the public discourse.

These unprecedented measures are a reflection of the unprecedented situation of public finances. Unlike earlier occasions when economic reforms have been announced only in form, this seems to be the beginning of a real process of change which, if sustained, will have serious implications for the economy in general, and the labour market in particular. For all the political benefits that the authorities derive from the current economic development model, market forces seem to be pushing the economy towards a more sustainable structure. It will not be a coincidence if this process of transformation will go farthest and fastest in Bahrain first – of all the GCC countries, it has the smallest reserves of oil, the smallest wealth fund and the most precarious fiscal position. With the right policy choices made by the government, these broader economic changes will have the potential to transform the current labour market model and set it on a more sustainable footing.

Another challenge looming on the horizon which will put further pressure on the labour market is the demographic structure of Bahrain's population. As chart 7 (below) shows, the population pyramid has a broad base which implies an upcoming youth bulge. Bahraini nationals from 0 to 19 represent the largest group in the population, which is about 30% larger than the 20 to 39 category. Such a population structure signals an ever increasing number of new labour market entrants who will have to be absorbed by the job market in the coming years. But as these new cohorts enter the labour market, they will demand employment opportunities that the public sector alone will not be able to provide. Even under most optimistic scenarios of revenue levels from the oil sector, it is hard to see how the government would be able to create the necessary number of jobs in the public sector. In all likelihood, the working age population will grow faster than the rate of public sector jobs the government will be able to create.

Chart 7: Population Pyramid for Bahraini Nationals in 2014

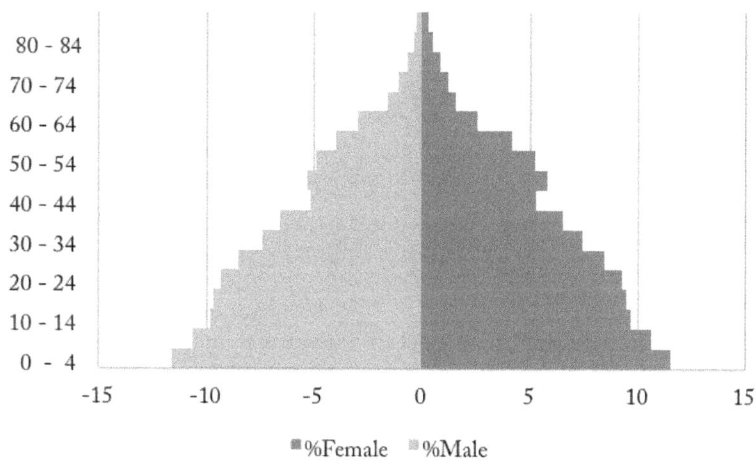

(Source: LMRA data website)

In light of the revenue and demographic challenges described above, the sustainability of Bahrain's current labour market model looks increasingly fragile. The current labour market model will be difficult to sustain in the face of such forces. Increasing pressures will require, amongst other things, adjustments in the size of the public sector and the wage bill relative to the economy. But if these adjustments are to take place without changes in the capacity of the private sector to absorb more Bahrainis, the result is going to be increased unemployment for Bahraini nationals. Therefore, the role of the private sector in the rebalancing of the labour market and the transformation of the structure of the economy cannot be emphasized enough.

The Path to Sustainability

Concerns about the effects of Bahrain's labour market imbalances on the competitiveness of the economy and its long-term sustainability are not something new. Labour market reform has been at the center of widespread and intense policy discussions and public debates since the early 2000's.[19] The government has prioritized the labour market as one of the key instruments for the creation of a more sustainable economic development model.[20] The increase of the nationals' share of employment in the private sector – a process called the *Bahrainization* of the workforce – has been one of the key objectives pursued by authorities over the last decade. The recognition of the risks associated with the lack of sustainability in the labour market has led to a number of fragmented reforms which have been introduced by the government. The following are some of the major policy changes that have been undertaken since the 1990's.

- Employment quotas for nationals in the private sector were introduced in the 1990's, but, as it turned out, they were not strictly enforced.
- A set of more comprehensive labour market reforms were introduced in 2006. An independent Labour Market Regulation Authority (LMRA) was established as part of this labour market reform wave. LMRA was initially charged with regulating and controlling work permits for expatriate employees and licensing of recruitment agencies and was further mandated to develop employment strategies and policies.[21] Also, an independent labour fund called Tamkeen was established and tasked to provide training and skill formation, financing grants and salary subsidies for Bahraini nationals and companies established by them.
- A tax on expatriate labour was introduced, intended to make the hiring of foreigners more expensive. Against considerable opposition from the business community, the government instituted a levy of BD 200 for a two-year working visa and an additional BD 10 monthly fee. 80% of the funds collected through this tax are used to fund the operations of Tamkeen.
- In 2009 Bahrain loosened the sponsorship (kafala) system by abolishing the mandatory "*No Objection Certificate*" (after one year of employment) that restricted the expatriates' job mobility by tying them to a specific employer who sponsored their stay in the country.

Although these reforms carried a great deal of ambition when they were announced, their impact has not met the expectations of the government. Certainly, there have been improvements in some areas, such as the number of Bahrainis who have started new businesses, an increase in the number of women engaged in employment, and so on. But overall, as the evidence provided in the previous sections of this paper shows, the labour market remains imbalanced – the number of Bahrainis employed in the private sector remains low, the rate of labour force participation is low, the wage gap between expatriates and nationals is significant, labour productivity remains low, etc. Sustainability remains a pressing issue and has become even more alarming in light of the latest development in the oil sector and the challenges that have emerged from the drop in oil prices.

There are many reasons for the lack of significant change from the reform measures undertaken thus far. Shortcomings that are commonly identified by researchers are linked to the lack of robust enforcement of policy by government agencies, lack of strong interest by employers in the incentives provided by the government or lack of sufficient incentives for employees. For example, the reformation of the "*kafala*" system has not led to the desired increase in the mobility of foreign workers. Data by LMRA show that by the 4th quarter of 2015 only 2% of expatriates had changed jobs without the employer's consent, despite of the abolishment of the rule that expatriates cannot move to a new job without the consent of their existing employer[22]. Similarly, the system of quotas for nationals in the private sector has not been strictly enforced by the authorities. Companies have found creative ways around the rules, leading to widespread evasion and abuse (Hertog 2014a: 11). The policy has ultimately had little effect on the employment of Bahrainis in the private sector.

Even major initiatives, like the establishment of Tamkeen, have not managed to transform significantly the structure of the labour market. Tamkeen's mission and activities are commendable and Tamekeen is exactly the kind of institution that Bahrain's labour market needs. But Tamkeen alone cannot bring about the type of readjustment in the labour market that is required. For all the training and private sector jobs that Tamkeen offers to Bahraini workers, why would they still want to give up their jobs in the public sector? Training and skills alone are not going to change Bahrainis' preference for the public sector. Unless the benefits provided by government jobs are brought more in line with those in the private sector, it is hard to see how measures related to skills and qualifications alone could work.

The main drawback of these reform initiatives is that they have been implemented while the public sector has continued to remain overstaffed and offer generous benefits relative to the private sector. By not addressing the imbalances' root cause – the availability of a large number of government jobs and the wage differential between the public and private sectors – the reform has not been able to radically change the incentives for Bahraini nationals to join the private sector.

Tackling the size of the public sector is one of the most difficult reforms to undertake because of its political implications. A significant shift toward more employment of Bahrainis in the private sector will require a change in the way state revenue is distributed in the society. Furthermore, an increase in the role of the private sector in the economy, accompanied by an increase of its contribution to public revenues, will imply a greater role for it in politics and society. Given the political sensitivities and risks that such reforms carry, in times of plenty it is easier to put them off until a future time. But with the ongoing fiscal pressures forcing the authorities to limit the size of the government and the public sector wage bill, there is now an opportunity to reassess the labour market reform agenda and undertake a set of policy measures that have the capacity to transform the labour market.

The key question now facing Bahrain is how to reform its labour market model without undermining social and political stability. Some key principles that can be drawn from Bahrain's experience with labour market reforms over the last decades are the following:

- If a larger share of the Bahrainis is to be employed in the private sector, it would mean that more people would enjoy less job security than in the public sector. In order to not let this undermine the social contract, the government could compensate the loss of security with more social protection. This will require a strengthening of the social security system, including mechanisms such as guaranteed minimum income, unemployment insurance and benefits, etc. Such measures will facilitate the development of the private sector and help make the state bureaucracy leaner and more effective, while supporting the social contract at the same time.
- The piecemeal approach to reform has been ineffective. A comprehensive approach tackling both demand and supply sides of the labour market is necessary. For example, measures targeting the number of employees and wage levels in the public sector should be combined with more effective measures to strengthen the capacity of Bahraini nationals to participate in the private sector. Failure to recognize this will doom the reform because if the public sector is to shrink significantly in the face of fiscal constraints and the private sector is unable to absorb the flow of public sector employees and the new entrants into the labour market, unemployment could escalate and lead to increased social tensions.
- The ultimate focus of Bahrain's labour market policy should be on the development of the human capital (as opposed to its present focus on cheap and unskilled labour). Bahrain should concentrate its investments in productivity-enhancing human capital development. The focus of government policy should be on building an educational sector that is driven by the goal of developing the country's human capital and supporting the process of structural transformation towards higher productivity and competitiveness. It will be also important to connect universities more closely with businesses and encourage the flow of knowledge and information between them. Moreover, immigration policy could be gradually reformed to attract higher-skilled foreign workers into the country. Bahrain could follow the example of Singapore in the way it has made its labour market policy a key instrument for the attraction of worldwide talent and entrepreneurs who contribute to the productivity and competitiveness of the economy.
- The pace of reform should be gradual and measured. Measures forcing the private sector to abruptly absorb more national workers will erode the cost-competitiveness of present activities and might drive existing firms out of business and scare away foreign investment. The nationals' shift of employment from the public to the private sector should take place in a gradual way and without undermining the viability of existing

activities. Competitiveness-enhancing measures, such as investments in human capital, should go hand-in-hand with the labour market reforms.

- Best reform measures are those that create the right market incentives for stakeholders. The enforcement of administrative restrictions (such as quotas for Bahraini nationals in the private sector) do not work well because they do not address the root causes of imbalances.
- The challenge that Bahrain faces with the employment of its young people can be turned into an opportunity if the country will capitalize on the youth bulge and direct its energy and creativity towards new economic activities, innovation and further economic growth.
- A more systematic effort to get women to participate more actively in the labour force will provide an additional boost to the economy.

Conclusion

As already discussed in this paper, the labour market model chosen by Bahrain (and other GCC countries) has resulted in a number of paradoxes:

- Strong economic growth has coexisted with a decline in labour productivity (IMF 2013).
- High level of underemployment of nationals has coexisted with rapid expansion of jobs for expatriates.
- High economic growth rates have coexisted with unemployment for Bahraini nationals.

The abundant use of cheap and low-skilled expatriate labour has been a double edged sword. It has greatly contributed to growth and has ensured price stability, which has led to considerable improvements in living standards, but at the same time, it has kept down productivity and skill formation. Ironically, longstanding efforts by the government to diversify the economy away from oil have been undermined by the labour market policies. Moreover, with Bahraini nationals largely outside the private sector as a result of an outsize public sector and well-paid government jobs, the labour market model that Bahrain has built has not facilitated economic diversification (IMF 2013). The need for reforming the labour market model has been widely understood for quite some time now, but attempts to undertake serious reforms have been fragmented.

Bahrain's labour market model appears largely unsustainable in the face of a youth bulge entering the job market in the next few years and decreasing oil revenues. The pressures on the existing model seem to have built up considerably recently, especially in the aftermath of the oil price collapse in the second part of 2014. A restructuring of the labour market seems inevitable, if the low oil prices are going to be sustained. The fiscal adjustment process that Bahrain is going through represents an opportunity which the authorities should capitalize on to carry out their labour market reforms. Addressing the labour market imbalances outlined in this paper will require policy measures that ultimately make employment in the private sector more attractive for Bahraini nationals.

References

Akbari, Reza H. and Jason Stern (2012). The triangle of conflict: how Bahrain's internal divisions inhibit reconciliation. IMES CAPSTONE PAPER SERIES, May 2012.

Assaad, Ragui (2013). Making Sense of Arab Labor Markets: The Enduring Legacy of Dualism, Institute for the Study of Labor, Discussion Paper No. 7573, August 2013.

De Bel-Air, Françoise (2015). Demography, Migration, and the Labour Market in Bahrain. Explanatory Note No. 6/2015. Gulf Labour Markets and Migration. GLMM - EN - No. 6/2015.

EIU (2015). Bahrain – Country Forecast. The Economist Intelligence Unit, December 2015.

EDB (2013). Economic Yearbook 2013, Publication of Bahrain's Economic Development Board, 2013.

EDB (2015). Economic Yearbook 2015, Publication of Bahrain's Economic Development Board, 2015.

EDB (2016). Bahrain Economic Quarterly, Publication of Bahrain's Economic Development Board, March 2016.

Hertog, Steffen (2014a). "Arab Gulf States: An Assessment of Nationalisation Policies", GLMM - Research Paper, GLMM - RP - No. 1/2014.

Hertog, Steffen (2014b) "Rent Distribution, Labour Markets and Development in High-Rent Countries," Working Paper, London 2014; International Monetary Fund, Labor Market Reforms to Boost Employment and Productivity in the GCC.

IMF (2013). Labor Market Reforms to Boost Employment and Productivity in the GCC, Annual Meeting of Ministers of Finance and Central Bank Governors, October 5, 2013.

UNDP (2015). Human Development Report 2015, 'Work for Human Development', United Nations Development Programme, 2015.

Notes

1 The 2015 Human Development Report of the United Nations Development Programme (UNDP 2015) placed Bahrain in its "very high development" category in the Human Development Index which measures three dimensions of human development: long and healthy life, access to knowledge, and decent standard of living. In the report's global ranking, Bahrain was positioned in the 45th place.

2 Bahrain Labour Market Indicators.

3 Working age in this case is defined as between 15 and 64.

4 OECD statistics - http://stats.oecd.org/Index.aspx?DatasetCode=LFS_SEXAGE_I_R (accessed on 17 May 2016).

5 2013 is the latest year for which data is available by age groups which allows the calculation of the size of the 15-64 age group.

6 The data presented in charts 1, 2 and 3 are from the fourth quarter of 2015.

7 This figure could vary from 35% to 40% depending on the unemployment rate for Bahraini nationals which is not reported consistently in the statistics publicly available.

8 The figures and charts in this section do not include state-owned enterprises in the calculation of the public sector because they are considered as part of the "commercial" sector in the Labour Market Regulatory Authority (LMRA) statistics.

9 This figure was reported for 2011 by OECD. See source here: http://tinyurl.com/y935kqwx (accessed on 16 May 2016).

10 Bahraini Dinars.

11 Bahrain Labour Market Indicators for the fourth quarter of 2015 - from the dashboard of the Labour Market Regulatory Authority (http://blmi.lmra.bh/2015/12/mi_dashboard.xml#key-messages-box – accessed on 16 May 2016)

12 Ibid.

13 Economic Yearbook 2013, Bahrain's Economic Development Board, page 10.

14 The role of the labour market as an instrument of the social contract is discussed in more detail in the context of the Middle East and North Africa region by Assaad (2013).

15 Based on calculations from IMF staff (see IMF 2013).

16 Bahrain and Saudi Arabia have signed a treaty on the shared offshore oil field Abu Safah which is operated by Saudi Arabia. This oil field is of the highest strategic importance for Bahrain because Bahrain derives from it 80% of its oil production and 70% of government revenues (Akbari and Stern 2012: 12). Without access to this oil field, it would have been impossible for Bahrain to maintain its current structure of government spending.

17 Subsidies for fuel, electricity, meat, etc., have already been cut down (EIU 2015).

18 These measures include: transferring the functions of the Supreme Council for Vocational Training to the Tamkeen labour fund, merging the Ministry of Labour with the Ministry of Social Development, merging the eGovernment Authority with the Central Informatics Organisation, upgrading the General Organisation for Youth and Sports to the Ministry of Your and Sports Affairs, incorporating the National Health Regulatory Authority into the Supreme Health Council, etc. (EDB 2015: 27).

19 Bahrain was the first country in the GCC region to initiate a serious and comprehensive public discussion of labour market reforms (Hertog 2014b: 10).

20 The Bahraini government launched in 2009 the "Economic Vision 2030" - a package of reforms aimed at reducing the dependency of the economy from oil and gas revenues and foreign labour. Private sector development and competitiveness are central objectives of the reform agenda.

21 LMRA website (http://lmra.bh/portal/en/page/show/56#.V1Iy4pFrjIU) – accessed May 4, 2016.

22 Bahrain Labour Market Indicators dashboard. (http://blmi.lmra.bh/2015/12/mi_dashboard.xml#key-messages-box – accessed 3 June 2016).

5

Business Sector and Labour Policies in Kuwait

Anastasia Nosova

Abstract

Since the implementation of the first welfare state measures in Kuwait in the 1960s, government employment has been one of the important means of wealth distribution, as it is coming with significant financial incentives, and is in general less demanding compared to the private sector. As such, it has long ceased to be seen as a privilege, but is rather considered an inherent right and a part of the social contract. This policy has led to the bulging of the government sector and the subsequent fast increase of budget spending on wages, which has become a serious economic burden expected to result in budget deficit and fiscal crisis in the not so distant future. Shifting the part of the burden of employment to the private sector is generally seen as a solution recipe for the problem. The patterns of reaching this goal have been more or less uniform in all GCC states and have been based around labour nationalisation, supporting entrepreneurship and widening the scope of private sector operation. Although various policies have been implemented in Kuwait to promote all three aspects, so far the success of those policies has been quite limited. The blame for the failure of labour reforms is often put on the national population itself, which is deemed neither qualified enough, nor willing to work in the private sector. The present paper, however, looks at the other angle of the problem, that is – the role of Kuwait's existing private sector and its prominent business players in the progress of labour reform policies. We argue that the unwillingness of the established business community to support national labour force, and more importantly, its ability to dodge the meaningful fulfillment of the labour policies' requirements, is one of the major stumbling blocks for the progress of those policies. We illustrate our argument with two policy case studies – the national labour quotas requirement and the support of small and medium enterprises. We will show that in the first case, the private sector companies utilise various means to avoid the genuine implementation of quotas, while in case of the SMEs development, they are not willing to contribute to the government's efforts in promoting new businesses, not least because they do not want any significant competitors to emerge.

Introduction

Kuwait's Labour Law No. 18/1960 stipulates that every citizen has the right to a job in the public sector[1]. Since the implementation of the first welfare state measures in Kuwait in the 1960s, government employment has been one of the important means of wealth distribution, as it is coming with significant financial incentives, and is in general less demanding compared to the private sector. As such, it has long ceased to be seen as a privilege, but is rather considered an inherent right and a part of the social contract.

This policy, however, has led to the bulging of the government sector and the subsequent fast increase of budget spending on wages, which has become a serious economic burden expected to result in budget deficit and fiscal crisis in the not so distant future. Such scope and pattern of spending have long been proclaimed unsustainable, and multiple recommendations from various international organisations and consultancies have been continuously issued stating the necessity for Kuwait to rationalise the spending through restructuring of employment patterns and reduction of subsidies on commodities and services.

Shifting the part of the burden of employment to private sector is generally seen as a solution recipe for the problem. The patterns of reaching this goal have been more or less uniform in all GCC states and have been based around labour nationalisation, supporting entrepreneurship and widening the scope of private sector operation. Although various policies have been implemented in Kuwait to promote all three aspects, so far the success of those policies has been quite limited.

The responsibility for the slow pace of those restructuring policies has been largely put on the government for being too reluctant to enforce them and opting for keeping the status quo for the sake of regime security. Like any other distribution mechanism in a rentier state system, government employment also serves to foster the economic dependency of the population on the state, thus enabling the latter to keep the national labour in check and providing it with an effective leverage tool in case of political discontent. By acquiring such a big role in the provision of day-to-day means and benefits to its citizens, the state also reserves the right to revoke them when necessary. Employment in government sector forestalls and de-legitimises political discontent. The provision of national employment in Kuwait, as it is actually the case in the rest of the GCC states, is therefore not only an economic requirement, but also a sensitive political matter.

At the same time, the blame for the failure of labour reforms is also often put on the national population itself, which is deemed neither qualified enough, nor willing to work in the private sector, which is considered more demanding.

The present paper, however, looks at the other angle of the problem, that is – the role of Kuwait's existing private sector and its prominent business players in the progress of labour reform policies. It is clear that there is little economic incentive for the private sector actors in Kuwait to substitute cheaper foreign workers with nationals. Thus, we argue that the unwillingness of the established business community to support national labour force, and more importantly, its ability to dodge the meaningful fulfillment of the labour policies' requirements, is one of the major stumbling blocks for the progress of those policies.

We illustrate our argument with two policy case studies – the national labour quotas requirement and the support of small and medium enterprises. We will show that in the first case, the private sector companies utilise various means to avoid the genuine implementation of quotas. Even if they do meet the quota or even exceed it, this does not necessarily mean that they are dedicated to developing the national workforce or integrating it in business operation. In case of the SMEs development, the government has recently made several attempts to encourage and support national small business. However, the existing and established private sector contributes relatively little to the government's effort, not least because the business actors do not want any significant competitors to emerge.

The paper will start with providing the analysis of the main features of the nature of business community in Kuwait and with briefly explaining the history of its formation. It will further focus on the labour nationalisation policies and the role of business in their implementation, while the next part will describe the case of small and medium enterprises development in Kuwait. In general, the paper aims to illustrate the direct and indirect (passive and active) role that the private sector in Kuwait is currently playing in the country's labour policies, and to draw conclusions about the position of business community in the context of current socio-economic changes and shifting state-society relations.

The paper is mainly based on empirical material, which was gathered during several extensive fieldwork trips to Kuwait throughout the past year. The data was collected through multiple interviews with the representatives of Kuwaiti private sector, young entrepreneurs, members of the Parliament, officials in government bodies aimed at implementing labour policies, and members of the SME fund board of directors. The collected information could be divided into two main types – the opinions of the respondents about certain topics and issues related to labour policies, and the storytelling, i.e. the information, which the respondents presented as facts. The latter was naturally biased and was further verified through media, secondary sources and cross-checking with other respondents. However, I consider the bias itself to be a valuable source of information about the attitudes of the respondents and conflicting relations within the society. Most of the interviews were conducted under conditions of anonymity due to the sensitivity of the topic and therefore will be referenced throughout the text under description.

The Main Features of Business Sector in Kuwait

Since the pre-oil times Kuwait has been a clearly stratified society, with a merchant elite being the major economic power and having a strong leverage in the country's political affairs. The establishment of Kuwait's political and economic hierarchy occured in the middle of the 18th century, when the wealthiest merchant families controlled the trading and pearling industries – the main sources of income for Kuwait at that time. It was these families that, according to the established myth, selected the Al Sabah to rule the country. Moreover, the ruling family used to be financially dependent on revenue from the merchants in the form of customs dues, taxes and loans. This relationship ensured the elite's participation in policy-making and gave the merchants the ability to challenge the rulers and engage in the power struggle, at the time that the Amir began to monopolise political power and gain economic independence on the eve of the oil era.

This historically formidable position of merchants vis-à-vis the ruling powers eventually enabled them to get a significant "piece of cake" of the oil-generated wealth. Their substantial economic benefits and business opportunities were secured by protectionist legislation. The Commercial Companies Law (Law No. 15/1960) barred any foreign companies or individuals from operating in Kuwait, unless they have a local agent or a partner who retains at least 51% of company ownership, while the ownership of shareholding companies was restricted only to Kuwaiti nationals[2]. These regulations effectively created immense opportunities for local business actors and protected them from foreign competition. Agency is a particularly important fiefdom for private sector, as it does not require a local businessman "to do much apart from signing off a contract and getting a commission"[3]. At the same time, state contracts have become one of the most substantial sources of enrichment for business.

Despite all the structural changes that the Kuwaiti private sector underwent with the emergence of the oil economy, it has also retained its pre-oil elitist oligarchic composition. The pattern of distribution of wealth and protection to private sector ensured that the business opportunities, agency rights and financial support were channeled to a relatively small merchant elite group[4]. Its core consists of those who were prominent since the pre-oil times. However, those families were also joined by newcomers, some of them being directly supported by the ruling powers or certain members of the ruling family[5].

With the protectionist legislation and state support, those merchant families and individuals have been able to largely monopolise the business opportunities and exclusively occupy various niches and fields of private sector economy. Most business groups would specialise in one particular sector (for example, food and catering for al-Ghunaim, al-Wazzan, construction for al-Thuwainy, retail for al-Shaya, industrial manufacturing for al-Khalid, etc.). However, the biggest ones, like al-Kharafi, al-Ghanim, al-Saqr, al-Bahar, al-Marzouq, Bukhamseen, Boodai, are diversified and have interests in multiple sectors.

The existence of de-facto monopolies and division of sectors among business groups is acknowledged by the members of Kuwaiti business community themselves, however they would most often explain it by the fact that "those merchants just do it better"[6], as if the monopoly was a result of a fair competition rather than a timely reservation of opportunities.

Thus, the business elite in Kuwait has been successfully reproduced and upgraded by the oil rentier system and through the new type of dependency-based relationship with the state. Its composition has been transformed. The criteria for being included in or considered a member of the merchant class are not solely based on origin anymore, as with the emergence of new business groups, the pre-oil family prominence has lost ground to assets. However, neither is the inclusion purely based on assets, as there are also plenty of rich individuals in Kuwait, who are to a certain extent involved in business, but who would not be considered or consider themselves members of the business class[7]. The membership is in a way a combination of both assets and origin, along with another important criterion – the proximity to the ruling powers, which ensures the channelling of preferential treatment. This proximity is often sustained through establishing joint business with (or managing business for) the ruling family members, as well as intermarriages with the ruling family.

To sum up, the business community in Kuwait represents a small elitist stratum of society with high barriers of entry, that owns a disproportionately large amount of wealth and opportunities compared to the rest of the population, and whose economic benefits are secured both legislatively and through close informal ties with the ruling powers. Such kind of business community has vested interests in preserving its privileged position and sustaining beneficial state policies, and therefore it also has incentives to interfere in policy-making, when its interests are endangered. The wealth and informal proximity to ruling powers provide the resources and means, through which this influence in channeled.

With the absence of almost any other type of national business activity, this is the sole representation of the private sector in Kuwait. Hence, its essential features should be necessarily taken into account when talking about the country's labour reforms and challenges to their progress. In the next two parts we will illustrate the obstructive role the established business community plays in the implementation of nationalisation of labour force in private sector and in fostering new business enterprises and SMEs.

Business Sector and the Policy of Labour Nationalisation

According to official statistics nearly 302,000 Kuwaitis work in the public sector, as opposed to around 82,000 in the private sector[8], while public sector salaries and subsidies increased by 540% within 2001-2011 period[9]. The important factor that contributes to the aggravation of situation is the rapid rise of the population that Kuwait has been witnessing since the 1980s[10]. It is estimated that 51% of the population is currently under 21 years old[11], which means that the number of new labour market entrants will be ever growing in the coming years, while the oversaturated public sector already has little capacity to accommodate them.

Nevertheless, the unemployment rate in Kuwait has been kept low (3.6% in 2008)[12], while the government sector has been expanding at an annual rate of 9% since 2005[13]. This clearly means that the government is still putting effort to create jobs, which leads to the development of redundant and un-/counterproductive workforce. The latter has come to be known as "disguised unemployment" (*batala muqanna'a*)[14]. Some respondents jokingly referred to a local anecdote, which claims that the average productivity of a Kuwaiti public sector employee is 20 minutes per week[15].

Therefore, the problem is not only in providing the population with whichever jobs the government can create. As the average education level is rising, young people are becoming disillusioned and frustrated by being allocated jobs that do not actually need to utilise their education and skills. Even according to official government procedures, PhD holders and foreign university graduates do not get any preferential treatment in terms of jobs allocation[16], and the distribution of job opportunities has been also heavily eroded by nepotistic practices, which further aggravates the frustration of young would-be employees who lack necessary informal connections. According to an interview with two young Kuwaitis, it is problematic to find a decent job in either public or private sector without having a proper "wasta" (i.e. a connector or informal relation)[17]. It is indicative that one of the respondents was on a waiting list for a government job for more than half a year, and was eventually assigned a job in the Ministry of Higher Education, which has nothing to do with his degree in logistics; another one has a PhD in engineering from a UK university, but has a nominal job where he does not even need to show up and is just receiving a salary.

Thus, the population is getting harder to appease and the discontent over the scarcity of jobs perceived as rewarding and the unequal distribution of opportunities is growing, while it is getting both financially and structurally difficult for the government to fulfill its employment obligations. Therefore, the labour issue represents one of the most serious structural challenges for both economic and political sustainability of all Gulf regimes, including Kuwait, and the urgency to resolve it has sharply increased.

Shifting the part of the burden of employment to private sector is generally seen as a solution, which has been continuously prescribed to the GCC governments by various international organisations and consultancies. The patterns of fulfilling those prescriptions have been more or less uniform in all GCC states and have been based around labour nationalisation, supporting entrepreneurship and widening the scope of private sector operation. Labour nationalisation policies, on one hand, aim to decrease the demand and supply of immigrant workers, and on the other hand – to increase the demand of national workers. Naturally, in none of the six Gulf states the attempt has been welcomed by the private sector, which perceives it as "tax on business", because of higher cost and lower productivity of local employees[18].

Remarkably, Kuwait was the first in the GCC to mull labour nationalisation policies in as early as 1978[19]. However, the idea was approached more seriously only in the 1990s. In 1993 a bill was passed proposing a quota of 30% private sector jobs for nationals, with incentives (such as government contracts) and penalties for companies, if they comply with the regulation and if they do not. The quota was later reviewed and adjusted for each sector. Companies in some sectors, mainly labour-oriented ones, were almost exempted from labour nationalisation requirement, as with the quota, they would simply become loss making[20]. For example, agriculture and manufacturing sectors have only 3% national employees quota. Other sectors, such as banking, financial services, communications, were assigned much higher quotas ranging from 15 to 66%, as they are less qualitatively affected by labour nationalisation and can afford paying higher salaries[21]. Penalties for not meeting the labour requirement are quite serious and include bans on importing foreign workers, barring from government contracts and government lands[22].

In 1997 the government also established a specialised entity, the Manpower and Government Restructuring Program (MGRP), which is aimed to develop policies to encourage the transfer of national labour from public to private sector. In 2000 the MGRP was authorised to pay salary subsidies to national private sector employees (as per Law 19/2000)[23]. Kuwait is the only GCC state which provides such salary subsidies on consistent basis[24], and this is arguably the major factor that explains relative success of labour nationalisation policies in the country.

It is clear that apart from subsidies and the prospect of penalties there is little incentive for private sector actors in Kuwait to substitute foreign workers with national labour force. Although the owners of large family corporations and members of established business elite claim that they wholeheartedly support labour nationalisation, which they see as a "social obligation", and even if their companies meet the quota or even exceed it[25], this does not necessarily mean developing the national workforce or integrating it in business operation. In reality there are multiple ways that the private companies utilise to avoid meaningful fulfillment of quota requirements. According to one of MGRP senior officials, there are two major schemes of quota manipulation[26]. One is based on increasing the amount of national employees in a company's subsidiary or sector, which is not directly related to its major business activity. For example, a bank, which needs to meet a high quota can sign a contract with a call centre company and employ 66% Kuwaitis there, claiming it to be a quota met by the bank. The alternative way is to reduce the national/expatriate employees' ratio by formally transferring the employment contracts of foreign workers to another subsidiary.

Another method, which is used to meet the quota on paper and which has become particularly widespread with the introduction of salary subsidies, is "phantom employment", i.e. employing nationals, but not requiring them to do any work, with the sole aim to meet the quota and collect the subsidy, which is then divided between the employer and "phantom employee". Companies often keep a desk in the office, so in case there is an inspection they could always claim that "the employee is in the field"[27]. They also show fake salary payrolls through bank account statements, but then withdraw all the money back. According to various accounts, both from business sector and government, the vast majority of companies, regardless of size, are involved in those practices, and a study by Markaz estimates that there are most likely tens of thousands of phantom employees in Kuwait[28].

One of the major problems that have been associated with the spread of fake employment is the lack of government's monitoring and ability to prosecute the wrongdoers. As it was emphasised in the interview with the MGRP official, although the body is responsible for the provision of subsidy, it has no authority to supervise the fulfillment of regulations and prevent the misuse of the subsidised money[29]. The monitoring is instead carried out by the Ministry of Labour and Social Affairs, which has no resources to inspect the companies efficiently or verify the data disclosed by business[30]. Arguably, punishment practices have neither been particularly effective. There are currently two main approaches to target fake employment: religious, i.e. shaming and blaming the practice itself based on the fact it is sinful and contradicts Islamic principles, and legislative, i.e. requiring the accused employer to return all the money he collected from subsidies. It has been claimed that about 1.2 mln KD has been returned so far[31], and 1500 companies have been prosecuted, while a small number of grossest violators have been given jail terms[32], although, it must be mentioned here, the names of the prosecuted companies are never made public.

Thus, as Baldwin-Edwards rightly mentions, the quotas and salary subsidies have been "quick-fix solutions which seem to create as many problems as they solve"[33]. Indeed, in terms of statistics, the number of nationals in private sector has increased quite fast in Kuwait: it is estimated that there are five times more Kuwaitis in the private sector now than in 2001[34]. However, taking into account the earlier mentioned means by which the private sector has been able to evade the regulations and in fact to take advantage of them, the quality and genuineness of this employment comes into question.

Some of the top business individuals argue that regardless of those labour nationalisation efforts, "the private sector still cannot compete with the state as employer of Kuwaitis", and in any case "cannot take all of them", and it is the structural flaws of the rentier system that should be addressed[35]. During the recent oil boom (starting from 2008), the outflow of private sector employees leaving their jobs to seek for public sector employment, when the salaries in government sector were increased, seems to corroborate this claim[36].

The baseline aim of the labour nationalisation policy is supposed to be the decrease of the dependency of the population on state, which would relieve the government from part of its expenses and obligations. However, keeping in mind the political nature of employment in Kuwait, in reality this economically long-term aim contradicts the regime's rentier foundations and shorter-term goal of political stability. In this entire situation, the private sector in its present shape and form is failing the effort in the most important aspect. By following its rent-seeking interests, it contributes to the lack of any meaningful development and productive integration of national labour force, which could indeed decrease its overall state-dependency. In this way, such nominal private sector employment of nationals serves the aim of the government, that is – to retain the population's state-dependency through distributing jobs regardless of their quality in order to avoid unemployment, as the latter poses a direct political threat. In the short term, the government can sustain phantom or nominal employment, but not unemployment[37].

Therefore, the means by which the labour nationalisation policy has been implemented have in fact dodged its initial aim, and what we currently observe is the substitution of one rent-seeking state dependency by another, only with more diversified means of rent distribution. Moreover, the subsidy and unemployment assistance schemes, which are administered by MGRP, are financed by 0.5% of the profits of listed companies, which is way too insufficient to cover the total costs, so a much larger part is paid in by the state[38]. Thus, the salary subsidies are in reality yet a new burden on the state budget.

Business Sector and the Support of Small and Medium Enterprises

Another policy, which goes hand in hand with the labour nationalisation and is also aimed at empowering national labour force in private sector, is the support to small and medium enterprises (SMEs) in Kuwait. The country is home to several dozens large business corporations, some of them being prominent on the regional level. At the same time, they constitute no more than 15% of the total number of private enterprises in Kuwait, while the rest are small businesses, the vast majority of which employ and are operated by non-Kuwaitis[39], while only 1% of national labour force is involved in them[40]. Therefore, increasing participation of Kuwaitis in small business has also been considered a potential contribution to the restructuring of national employment.

So far the government has made several attempts to encourage and support national SMEs. As it is known that SMEs find it hard to raise funds and obtain bank loans, due to the unwillingness of banks to take risks[41], the government has designated two separate bodies to support SMEs financially – the Kuwait Small Project Development Company and the Kuwait Industrial Bank. The former was established in 1996 with a capital of 100 million KD by Kuwait Investment Authority[42]. The portfolio of Kuwait Industrial Bank was established in 1998 and was worth 50 million KD. Despite the substantial capital, both of these bodies have been criticised in media for "just pumping money" without planning or proper technical and training support to the new business enterprises [43].

The most recent and significant attempt in this direction was the launching of a 2 billion KD fund in March 2013 "to achieve the objectives of the Small and Medium Enterprises"[44]. The government officials have proclaimed their grand hopes with regards to the new effort, which is aimed to ensure "a bigger role for the SMEs to give impetus to the national economy and to diversify its resources away from oil industry to achieve sustainable development and welfare"[45]. Unlike the past experiments, the current fund will also provide training, and is likely to allow the would-be entrepreneurs to apply for funding while still holding a government job[46] – the restriction that prevented many from approaching the funds previously[47].

It is remarkable that the existing and established private sector, i.e. leading companies and prominent business individuals, contribute relatively little to the government's effort to support small and medium businesses. The role of Kuwait Chamber of Commerce and Industry, the stronghold of the old merchant elite, is limited to providing paid courses and workshops about small business and self-employment, and it is often accused by government officials of being focused on the interests of big businesses only[48]. In general, the provision of private SMEs-related training courses has become a business on its own, which can bring good income, while there is little investment in training from the side of private sector.

All in all, there is little genuine will from the part of the big business to help small and rising one, not least because the established private sector actors do not want any significant competitors to emerge. Neither does the state's legislation provide for integrating small businesses in the activities of the established ones[49]. As one of the employees in the SME promotion department of MGRP put it, "there is no real support … If there was genuine support [from big business] we would see a completely different picture"[50]. This lack of action, however, is already indicative of the merchants' stance on the issue of small business, as according to C. Wright Mills, the "failure [of elite] to act, their failure to make decisions, is in itself an act that is often of greater consequence than the decisions they do make"[51].

In a way, however, big businesses still have to show some formal support for SMEs out of "social responsibility" or publicity reasons[52]. There have been attempts to engage prominent merchant elite members in various SME-related events as role models to share their experience in entrepreneurship and motivate young people to consider private sector career. However, such "motivational" support from businessmen, who have semi-monopolised whole sectors of economy, is hardly relevant to the experiences of SME entrepreneurs[53]. It is obvious that the problems that the latter is normally complaining about in Kuwait's business environment, such as licencing procedures, high rent, visa restrictions and quotas on foreign labour etc., are quite different from the concerns of large monopolist businessmen, "who can cut the red tape with a phone call"[54].

Indeed, inefficient predatory bureaucracy has most often been called the major factor obstructing the development of small business in Kuwait. The bureaucratic procedures are seen so overly lengthy and complicated, compared to other Gulf countries, that Kuwaitis joke that "if you could start a business in Kuwait, you can start it anywhere in any environment"[55]. Young entrepreneurs believe that these burdensome expenses at establishing a business might even deplete the whole state-awarded initial capital before the business even starts operating. For this reason, there is already a lot of scepticism about the new 2 billion KD fund, as the funding by itself is not seen as a panacea that would bring any drastic changes to the situation. Many also expect that the fund would suffer from corruption and nepotism as much as the previous funding portfolios did, which means that it would only support applicants with prominent family names and high-profile connections[56]. In essence, this restricts the funding almost exclusively to the offspring of the same merchant elite and prominent individuals.

Furthermore, there is lack of legislation that would ensure state support to small and medium companies during the initial stages of their operation, for example through government contracts, which would play a role of guaranteed "market" and protect them from competition from larger and established players[57]. For this reason, SMEs in such sectors as manufacturing are very difficult to operate, and are almost non-existent in Kuwait.

All these factors result in a very poor situation of national SMEs in Kuwait. The two funding portfolios mentioned earlier – Kuwait Small Project Development Company and Kuwait Industrial Bank – are known to have allocated no more than 70 million KD throughout the whole period of their operation, which is less than half of their total capital[58]. They have also been criticised for funding companies without prior feasibility studies, which have therefore subsequently failed, as well as businesses that ultimately did not employ Kuwaitis[59]. Indeed, most small businesses emerge in sectors like catering (restaurants, small-scale food production), services, accessories production, etc. Very often the owners of those businesses retain jobs in public (or even private) sector[60]. For this reason, national small business is often looked down upon and even not considered as genuine small business at all[61].

The preference towards those sectors, however, is also a result of the absence of protective legislation mentioned earlier and the fear of competition: "All small business goes to restaurants at cetera to be away from big giants ... It is a comfort zone [for them] ... No young Kuwaitis think of challenging them, they will destroy you through the government ... Big business does not want new ones to grow, they want the market to be fixed ... [This explains why] successful small businesses are often acquired by big ones"[62]. These reasons – bureaucracy and dominance of established businesses – push the small business to search for better environment outside Kuwait. It is indicative that the country is the second biggest investor (in terms of SMEs) in the UAE[63].

There is no doubt that big business in Kuwait also suffers from red tape, which they see as the result of "jealousy from a parasitic public sector"[64]. However, the social position of business elite individuals (their close connections with top officials and ruling powers), as well as the availability of sufficient funds to buy off public sector officials when necessary, enables them to overcome the red tape roadblocks. "They do not wait in line" for months, like small business entrepreneurs, but "go [straight] to officials to cut through red tape"[65]. According to an anecdotic reference, the top family companies and private sector individuals "have their own people in all main [official] bodies", who are added to payrolls and are paid "almost monthly salaries". One of the examples of the effect of such public-private relations was given by a young Kuwaiti businessman working in the sphere of mobile accessories retailing. According to him, he constantly faces delays with shipments of his goods at customs, which is very harmful for his business, as the price of these particular goods is very dependent on the time they go on sale; at the same time, he can witness how the goods of bigger and more prominent retailers are never subject to any delays and go through customs straight away[66]. A widespread Kuwaiti joke, which reflects the extent of public-private corruption and informality of relations, says that "even if the government stops paying public officials, they will still be working because of those unofficial salaries"[67].

The corruptive pattern of public-private relations creates an opportunity for mutual benefits and a shadow economy of its own, hidden behind inefficient bureaucracy. On one hand, it allows public sector officials to prey on business and make profit just from creating obstacles, on another, it keeps a high barrier for entrance and operation in the private sector, restricting it to a small circle of established business players. Even though it might be also costly and time-consuming for them too, it pays off by turning away new players and potential competitors, preserving the established monopolies. This symbiosis steers the wheel of corruption.

Thus, as long as their interests are protected, the major business players have little incentive to change the situation. In fact, the improvement of business environment, reduction of red tape and corruption in public sector, and promotion of the emergence of new business contradict the rent-seeking interests of the existing private sector. Therefore, its very nature and mode of interaction with public sector would obstruct any policies aimed at nourishing new business players and companies.

The position of the dominant business players towards newcomers in the private sector is further evident in the fact that the current (2013) National Assembly, which is dominated by pro-business interests and is actively promoting policies that would benefit merchants, has done very little in terms of the support for the SMEs. It is indicative that, despite being launched in 2013, the afore-mentioned 2 billion KD fund to support SMEs and young entrepreneurs is still barely functioning, and there has been little pressure from the Parliament to speed up the development.

Conclusion

The paper has attempted to analyse the attitude of Kuwait's business sector towards government's efforts to restructure the national labour force. It has shown that the stance of the existing business community on various government policies and initiatives is largely defined by its rent-seeking self-interests, which stem from the very nature of a rentier system-based private sector – elitist, oligarchic and monopolistic, and in case of Kuwait, with a long history of protecting and expanding its economic interests and privileges.

We have argued that some of the major policy steps that have been taken by the government towards reforming the national labour are either of little interest to the dominant business players, or openly oppose their economic preferences. Thus, their natural response to such policies is to resist them actively or passively. It has been shown that Kuwaiti merchant community retains significant means of influence, which can be utilised to reverse or stall the implementation of the policies that compromise its vital interests. The latter, in their turn, are concentrated around the preservation of the elitist, monopolist nature of private sector with high entry barriers and special relations with the ruling powers. Hence, the preference of the status quo, however dysfunctional and inefficient it might seem. Thus, the discourse of labour reforms, which is indiscriminately offered by dominant international institutions and which assumes that the private sector should play the leading role as the main employer of national labour force, is hardly implementable on the ground.

The factors, which define the behaviour of business community with regards to the labour policies, also point to the major reasons behind the growing antagonism of the larger population towards the merchant elite. Its monopolist nature, ability to navigate bureaucratic environment, involvement in corrupted practices, ability to influence political discourse, and as a result, secure its rent-seeking interests – all reveal the huge disparity between the established business community and less privileged and more numerous stratum of population, which feels that it "is getting the crumbs of the piece if cake that merchants and ruling powers are dividing between themselves"[68]. Such antagonism and unfolding socio-economic conflict, in its turn, means that it is getting increasingly difficult for the government to promote and justify large-scale austerity measures in public sector for the sake of sustainable development, while a small merchant elite preserves its privileges and is able to evade imposed regulations.

References

Abdalla, I. and Al-Homoud, M. (2012) 'Foreign faces in Kuwaiti places: the challenges of human capital utilization in Kuwait', *International Journal of Business and Management* 7(20), Canadian Center of Science and Education.

Al-Awadhi, I. (2014) 'Kuwaiti nationals waiting for a job', *Kuwait Times*, 11 January; accessed at http://news.kuwaittimes.net/kuwaiti-nationals-waiting-job/

Al-Baghdādī, R. (2014) 'Fī al-Kuwait laisa bi al-māl al-wahdi tuḥiyā al-mashārī' aṣ-ṣaghīra' [In Kuwait it is not only money that bring to life small enterprises], *Al-Ḥayāt* (Arabic), 16 February; accessed at http://alhayat.com/Articles/659659/في-الكويت-ليس-بالمال-وحده-تحيا-المشاريع-الصغيرة

Al-Kuwari, D. (2013) *Mission Impossible? Genuine Economic Development in the Gulf Cooperation Council Countries*, London School of Economics Kuwait Programme Research Papers.

Al-Nakib, F. (2014) 'Revisiting Hadar and Badu in Kuwait: citizenship, housing, and the construction of dichotomy', *International Journal of Middle East Studies* 46: 5–30.

Al-Tamimi, A. T. (2013) 'Plan to support small businesses in Kuwait lacks clear vision', *Al-Monitor*, 15 March; accessed at http://tinyurl.com/ydcc7yoq

Al-Yaqout, A. (2013) 'Door to total foreign ownership in companies opened in Kuwait', *Kuwait Times*, 3 November.

Al-Zumai, F. (2013) *Kuwait's Political Impasse and Rent-Seeking Behaviour: A Call for Institutional Reform*, London School of Economics Kuwait Programme Research Papers.

Arab Times (2013) 'Kuwait SMEs Fund Could Boost Jobs', *Arab Times*, 26 April, accessed at http://tinyurl.com/yd2m4z9r

Azoulay, R. (2013) 'The politics of Shi'i merchants in Kuwait' in S. Hertog, G. Luciani, M. Valeri (eds) *Business Politics of the Middle East*, 67-100. London: Hurst.

Baldwin-Edwards, M. (2011) *Labour Immigration and Labour Markets in the GCC Countries: National Patterns and Trends*, London School of Economics Kuwait Programme Research Papers.

Central Statistical Bureau, 2015.

Hertog, S. (2013) *The Private Sector and Reform in the Gulf Cooperation Council*, London School of Economics Kuwait Programme Research Papers.

Hertog, S. (2014) 'The GCC's national employment challenge', *The Washington Post*, 31 July; accessed at http://tinyurl.com/y8qe7k2z

Ibrahim, A. A. (2014b) 'Equal indemnity for govt, private sectors, says law', *Arab Times*, 6 July; accessed at http://tinyurl.com/y8okpcdp

Kuwait Economic Society (KES) (2013) 'Blueprint for public sector good governance in Kuwait: four policies for administrative reform', July 2013.

Kuwait News Agency (2013) 'SMEs Fund, step forward to diversify Kuwait economy', *Kuwait News Agency*, 24 February; accessed at http://tinyurl.com/ybwajsde

Kuwait Times (2014a) 'National labor quotas increased in private sector', *Kuwait Times*, 25 August; accessed at http://tinyurl.com/yc2vs3yz

Kuwait Times (2014b) 'Government to implement development plan projects: Minister', *Kuwait Times*, 15 December; accessed at http://tinyurl.com/yacf3aol

Markaz (2012) 'Towards sustainable economic development: policies towards involving Kuwaitis in the Private labour market', *Kuwait Financial Centre S.A.K. (Markaz)*, May 2012.

Mayenkar, S. S. (2014) 'UAE business climate top draw for GCC nationals', *Gulf News*, 30 September; accessed at http://tinyurl.com/ybhlvd6s

Mills, C. W. (1956) *The Power Elite*, London: Oxford University Press.

Oxford Business Group (2014) 'The Report: Kuwait 2014', accessed at http://tinyurl.com/y974nhpa

Randeree, K. (2012) 'Workforce nationalization in the Gulf Cooperation Council states', *Occasional Paper No. 9*, Doha: CIRS, Georgetown University School of Foreign Service in Qatar.

Tétreault, M. A. (2000) *Stories of Democracy: Politics and Society in Contemporary Kuwait*, N.Y.: Columbia University Press.

Notes

1 I. Abdalla and M. Al-Homoud (2012) 'Foreign Faces in Kuwaiti Places: The Challenges of Human Capital Utilization in Kuwait', *International Journal of Business and Management* 7 (20) (Canadian Center of Science and Education), p. 5.

2 Al-Yaqout, A. (2013) 'Door to total foreign ownership in companies opened in Kuwait', *Kuwait Times*, 3 November: http://news.kuwaittimes.net/door-total-foreign-ownership-companies-opened-kuwait/

3 Personal interview with a teaching member of staff in Finance Department, Kuwait University; Kuwait, November 2014.

4 According to the views of the respondents from of the merchant background, there are approximately 50 large business groups.

5 See R. Azoulay (2013) 'The politics of Shi'i merchants in Kuwait' in S. Hertog, G. Luciani, M. Valeri (eds) *Business Politics of the Middle East*, 67-100. London: Hurst..

6 Personal interview with a member of an old Sunni merchant family; Kuwait, May 2014.

7 Personal interview with a professor in Public Policy Department, Kuwait University; Kuwait, May 2014.

8 Al-Awadhi, I. (2014) 'Kuwaiti nationals waiting for a job', *Kuwait Times*, 11 January: http://news.kuwaittimes.net/kuwaiti-nationals-waiting-job/

In 2013 total national population of Kuwait was estimated to be 1,159,787 (33.6%), while the amount of non-Kuwaitis reached 2,288,352 (66.4%). The number of non-Kuwaitis working in private sector is 1,249,033, which means that Kuwaitis (56829) constitute only 4.4% of private sector labour force (Central Statistical Bureau, 2015).

9 F. Al-Zumai (2013) *Kuwait's Political Impasse and Rent-Seeking Behaviour: A Call for Institutional Reform* (London School of Economics Kuwait Programme Research Papers), p. 9.

10 In case of Kuwait, the improved healthcare, high birth rate and growing welfare of the population are not the only reasons behind such a sharp increase in numbers: the current population rate is also the result of the government's naturalisation policies, particularly throughout the 1980s (Tétreault, 2000: 108; F. Al-Nakib, 2014). Arbitrary naturalisation (as much as arbitrary revocation of citizenship) has been a tool the Kuwaiti ruling powers utilised in times of the rise of political opposition to increase the physical number of its allies and supporters in exchange for citizenship and welfare, which comes along with it.

11 Estimates by Kuwait Finance House quoted in 'The Report: Kuwait 2014', Oxford Business Group, 2014: http://tinyurl.com/y974nhpa

12 M. Baldwin-Edwards (2011) *Labour Immigration and Labour Markets in the GCC Countries: National Patterns and Trends* (London School of Economics Kuwait Programme Research Papers), p. 19, 21.

13 'Blueprint for Public Sector Good Governance in Kuwait: Four Policies for Administrative Reform', Kuwait Economic Society, July 2013, p. 14.

14 Personal interview with one of the senior officials in MGRP; Kuwait, November 2014.
15 Personal interview with a member of an old Sunni merchant family; Kuwait, May 2014.
16 Kuwait Economic Society (2013), p. 15.
17 Personal interviews; Kuwait, March 2014.
18 Hertog, S. (2013) *The Private Sector and Reform in the Gulf Cooperation Council*, London School of Economics Kuwait Programme Research Papers, p. 16.
19 K. Randeree (2012) 'Workforce Nationalization in the Gulf Cooperation Council States', *Occasional Paper No. 9* (Doha: CIRS, Georgetown University School of Foreign Service in Qatar), p. 18.
20 Personal interviews with a member of an old Sunni merchant family and a member of Kuwait Economic Society who is working in banking industry; Kuwait, May 2014.
21 The quotas have also been recently slightly increased (for example, from 2 to 3% in agriculture and from 60 to 66% in banking) ('National labor quotas increased in private sector', Kuwait Times, 25 August 2014): http://news.kuwaittimes.net/national-labor-quotas-increased-private-sector/
22 Markaz (2012) 'Towards sustainable economic development: policies towards involving Kuwaitis in the Private labour market', *Kuwait Financial Centre S.A.K. (Markaz)*, May 2012, p.17.
23 The same decree (No. 19/2000), which introduced the salary subsidies, extended various social allowances to Kuwaitis working in private sector, while in July 2014 the Parliament has also agreed to extend ends-of-service indemnity rights to all Kuwaiti employees ('Equal Indemnity For Govt, Private Sectors, Says Law', Arab Times, 6 July 2014): http://tinyurl.com/y8okpcdp
24 S. Hertog (2014) *The GCC's national employment challenge*, The Washington Post, 31 July 2014.
25 Personal interview with a member of an old Sunni merchant family, which is one of the wealthiest in Kuwait and also has consistent presence on political arena; Kuwait, November 2014.
26 Personal interview with one of the senior officials in MGRP; Kuwait, November 2014.
27 Personal interview with a member of family business group operating in automotive field (medium rank); Kuwait, November 2014.
28 Markaz (2012), p. 24.
29 Personal interview with one of the senior officials in MGRP; Kuwait, November 2014.
30 Markaz (2012), p. 18.
31 1 Kuwaiti Dinar equals $3.31.
32 Personal interview with one of the senior officials in MGRP; Kuwait, November 2014.
33 Baldwin-Edwards (2011), p. 48.
34 Markaz (2012), p. 21.
35 Personal interviews with members of two prominent Sunni merchant families.
36 Abdalla and Al-Homoud (2012), p. 6; Kuwait Economic Society (2013), p. 18.
37 Personal interview with a partner of an international auditing company operating in Kuwait; Kuwait, November 2014.
38 Markaz (2012), p. 21.
39 A. Al-Tamimi (2013) *Plan to Support Small Businesses in Kuwait Lacks Clear Vision*, Al-Monitor, 15 March 2013, http://tinyurl.com/ydcc7yoq
40 'Kuwait SMEs Fund Could Boost Jobs', Arab Times, 26 April 2013: http://tinyurl.com/yd2m4z9r
41 D. Al-Kuwari, D. (2013) *Mission Impossible? Genuine Economic Development in the Gulf Cooperation Council Countries*, London School of Economics Kuwait Programme Research Papers, p. 26.
42 The portfolio was managed by KAMCO, the assets management arm of Kuwait Projects Company – an investment holding owned by Sheikh Hamad, the son of the current Amir.
43 Al-Baghdādī, R. (2014) 'Fī al-Kuwait laisa bi al-māl al-wahdi tuḥiyā al-mashārīʿ aṣ-ṣaghīra' [In Kuwait it is not only money that bring to life small enterprises], *Al-Ḥayāt* (Arabic), 16 February: http://alhayat.com/Articles/659659/في-الكويت-ليس-بالمال-وحده-تحيا-المشاريع-الصغيرة
44 'SMEs Fund, step forward to diversify Kuwait economy', Kuwait News Agency, 24 February 2013: http://tinyurl.com/ybwajsde
45 'Government to implement development plan projects: Minister', Kuwait Times, 15 December 2014: http://tinyurl.com/yacf3aol

46 Oxford Business Group (2014).
47 Personal interview with a member of family business group operating in automotive field (medium rank); Kuwait, November 2014.
48 Personal interview with one of the senior officials in MGRP; Kuwait, November 2014.
49 Personal interview with a member of a prominent Shi'i merchant family, who however considers himself a businessman of a small/medium rank, and who has started an organisation aimed to help SMEs by providing training and skills and organising relevant events; Kuwait, January 2014.
50 Personal interview with one of the senior officials in MGRP; Kuwait, November 2014.
51 C. Wright Mills (1959) *The Power Elite*, p. 4.
52 Personal interview with a member of a prominent Shi'i merchant family, who has started an organisation dedicated to assist SMEs in Kuwait; Kuwait, January 2014.
53 The observation is based on experience of attending one of such events.
54 Personal interview with a professor in Political Science Department, Kuwait University; Kuwait, April 2014.
55 Personal interview with a young Kuwaiti businessman operating a small firm in phone accessories industry; Kuwait, November 2014.
56 Al-Baghdādī, R. (2014).
57 Personal interview with a Kuwaiti businessman who tried and failed to launch an SME business in Kuwait and had to move to work in another Gulf state because of better business environment; Kuwait, November 2014.
58 Ibid; Al-Baghdādī, R. (2014); Al-Tamimi (2013).
59 Al-Tamimi (2013).
60 Personal interview with a partner of an international auditing company operating in Kuwait; Kuwait, November 2014.
61 Ibid; multiple interviews with business owners, Kuwait, November 2014.
62 Personal interview with a member of family business group operating in automotive field (medium rank); Kuwait, November 2014.
63 'UAE business climate top draw for GCC nationals', Gulf News, 30 September 2014: http://tinyurl.com/ybhlvd6s
64 Personal interview with a senior member of a prominent Sunni merchant family; Kuwait, November 2014.
65 Personal interview with a member of family business group operating in automotive field (medium rank); Kuwait, November 2014.
66 Personal interview; Kuwait, November 2014.
67 Personal interview with a member of family business group operating in automotive field (medium rank); Kuwait, November 2014.
68 Personal interview with a teaching member of staff in Literature Department, Kuwait University; he was previously involved in politics and is currently closely connected to opposition-leaning media outlet; Kuwait, March 2014.

6

The Future of Learning in the GCC: An Analysis of the Current State and the Way Forward to a More Positive Approach to Education and Organisational Learning

Radhika Punshi and Elizabeth Topolskaya

Abstract

According to a recent report by the World Economic Forum "in the context of an increasingly competitive global economy, the transition from education to productive and rewarding employment is challenging for young people everywhere". However, the situation is even more profound in the MENA region, including the GCC with its persistent levels of high youth unemployment and under-employment and expanding population where "2.8 million young people are entering the labour market every year." (WEF, 2014). Developing the skills, capabilities and mindset of youth is absolutely crucial both within and without the formal education system. The total number of students in the GCC region is expected to grow from an estimated 10.2 million in 2011 to 11.6 million in 2016, a compound annual growth rate of 2.7% (Khaleej Times, 2015).

The effective learning and transmission of knowledge, skills and culture has always been a critical means of achieving human development. Since the establishments of civilisation, this has at least partly been achieved through formal education for academic or vocational purposes and new technology challenges existing methods and provides greater opportunities to enhance the effectiveness and efficiency of learning. Our world is increasingly being recognised as a VUCA world (volatile, uncertain, complex and ambiguous), whether from an environmental, economic or employability perspective. As the recent decline in oil prices and the increasingly chaotic regional geo-political situation has demonstrated, there has been no time more urgent that today to skill, upskill and reskill our population to diversify our economies and build the knowledge-based hubs which are crucial to every GCC nations strategic vision.

For some time now, the region's policy-makers have committed to the establishment of 'knowledge-based economies" which will accelerate the continued development of their societies beyond their reliance on energy revenues and the dependence on government employment and rent-seeking behaviour which results. In addition, recent work by Ridge (2014) and Jones, Le Ray and Punshi (2016) has cited the cultural preference for more passive, didactic forms of learning, the differential roles of nationals and expatriates as positive teaching role-models amongst boys and girls in determining their drastically different levels of average performance. Within the GCC in general, girls outperform boys in all subjects, whereas in most of the rest of the world, boys still outperform girls in STEM subjects.

The question remains as to how? How can skills and talents been developed at the national level targeting impact and change across millions of youth. What practices does technology impact how knowledge is imparted, both within the classroom and outside? And finally, what practices are employers adopting towards accelerating their learning and development strategies? In sum, contemporary socio-cultural, scientific, and technological advances are transforming the very essence of learning - both within our education systems and more so in the workplace.

This paper will focus what is the future of learning in the GCC and what are the challenges and opportunities towards skill development for policy-makers, employers and educators, using an evidence-based approach.

The first part of the paper will set the theoretical context on the topic under discussion, highlighting key demographic and learning trends, both from a local and global perspective. The second section of the paper will focus on providing empirical data from an online research survey on the future of learning conducted with over 200+ L&D professionals representing public and private sector organisations from the GCC. The quantitative research will shed light on the perspectives and practices of senior human capital and learning professionals on the current and future state of learning, focus on national talent development, and views on alternative forms of learning such as gamification and e-learning. The third and final section will provide a comprehensive case study analysis on three particular developments in learning at the macro level – the rise of government-funded and supported MOOC's with nation-wide platforms such as Edraak Jordan, funded by the Queen Rania Foundation and Doroob in Saudi Arabia, supported by the Ministry of Labour and the Human Resource Development Fund, both impacting 1000's of learners in the Arab world every year. The case study section will also focus on the launch and progress of the Smart Schools initiative in Dubai, known as the he Mohammad Bin Rashid Smart Learning Program. The paper will conclude by providing a critique of the empirical and qualitative data presented with some clear recommendations on what the future of learning and skill development may look like up to 2020 and beyond.

Literature Review

Scholars have been studying the concept of learning for a significant amount of time, coming up with various definitions and theories of learning. One very important concept that commenced the development of many sub-theories, is behaviourism, where scholars focus on objective and observable part of acting – behaviour, omitting the cognitive processes that happen alongside the acts of an individual (Leahey, 2000, p.686). Behaviourists are yet to agree on a single definition for the concept (Mills, 1998); however, several distinct movements have stemmed from behaviourism, including classical conditioning (Watson & Rayner, 1920), operant conditioning (Skinner, 1968) and social learning theory (Bandura, 1969).

Another learning theory worth looking at and considering, that has had a significant impact on academia, is Bloom's taxonomy (Krathwohl, 2002) with cognitive, affective and psychomotor domains (Krathwohl, Bloom & Masia, 1964), casting light on why some objectives are less conducive to the critical cognitive processes than others. In general, traditional learning settings typically rely on memorizing facts, rather than encouraging the use of analytical or creative skills (Boumova, 2008). Powell and Tod (2004) have also pointed out, that the current education system can be referred to as discouraging and demotivating. Generally speaking, the taxonomy is represented by a pyramid of levels, that build upon one another, leading to the topmost - evaluation (in the older version) or creativity (in the new interpretation) (Krathwohl, 2002; Pohl, 2000). The levels are arranged from the most basic to the most challenging objectives, starting from knowledge, followed by comprehension, application, analysis, synthesis and evaluation (Krathwohl, 2002; Pohl, 2000). The application of this theory to the sphere of employee education would be to ensure the creators of the program value the most important objectives that motivate employees to think creatively and critically, rather than a mere memorization of facts or technical details.

Bloom has also presented the academic world with the affective domain of learning, which is composed of five stages: receiving, responding, valuing, organization and characterization (Krathwohl et al., 1964). Affective domain describes objectives, which focus on tone, emotions, acceptance of values or concepts and an overall emotional consonance or dissonance with an idea (Krathwohl et al., 1964). In order to properly integrate the new idea into the employee's system of values, it is vital to encourage not just accepting the idea, but also to evaluate it, placing it relative to their personal values or even to maybe characterize the self by the idea, through consistent acting upon one (Koballa & Glynn, in press).

Overall, although it is important to look back and base the decision regarding the curriculum on the well-researched and empirically established base, it is crucial to remain flexible and integrate the newly available effective methods into the employee training. One of such methods is known as "70-20-10" method (Jennings, 2013), which has been adopted in many organizations as the new mantra in order to transform and "flip" the traditional or "classroom" view on learning. The framework suggests that effective learning does not necessarily need to take place in the traditional didactic setting in order to happen, as 70%

of what people learn typically occurs during the normal workflow, 20% through talking to colleagues and sharing experience, and only 10% in a classroom (Jennings, 2013).

Therefore, leaders should consider organizing daily workflow in a way that will be challenging enough for the employees to remain motivated and gain valuable experience, or "adding learning to work" (70:20:10 Forum Pty Ltd, 2015). Learning needs to be integrated within the workflow, through supporting the employees in their challenges, as well as through the efficient utilization of the networks (70:20:10 Forum Pty Ltd, 2015). This method is a great illustration that the challenging work environment can yield a productive, motivated and engaged workforce, as only a task that is difficult enough can produce the state of flow, which is the enjoyable state of complete focus and absorption by the just manageable, yet challenging task (Csikszentmihalyi, 1990; Nakamura & Csikszentmihalyi, 2002).

For workers, the concept of 70-20-10 learning can present significant benefits not only through the potential achievement of the state of flow (Csikszentmihalyi, 1990), but also through personal development. This framework implies that creation of a "high performance culture" in the organization (Corporate Learning Council, 2003), requiring individuals to be continuously involved in the learning process, which leads to self-development, engagement and higher job satisfaction (70:20:10 Forum Pty Ltd, 2015). Engagement is a very pressing issue in the Middle East, as, according to the Gallup study, the region stands the lowest in the world, where only about 10% of the employees are engaged in the Middle East (Gallup, 2012; Jones & Punshi, 2013, p.146). It has also been noted, that the GCC region has a significant gap between the engagement levels of nationals and expatriates, with only 43.7% engagement amongst local citizen, and 56.1% in expats (Jones, 2015, p. 130). As Jones and Punshi (2013) pointed out, it is crucial to achieve higher levels of engagement in the Middle East in order to develop the workforce that is able to achieve economic progress. The new learning and development strategies should focus on improving the engagement through informal and more involving learning, such as gamification.

Furthermore, informal learning trends illustrated by the 70-20-10 framework, can significantly influence the mindset of individuals through continuous education. Growth mindset presumes that the intelligence is malleable and can be developed, opposite to fixed mindset, where intelligence is considered to be unchangeable (Dweck, 2006). Therefore, if the company establishes the culture of incessant learning and self-development, it is highly unlikely that employees will be able to maintain the fixed mindset. Individuals with growth mindsets tend to focus more on learning objectives, rather than performance goals, or creating a certain image to impress the colleagues (Grant & Dweck, 2003). Growth mindset also contributes to higher motivation and engagement in the educational activities as well as better learning strategies after a setback or failure (Dweck, 2008; Blackwell, Trzesniewski & Dweck, 2007), as learners are willing to absorb new information, even in the face of hindrances. Non-conventional ways of delivering information are able to increase motivation and even further, making the learning process involving and enjoyable for employees, e.g. gamification increased employee engagement by 48% and reduced the employee turnover by 36% in Aberdeen Group (Pflug & Jara, 2014).

Apart from the informal learning, relationships play a crucial role in the effectiveness of learning; it is vital to establish positive connections with those who deliver the information (Evans, 1996; Powell & Tod, 2004). Positive education, if set up correctly, can contribute to higher engagement levels and well-being (Geelong, 2012). Positivity, in general, be it in the workplace or in the classroom, should be adopted as part of the culture, as it has been frequently linked to increased success (Achor, 2010; Staw, Sutton, & Pelled, 1994). Due to the fact that employees working in an organization with an overwhelmingly positive culture tend to be more engaged, motivated and are less vulnerable to "burnout" (Lyubomirsky, King & Diener, 2005), such workforce is especially beneficial for the company. Happy employers are lucrative for the organization, they are capable to make wiser choices, assess the broader picture, be effective leaders and come up with creative solution to challenging problems (Cabrera, 2012; Fredrickson & Branigan, 2005; Staw & Barsade, 1993), hence all educational initiatives must be conducted in a positive, non-pressurizing atmosphere, if, in fact, it has been decided to use the conventional methods.

Traditionally, employee education has been associated with formal courses in a classroom setting, delivering mostly knowledge necessary for the technicalities of the job one is performing, as it has been reflected in several research papers (Gerzon, Heuer, Kibbee, Nielsen & Veal, 2006; Scott, 2010; Harvard Business Review Survey, 2015; Australian Public Service Survey, 2012). Technical skills, although being located on the lowest level of Bloom's taxonomy, hence not conducive to the utilization of critical thinking capabilities, are currently prioritized for training programs in the GCC region (Jones, Punshi & Griffiths, 2015). Employers all over GCC are reporting that around 49% of graduates (specifically in Bahrain) lacked the required "soft skills" (Punshi, Mirza & Gupta, 2015), which contributes to the workforce that is not developed enough to truly utilize the potential. However, employee training could potentially solve the problem by providing the courses and guidance to fill in the skill gap. Soft skills must be prioritized, as many of them, including resilience, can and should be developed through specifically selected interventions, opposite to the idea that they are a part of the fixed personality traits (McAllister and McKinnon 2008; McDonald et al. 2012 & 2013; Beddoe et al. 2013). Many of valuable skills can be integrated into the training programs, including "communication, teamwork, resilience, self-confidence, negotiation, self-expression etc." (Punshi, Mirza & Gupta, 2015). That leaves employers with tremendous opportunities to develop the workforce that has the strengths required to successfully work in the company, e.g. tailor the employees to the company needs. Taking the concept further, with the strategically targeted positive psychology interventions, it is not at all impossible to switch the mindsets of the employees to the "growth" direction (Dweck, 2008).

Further, although predicted earlier, innovative learning practices are not replacing the traditional ones as quickly as was previously expected. Gartner Group (2012) forecast that by 2015 nearly half of the organizations would transform their learning by utilizing gamification. However, the claim has not been fulfilled, and it is likely due to the fact that such implementation requires profound change management, and organizations are reluctant to implement it. This may be if the organization was successful in the past, there is no objective need for a fundamental change, and several traditional universities well exemplify this idea, including Oxford University (Davidson & Goldberg, 2009). Thus, it is important to evaluate the empirical evidence regarding whether such methods are indeed useful and beneficial to the learners.

MOOCs, or Massive Open Online Courses, have been thoroughly researched by universities, which are actively implementing the initiative on various platforms, including "edX", "Coursera" and "Lynda". Research, conducted by MIT RELATE group has revealed, that, although students indeed learnt more that they would have in a classroom, they have benefited even further from an interactive delivery method (blended learning) (Colvin, Champaign, Liu, Zhou, Fredericks & Pritchard, 2014). Interestingly, the same paper indicated, that students were able to learn regardless of their level – no matter the background, students with minimal knowledge in the field were able to perform almost as well as more advanced ones (Colvin et al., 2014). Further, it has been pointed out that teachers were able to gain new information from the learning platforms and benefit from the courses (Colvin et al., 2014). These findings suggest that, although online learning may not be the most effective way of delivering the information, it is certainly beneficial for the wide range of students and even professors.

Another empirical study points out, that although MOOCs have a great potential for learning, the way it is best utilized is yet to be well understood (Anderson, Huttenlocher, Kleinberg & Leskovec, 2014). The paper suggests, that various students engage on different levels, each pursuing different goals from the online courses, e.g. learners have been classified into "viewers, solvers, all-rounders, collectors and bystanders" (Anderson et al., 2014), indicating that the online courses effectiveness can only be proven if learners are particularly motivated and engage to the maximum level. Given the aforementioned engagement crisis in the GCC (Gallup, 2012), it might be difficult to fully exploit the potential benefits of MOOCs.

MOOCs are capable of improving the students' performance along with reducing the costs of learning, given that they are not a sole delivery method (blended learning) (Griffiths, 2014). Therefore, a good practice in terms of employee education would be to integrate learning in the daily routine activities, by facing the workers with challenge, and providing support by granting access to the related courses. However, it is important to maintain face-to-face communication, along with building positive relationships, as students that had the least interaction with instructors reported dissatisfaction with their learning experience (Griffiths et al., 2014; Israel, 2015), which may significantly affect the retention of information, as well as overall attitude of learners (Mill, 1960).

Previously briefly referred to innovative method of education, gamification, has been defined as the use of game elements in order to translate such experience into the desired behavioural or psychological outcomes (Huotari & Hamari, 2012; Hamari, 2013). The rising popularity of gamification can be observed in the growing number of academic papers as well as the increased number of start-ups (Hamari, Koivisto, Sarsa, 2014). In the majority of the academic papers, it was reported that gamification does indeed yield a positive effect on performance (Hamari, Koivisto, Sarsa, 2014). And although not all of the tests reported positive results, a lot of papers highlighted the improved motivation, attitude and enjoyment and none of the researches claimed that all findings were insignificant (Hamari, Koivisto, Sarsa, 2014). However, there is a concern, that the effects may dwindle in the long run (Hamari, 2013; Farzan, DiMicco, Millen, Brownholtz, Geyer & Dugan, 2008a; Farzan et al., 2008b; Thom, Millen & DiMicco, 2012), the improvements could have also been due to the "novelty effect" (Hamari, Koivisto, Sarsa, 2014).

Several negative implications caused by gamification may be associated with a competitive climate in the company (Hakulinen, Auvinen, & Korhonen, 2013), problems with understanding the required time to complete the task (Domínguez, Saenz-de-Navarrete, de-Marcos, Fernández-Sanz, Pagés, & Martínez-Herráizas, 2013) as well as design features of the game itself (Dong, Dontcheva, Joseph, Karahalios, Newman, & Ackerman, 2012). Therefore, in order to effectively implement gamification for employee training, it is vital to achieve effective design, clearly define the tasks and maintain a positive climate in the organization to reduce rivalry.

Just-in-time (JIT) learning is developed to reach employees on the go and deliver information wherever and whenever convenient (Iannarelli, 2009). Such innovative delivery method has already been applied in the medical, technological and military fields (Iannarelli, 2009). Yet again, it was found that mobile learners were able to outperform the students to whom the information was delivered via a classical model, however, the value of the blended approach proved to be much higher than M-Learning (Williams, 2009). Overall, it has been confirmed, that regardless of the kind of the innovative delivery method, therefore, it is important to use non-traditional method in conjunction with a face-to-face communication.

In conclusion, it becomes evident, that although the new trends are extremely promising, it is yet too soon to replace the traditional learning completely. When it comes to employee training, utilizing innovative content delivery methods may prove effective in terms of motivation and engagement, however, continuous guidance and support is also necessary. Although it might supposedly lead employers into thinking that the classroom learning is the best solution, it is not necessarily the case. New methods are typically more integrated into workflows. Given the latter, a company may be transformed into a learning organization, employing workers with more psychological resources and character strengths. Further, if learning is prioritized in the organization, new tools may serve as a support resource for the employees trying to overcome a challenging task, alongside with productive and positive relationships with the management and colleagues.

Research Analysis

Method and Participants

The analyzed research has been conducted by The Talent Enterprise and Informa Middle East. The results are adapted from the white paper written by Jones, Punshi and Griffiths, 2015.

An online survey was designed that contaned 27 questions in order to assess the current state of the organizations in terms of L&D, as well as try to gather strategic information that will help to forecast the future of learning. From 226 participants, located across the GCC region, 30 did not complete any question and were therefore removed from the data presented. The analysis of data was completed on 196 responses acquired, of which 84 participants completely filled in the questionnaire.

The questions of the survey are provided below:

1. Your primary location of work/operation
2. Primary industry classification
3. Total number of employees
4. What best describes the influence that the L&D function has within your organisation?
5. Our organisational learning and development priorities are determined by: (Please drag and drop options to rank in order of priority)
6. How is your learning currently delivered? (Assign percentages to each option so that the total sums up to 100%)
7. Please rank in order of priority your L&D areas of focus for the next 12 - 36 months? (Please drag and drop options to rank in order of priority)
8. Approximately what percentage of your L&D delivery is managed by external training providers?
9. Which level of training is most commonly led by external providers? (You can choose up to 3 options)
10. Could you please share your overall L&D budget?
11. Approximately how is this budget allocated amongst the various levels? (Assign percentages to each option so that the total sums up to 100%)
12. Does your organisation offer the following development opportunities? If yes, approximately what number do you expect to take in for each program over the next 12 months?
13. As part of your L&D strategy for nationalisation, which work levels are the most important for you to focus on? (Please drag and drop options to rank in order of priority)

14. What statements would best describe your philosophy and approach for national talent development?
15. What are the key areas that need more focus in developing national talent? (Please drag and drop options to rank in order of priority)
16. What is your average per person training cost for: (USD)
17. Which areas will witness significant increase with regards to L&D spending by 2020? (Please drag and drop options to rank in order of priority)
18. Q18 In your understanding, which techniques for learning and development could attract the biggest growth in spending by 2020? (Assign percentages to each option so that the total sums up to 100%)
19. Virtual classrooms could replace tradition training rooms by 2020 (strongly agree to strongly disagree)
20. Will the workforce determine their own learning paths by 2025 (strongly agree to strongly disagree)
21. What percentage of L&D is delivered through e-learning in your/organisation?
22. How many online courses does your organisation offer?
23. What is the source for content for e-learning? (Assign percentages to each option so that the total sums up to 100%)
24. I believe that e-Learning delivers / can deliver considerable impact on meeting the L&D outcomes in our organization (strongly agree to strongly disagree)
25. Have you considered gamification as part of your L & D strategy?
26. Which are the most common topics covered / being considered through gamification?
27. I believe that gamification delivers / can deliver considerable impact on meeting the L&D outcomes in our organization (strongly agree to strongly disagree).

Results

Results have proven to be very interesting. In brief, so far organizations do not seem to utilize the modern approaches to information delivery. The findings revealed overreliance on the traditional educational methods, and contrary to the prediction about the innovative learning trends, so far the organizations do not seem to be willing to change their L&D strategy.

Respondents, for the most part, felt that the L&D function was responsive to their organizational needs, followed by 27% of participants saying that it is standard. Luckily, only 5% said that training was either minimal or non-existent, but less than 15% of employers only believed that L&D demonstrated a significant ROI, and should be a proactive initiative. Unfortunately, such attitude does not predispose to the integration of learning in the organization, as most leaders do not see the value in it.

How do you describe the L&D function within your organisation?

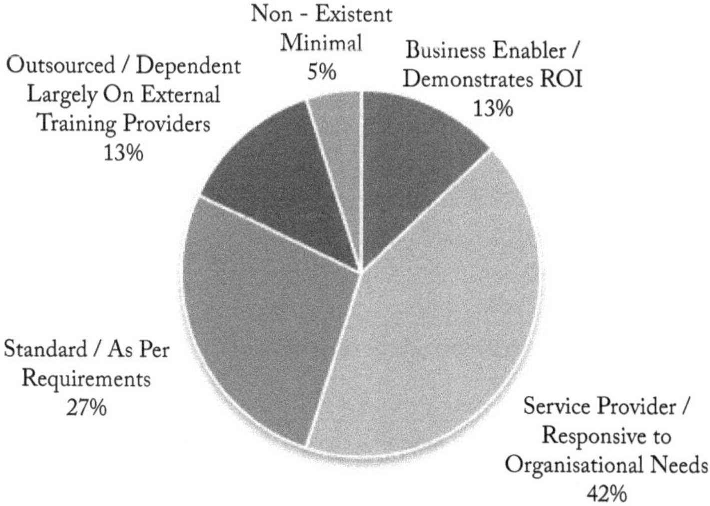

An alarmingly low percentage of respondents (24%) had a formal process of conducting the need analysis, and only 2% claimed that L&D priorities are driven by the hiring needs. However, 65% assured, that the learning process is integrated in their strategic priorities, yet less than 10% identified their priorities through industry and customer needs.

How are your L&D priorities currently identified?

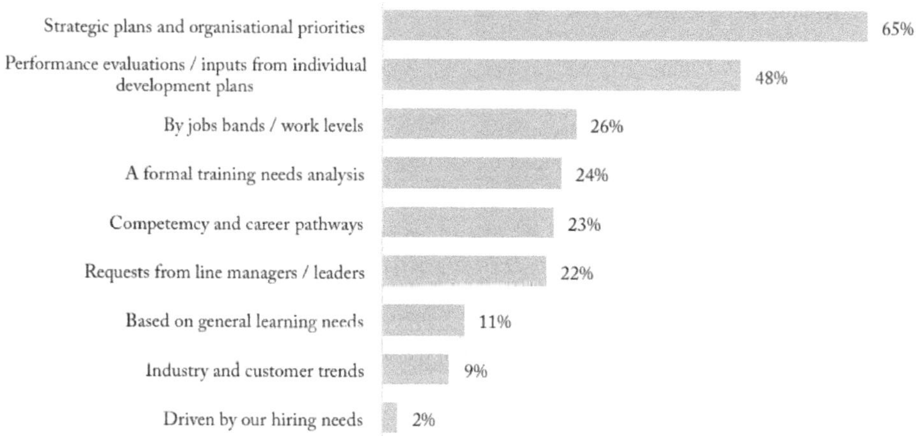

Source: The Future of Learning, Position Paper by The Talent Enterprise

Not at all surprisingly, the majority of organizations were utilizing traditional learning delivery methods, with only 22% of on-the-job training and little to no use of innovative techniques. It is clear, that the GCC-based companies do not believe in the power of blended learning, that has been globally adopted as a more effective way of education (Jones, Punshi & Griffiths, 2015) with the use of gamification, M-learning, virtual training etc. Unfortunately, there is much to be desired in terms of delivery methods; many employees tend to not embrace the profound change process (Zigarmi & Hoekstra, 2008; Schuler, 2003), therefore it is not unlikely, that such attitude will remain for quite some time in the GCC-based companies. Further, the current distribution of educational methods is almost opposite to the 70-20-10 model; hence, there is very little learning that is actively accommodated in the daily responsibilities of the employees.

What L&D delivery methods & techniques do you currently use?

	L&D in 2015
Instructor Led / mainly classroom based structured training	34%
On-the-Job Training	22%
Self-Learning	9%
Mentoring / Coaching	9%
Blended Learning	8%
e-learning	8%
Manager-led	6%
Simulators / virtual training	3%
Social Learning	2%
Gamification	0%
Mobiile / app-based	0%

Source: The Future of Learning, Position Paper by The Talent Enterprise

In regards to the content of learning, companies tend to prioritise technical skills, which doesn't match with the view that employers assured that graduates do not have sufficient soft skills required for the position (Punshi, Mirza & Gupta, 2015).

The priority emphasis tends to be placed on the technical, business, and leadership skills. The focus on the latter can indeed beneficial for employers, as there has been an observable challenge with leadership in the region (Jones, Punshi & Griffiths, 2015) – a mere 46% of workers agree with the decisions made by their leaders in terms of the company and human resources (Jones & Punshi, 2013). Further, managerial skills must be placed under the spotlight for the majority of the companies, as managers tend to be the reason for lower engagement rates, reduced productivity and positivity of the employees (given that they lack the appropriate "soft skills", are not committed to the organization or bully their subordinates) (Jones, Punshi & Griffiths, 2015; Emmott, 2006; Truss, Soane, Edwards, Wisdom, Croll & Burnett, 2006; Kular, Gatenby, Rees, Soane & Truss, 2008; Robinson, Perryman & Hayday, 2004). Further, more than half of the employees in the

GCC feel "they do not have supportive managers" (Jones, 2015). Further, along with the reduced trust in leadership, managerial effectiveness tends to be forgotten and placed much lower in the priorities.

What would be your priority area in terms of L&D for the next 18-36 months?

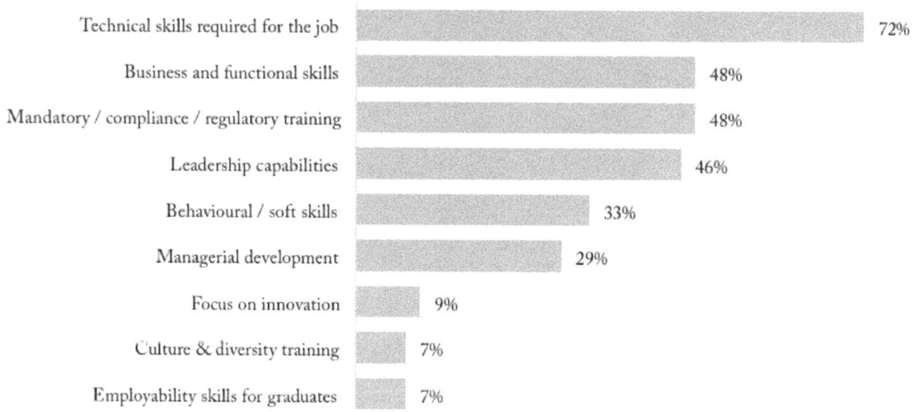

Source: The Future of Learning, Position Paper by The Talent Enterprise

Which type / level of L&D is most commonly delivered by external training providers?

Leadership	34%
Managerial	29%
Supervisor / Team Leader	18%
Front Line Staff / Operator	16%
Graduate Training / Induction (including national development)	5%

Source: The Future of Learning, Position Paper by The Talent Enterprise

When it comes to relying on external providers, most organizations responded that leadership, closely followed by managerial skills, are being delivered externally. Such decision might invoke resonance, considering the current situation with lack of confidence in both management and leadership reported by nearly half of employees (Jones, 2015). Therefore, the following responses might suggest that the external providers are neither effective nor successful enough in preparing good leaders and managers.

What proportion of your current L&D is delivered by external training providers?

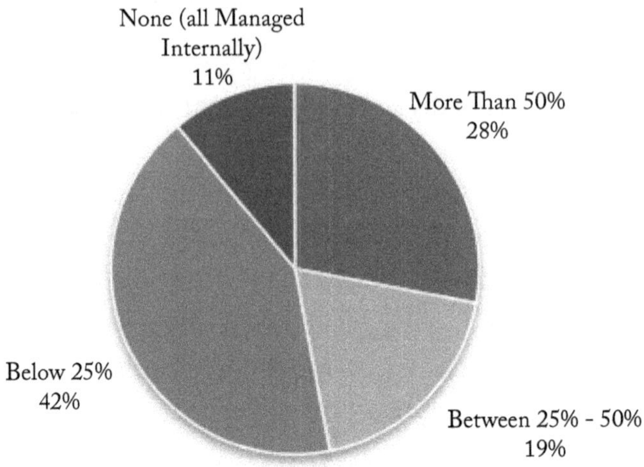

Source: The Future of Learning, Position Paper by The Talent Enterprise

Further, almost a third of the respondents indicated that they delegate more than half of their L&D programs to external providers. It appears that leaders are reluctant to commit to the implementation and ownership of learning (arguably best achieved internally), although are aware of it, hence they are looking for ways to achieve learning with the least resistance and effort. However, 42% of the participants assured that less than quarter of their L&D happens externally. Nearly half of the organizations which tool part in the survey do not rely heavily on external providers, but it does not necessarily imply that the rest of learning delivered is, in fact, of good quality, beneficial for the employees and provided in a blended technique. Therefore, it is crucial to understand that learning conducted internally is not a sole requirement for success: it needs to be organized correctly, integrated in the workflow, and sufficient support must be provided to the learners.

Globally, CEOs are on the quest to retain the most productive employees and attend to deficiency of industry skills, and even locally, in GCC, governments put a significant emphasis not only on nationalization, but also on the transitioning to knowledge-based economy by 2030. 70% of the surveyed admitted the room for innovation and improvement for their national learning and development program. Most of the organizations (60%) confirmed that attitude is the primary driver of their hiring decision, and that if there is a skill gap present – additional training can be conducted; the remaining companies were assured in the necessity of choosing the specific candidates with a predefined roles and skills set (Jones, Punshi & Griffiths, 2015). The classic model of delivery may be beneficial for the theoretical basis, but in order to truly shape the talents and create a culture of sustainable learning, the latter has to occur in the same setting as the application of learnt material – at a workplace. Moreover, the younger generation yearns for engaging and captivating modern learning methods, which incorporate high-technology and provides visual learning experience.

While focusing on your nationalisation priorities, which level is the most important in terms of L&D priority?

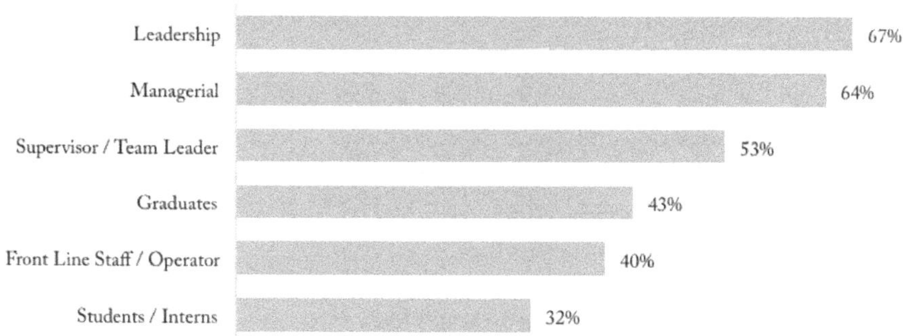

Source: The Future of Learning, Position Paper by The Talent Enterprise

Contrary to expectations, employers prefer to focus national talent development on existing top management levels, rather than placing an emphasis on younger generations comprised of graduates and interns. After nationalisation project has been deployed for quite some time, companies might feel confident about the number and quality of their internship programs. Further, 72% of leaders and HR managers confirmed the nationalization as their top priority, which is an overwhelming proportion requiring significant resources (Jones & Punshi, 2014). Moreover, as GCC is a region "where ambition meets opportunity" (Jones & Punshi, 2013; Jones, 2015, p.123), it is not at all unlikely that nationals tend to aim for higher steps on the career ladder, and these preferences, reinforced by the government's support, are reflected in the talent strategies within organizations. According to recent research conducted by Ernst and Young in 2016, 70% of the respondents shared, that the primary difficulty in retaining nationals is their high salary expectations (Gallagher, Cooper, Collins & Shahir, 2016), suggesting nationals would prefer higher managerial positions, with an accordingly higher salary. "Broader career management and succession planning may be considered pivotal in managing talent risk" – recommended Jones, Punshi & Griffiths (2015).

As for spending, graduate programs have the overall lowest of $19,395 annually, followed by managerial development $28,975 and exceeded by leadership development with a figure of $33,159 per year. Although most organizations do allocate a significant portion of their income to talent development, almost three quarters stated that their national learning programs require enhancement. Therefore, it would be unwise to conclude solely from spending patterns alone, that the education offered is effective and worth investing. Other indicators and further research must be developed to analyse the ROI and the effectiveness of the learning programs.

Learning programs for graduates, including internships, can benefit an employer with a higher ROI (Walter & Malhotra, 2014). Thus, a seemingly uncertain investment in future talent, not only provides the organization with the capabilities required by employers, it is also more beneficial for future leaders. Fortunately, given the youth bulge in the demography of the region, 70% of employers surveyed agreed with the statement and offer the internship programs in the GCC.

Internships can be beneficial to both employers and students, providing the graduates with an opportunity to network and potentially continue working in the organization full-time, for around 70% of candidates, according to Forbes and internship.com research (Smith, 2012; Jones, Punshi & Griffiths, 2015).

With regards to your nationalisation priorities, which of the following types of programs do you offer?

Source: The Future of Learning, Position Paper by The Talent Enterprise

Globally, vocational education is rising in popularity, as it supplies the market with employees with employer-led qualifications in a specific role currently demanded. With a growing demand and being largely composed of younger graduates, vocational training has proven to be most innovative in terms of learning methodology, utilizing techniques such as blended learning, flipped classrooms, e-learning, gamification etc. Despite the evident growing popularity of vocational programs, the GCC reports a relative aversion to this method of workplace learning. One reason is that academic educational methods can be perceived by employers as higher status, more desirable or a greater guarantee of competence compared to vocational education. Further, as discussed earlier, innovation is not always embraced by employers (Zigarmi & Hoekstra, 2008). Nevertheless, to promote sustainable economic development and greater employability in the region, the development of vocational education programs, which prepare highly specialist employees for faster growing fields of employment.

How much of your current L&D content is delivered through e-learning?

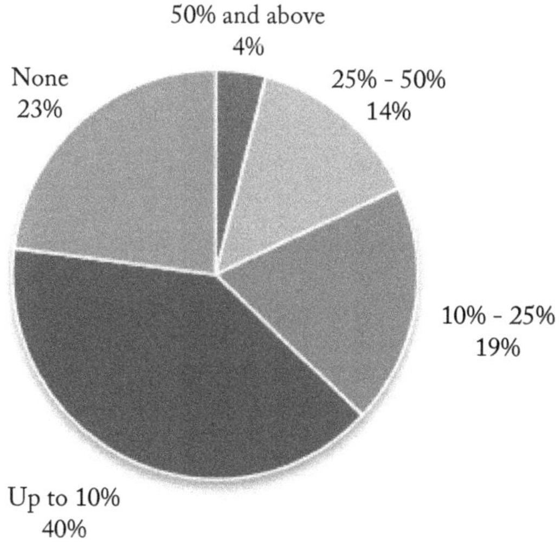

What is your most common source of content for e-learning?

Fixed content offered by external providers	32%
Home-Grown	25%
Free online resource	25%
Customized content development by external providers	18%

Source: The Future of Learning, Position Paper by The Talent Enterprise

Unfortunately, around 60% of the respondents did not embrace e-learning and do not fully exploit innovative delivery methods. This suggests that the GCC is behind the global preferences, as according to the CIPD research, 74% of employers confirmed using hi-tech learning in at least some areas of content delivery, whereas 91% were assured in the effectiveness of blended learning with elements of e-learning (McGurk & Belliveau, 2013).

Although there is a challenge in motivating employees to complete online courses (Colvin et al., 2014; Jones, Punshi & Griffiths, 2015), it is not an insurmountable barrier to utilize e-learning and exploit its benefits. It is important to design the courses in a way that is engaging and involving for learners (Dong et al., 2012; Jones, Punshi & Griffiths, 2015), to prevent the dropout rate as well as lack of engagement and positive experience associated with e-learning. 54% among the companies that do, in fact, use e-learning, offer only less than 50 online courses, with a modest 14% of respondents providing a wide array of more than 200 courses to choose from. Another way to tackle the lack of completion rate is to ensure greater interactivity from the user end, so that the courses do not resemble the initial approach of e-learning several decades ago. It is crucial to adapt these newly designed technologies and challenge employers to embrace the growth mindset to truly incorporate learning into the culture of the workplace, fostering greater interactivity and engagement through social learning and gamification methodologies.

The concept of gamification seems to be even less embraced by employers, with as little as 25% of employers believing it could be beneficial as one of the learning delivery methods, with around one third of respondents affirming that they have not considered integrating gamification into their learning strategy.

How much is gamification a part of your current L&D strategy?

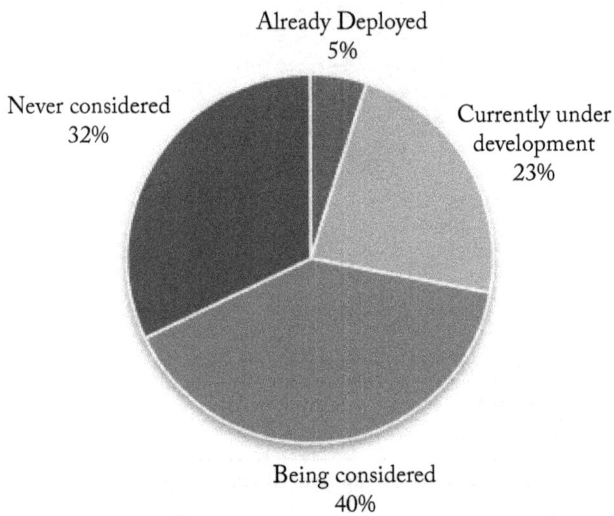

Source: The Future of Learning, Position Paper by The Talent Enterprise

As the graph shows, only 5% of organizations which took part in the survey respondent that they have already been utilizing gamification as one of their educational methods. And although a little less than half of participants are still thinking about the introduction of such method into the learning strategy, 23% reported, that they are currently designing a system for this delivery technique, giving hope that the region may accelerate towards this trend. Further, a difficulty in deploying such interactive system may lie within the technical provision of the company, i.e. the current interface may simply be incompatible with the operating system necessary to deploy gamification. Thus, in order to properly introduce gamified elements into learning, organizations will have to go through the profound process of change management, which may face resistance from employees and even leaders (Zigarmi & Hoekstra, 2008; Schuler, 2003).

Overall, the findings from the survey exemplify that the GCC lags behind global trends on e-learning, gamification and vocational education and is less eager to introduce them into organizational learning. The current picture represents lack of appreciation of the innovative methods of content delivery, that are widely used globally, have proven to be effective and engaging, which could potentially help overcome the engagement crisis in GCC. However, a lot of resources, including finance, time and talents need to be put to the process of development for the modern methods, which may be one of the reasons why companies decide to stick with traditional methods. Secondly, an "addiction to cheap labour" (Jones & Punshi, 2013) in the region may also be reflected in the resourcing models for HR and Training departments, with employers preferring labour-intensive, didactic methods as a reflection of unique labour market preferences. This may also be driven by the continued existence of economic rents in many industries, along with cultural preferences for face to face interaction (Jones & Punshi, 2016), although this would need to be studied further. Finally a tremendous amount of daily activities need to be redesigned in order to accommodate learning on-the-job delivered be blended method, which may face resistance and cause stress among employees. However, significant progress is not going to be made, until employers in the GCC embrace the new models and implement change management to implement them at a workplace.

Which areas do you believe will witness a significant increase by spending L&D in 2020?

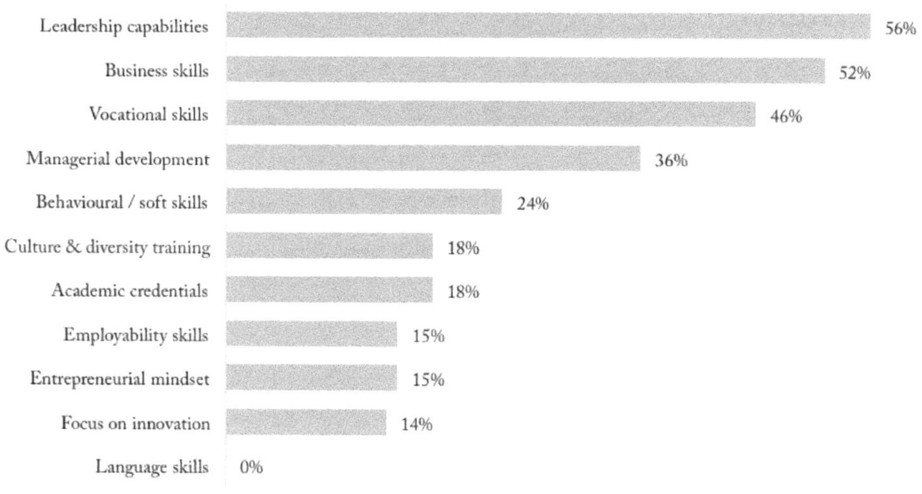

Source: The Future of Learning, Position Paper by The Talent Enterprise

Unfortunately, the future in terms of learning in GCC does not seem to be progressive – respondents, for the most part, feel a degree of confidence in the conventional delivery methods and learning content. Employers believe they are going to spend more on leadership, managerial and business skill training, generally more expensive, and arguably do not demonstrate clear learning impact. If organizations decided to use more engaging and involving technology-based methodologies, this could yield better results in terms of positivity and productivity in the region's workplaces, both low by international standards (Jones & Punshi, 2013). Only 14% of employers believe it is a good idea to focus on innovation, despite the stated strategic goals of most governments and employers in terms of promoting greater dynamism and new knowledge within the GCC's workplaces.

As the survey pointed out, the predicted overwhelming utilization of innovative methods (Gartner Group, 2012) is not likely to happen by 2020. Unfortunately, only 5% of respondents hope to use gamification as one learning method by 2020, with 19% predicting resolute preference for didactic classroom learning. However, e-learning is expected to almost double in percentage compared to the current situation, along with an increase in blended learning as well. Surprisingly, M-learning appeared almost at the very bottom of the list, which is counter-intuitive given the extent to which individuals are connected to multiple mobile devices in the region (Jones & Punshi, 2016).

What L&D delivery methods & techniques do you hope to use by 2020?

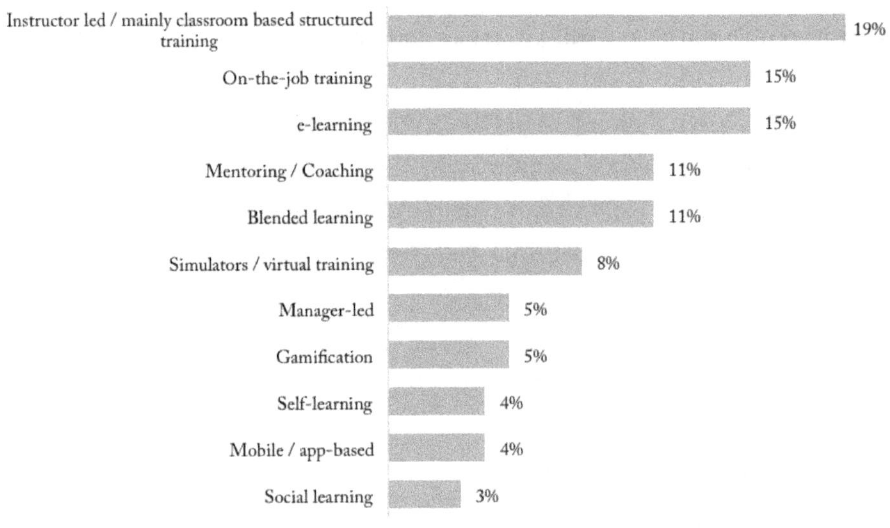

Source: The Future of Learning, Position Paper by The Talent Enterprise

Case Studies

Despite the fact that results have proven, that innovative delivery methods are yet to be embraced by the leaders and receive the attention they deserve in GCC, a few countries have proven to act progressively by setting up MOOCs to deliver knowledge help grow the economy. New platforms include Doroob in Saudi Arabia (https://www.doroob.sa/en/individuals/about/) and Edraak (https://www.edraak.org/en/about-us/) in Jordan, which are created to deliver online courses to ensure innovation and support the technological progress. Considering that not all areas of either country are equally developed, and some individuals may have difficulties accessing quality education, online-based platforms are a useful solution to provide equitable access to learning, especially for women, those in rural areas, thosewith disabilities and younger citizens generally, who have been marginalized from the region's labour markets (Jones & Punshi, 2013).

MOOCs in the Arab world are aimed at supplying labour market with highly skilled professionals, including women and younger graduates. Doroob is based on a larger MOOCs platform – EdX and is endorsed by HRDF. The website highlights, that anyone interested, not necessarily a Saudi national, may sign up for the variety of courses. The platform has received overwhelming support from the government, which believes that in order to accomplish the transition to knowledge-based economy, employees must be provided with means to gain necessary information – both theoretical and practical.

"In this context, individual and societal actions stand out as a necessity that can be achieved by integrating work and practical and theoretical knowledge." – Mofarrej Bin Saad Al-Hoqubani, Minister of Labour and Social Affairs. It is evident that the position of the government is based on incorporating learning into the daily activities of workers, which implies, that Saudi Arabia moves steadily towards the approach of blended learning and approves 70-20-10 ideology. The Minister has also mentioned that Doroob prepares individuals for the current labour market, considering its demands in order to achieve greater employability. Further, Doroob provides recognized certification, which allows workers to recognize their qualification, ensuring constant competence advancements in a competitive labour market. Therefore, this initiative is aimed at strengthening the foundations of the national economy, improving employability, as well as delivering quality education to all learners.

Edraak is an initiative of the Queen Rania Foundation, which seeks to ensure the constant progress and innovation in the Arab world. Edraak was also developed on the EdX platform, and it is the first ever non-profit Arabic MOOC platform. In order to achieve continuous education and technology-enabled Arab talent development, Edraak claims to feature renowned Arab professors, delivering content in Arabic and to give learners further insight into current themes and topics. However, Edraak also provides courses in English, which makes education accessible for international users as well. The platform has partnered with the leading providers of online courses to ensure the top quality of the education – HarvardX, MITX, and UC Berkeley. Further, Edraak has a mission in spreading the knowledge about the Arab community and culture to those who might be interested, as well as to encourage users to take advantage of new technology.

Dubai Smart Education Initiative (http://smarteducation.ae) is another example of interpreting technology-enabled education. It is said to be founded by qualified providers, utilizing blended information delivery methods, with a high inclusion of local materials. Smart education delivers both learning experience and materials to any educational institution willing to participate in the initiative.

It is laudable of government to set up such initiatives, it is increasingly recognized that the individual's character traits play a vital role in the effectiveness of all learning methodologies, including MOOCs, in general. In order for the e-learning to yield positive outcomes, it requires the learners to possess high levels of grit, resilience, growth mindset, optimism, self-efficacy and learning agility. The need to develop such character strengths may help to explain the high rates of non-completion of such courses, reducing their overall impact. This both employers and government institutions might want to consider not only investing in some form of e-learning, but also ensuring its positive effect through developing the receptiveness and the motivation of the learners.

Discussion, Conclusion and Recommendations

With the low preference towards innovate approaches to learning, there are indications of employers slowly but steadily embracing the new approaches as we head towards 2020. It is also evident that the region lags behind global trends of gamification, M-learning and, in general, stepping away from the traditional delivery settings.

The increasingly popularity and prevalence of MOOCs also needs to be examined further. Whilst great at "pushing" a large amount of learning content, arguably some of the new platforms may not yet fully appreciated that isolated students will need more grit, resilience and other character strengths than students with the potential for regular social support amongst colleagues and learning professionals. Arguably, there is an equal need to focus on greater interactively and networked, peer-to-peer social learning as a means of "pulling" learning from such platforms. As this review has shown, although innovative methods may have some drawbacks when focusing on utilizing them solely, overall, technology-enabled learning, which allows some face-to-face interaction, has proven to be the most effective (Colvin et al., 2014). Further, considering relatively low employee engagement rates in the region, it is vital to step in to design interactive system of content delivery, that will not only provide learners with information, but will also improve economic situation, thus strengthening the economy and increasing the quality of life.

For boys in particular, the adoption of truly engaging, gamified learning offers the opportunity to redress the balance of their underperformance in the region's education system.

In order to be the most effective, learning should be integrated in the workflow and supported with workplace feedback and coaching. Further, utilizing technology-enabled learning is outstanding, if coupled with personal support and interaction, which, in fact, could involve traditional classroom training. However, it must be kept in mind, that younger generation should be involved with more engaging and captivating delivery methods, which, if done right, may result in reducing the number of actively disengaged employees in the future.

It is crucial for organisational leaders and HR professionals to understand that without the development of individual character traits, such as grit, resilience, growth mindset, learning agility, self-confidence, optimism and hope, education initiatives may not be as effective as expected. With the volatile, uncertain, complex and full of ambiguity situation that the world is experiencing, it is crucial to develop the soft skills prior to technical requirements for the job. An employer or leader can utilize several simple interventions, like drawing attention to the meaning of the job through the connection to the bigger picture. Another beneficial practice would include showing social support from the management, yet providing employees with challenging tasks to encourage learning and the development of grit.

If we are moving towards an increasingly VUCA (volatile, uncertain, complex and ambiguous) world, then the character strengths of our youth and our employees will be critical. We will all need to demonstrate more consistent levels of grit, resilience, growth mindset, optimism, self – efficacy, resourcefulness, confidence and so on. This has only just started to be included in the curriculum of education institutions and employers under the label of "positive education" and their importance can only grow going forward.

Lastly, it is important to remember, that learning cannot be regarded as a one-time event, it cannot be taken lightly, either. Education has to become a part of the organization in order to support and challenge employees to become a more productive workforce. Learning has to be delivered in a way, so it is not noticeable by employees, as they have to search for knowledge to complete the task they are required to submit, for example. Further, it is extremely important to spread the awareness about the new educational techniques and methods of content delivery across the GCC region to inspire the leaders to give them a chance and potentially set an example for the rest of the companies to follow innovation and develop and grow for the better with education embedded in the core of the organization.

If the GCC is to move towards a group of sustainable knowledge – based economies, then the relative effectiveness and efficiency of our education and organizational learning practices will be critical to determining the sustainability of our economic and social well – being. The employability of individuals, the performance of our organisations and the contribution of our governments in this regard must be at least as good as those anywhere and everywhere else in the world to secure the promise of the future.

References

70:20:10 Forum Pty Ltd. (2015). 70:20:10 Workplace Learning That Really Works (pp. 2-10). 70:20:10 Forum.

Achor, S. (2010). The happiness advantage. New York, NY: Random House Inc.

Anderson, A., Huttenlocher, D., Kleinberg, J., & Leskovec, J. (2014). Engaging with Massive Online Courses. International World Wide Web Conference Committee (IW3C2). ACM 978-1-4503-2744-2/14/04.

Appendix B: Taxonomy of Educational Objectives (Bloom 1956; Krathwohl, Bloom and Masia 1964). (2009). AAHE-ERIC/Higher Education Research Report, 3(1), 59-60. http://dx.doi.org/10.1002/aehe.3640030109

Australian Public Service. (2012). Leadership, Culture and Conduct. Canberra, Brisbane, Melbourne, Sydney: Australian Public Service Commission. Retrieved from http://tinyurl.com/y9b7c2h5

Bandura, A. (1969). Social Learning Theory of Identificatory Processes. In D. Goslin, Handbook of Socialization Theory and Research (1st ed., pp. 213-261). Stanford: Rand McNally & Company. Retrieved from http://tinyurl.com/yd4uw23b

Bandura, A. (1978). The Self System in Reciprocal Determinism. American Psychologist, 33(4), 344-358. http://dx.doi.org/10.1037/0003-066x.33.4.344

Beddoe, L., Adamson, C. and Davys, A. (2013) Educating Resilient Practitioners. Social Work Education. 32 (1), 100–17. [DOI:10.1080/02615479.2011.644532]

Belkin, Gary, S. and Gray Jerry, L. (1977). *Educational Psychology: An Introduction.* Dubuque Iowa: Wm. C. Brown Company Publishers

Blackwell, L., Trzesniewski, K., & Dweck, C. (2007). Implicit Theories of Intelligence Predict Achievement across an Adolescent Transition: A Longitudinal Study and an Intervention. Child Development, 78(1), 246-263.

Boumova, V. (2008). Traditional vs. Modern Teaching Methods: Advantages and Disadvantages of Each (Master's Diploma). Masaryk University Faculty of Arts.

Cabrera, E. F. (2012). The Six Essentials of Workplace Positivity. People & Strategy, 35(1), 50–60.

Colvin, K.F., Champaign, J., Liu, A., Fredericks, C., Zhou, Q., & Pritchard, D.E. (2014). Learning in an Introductory Physics MOOC: All Cohorts Learn Equally, Including an On-Campus class. The International Review of Research in Open and Distance Learning.

Cooper, W., Gallagher, G., Collins, A., & Shahir, T. (2016). How will the GCC Close the Skill Gap? Ernst and Young Global Limited.

Csikszentmihalyi, M. (1990). Flow. New York: Harper & Row.

Davidson, C., & Goldberg, D. MacArthur Foundation. (2009). The Future of Learning Institutions in a Digital Age (pp. 9-20). Cambridge, London: The MIT Press. Retrieved from http://tinyurl.com/lr5mqyx

Dominguez, A., Saenz-de-Navarrete, J., de-Marcos, L., Fernandez-Sanz, L., Pages, C. & Martinez-Herraiz, J.J. (2013). Gamifying Learning Experiences: Practical Implications and Outcomes. Computers & Education, 63, 380-392.

Dong, T., Dontcheva, M., Joseph, D., Karahalios, K., Newman, M. W., & Ackerman, M. S. (2012). Discovery-Based Games for Learning Software. In Conference Proceedings - The 30th ACM Conference on Human Factors in Computing Systems, CHI 2012. (pp. 2083-2086). DOI: 10.1145/2207676.2208358

Dweck, C. (2006). Mindset. New York: Random House.

Dweck, C. (2008). Mindsets and Math Science Achievement. Institute for Advanced Study.

Emmott, M. (2006) 'Hear Me Now', People Management, 23rd November, pp. 38-39.

Evans, J. D. (1996). Straightforward Statistics for the Behavioral Sciences. Pacific Grove, CA: Brooks / Cole Publishing.

Farzan, R., DiMicco J.M., Millen D.R., Brownholtz, B., Geyer, W., & Dugan, C. (2008a). When the Experiment is Over: Deploying an Incentive System to All the Users, In Symposium on Persuasive Technology.

Farzan, R., DiMicco J.M., Millen D.R., Brownholtz, B., Geyer, W., & Dugan, C. (2008b). Results from Deploying a Participation Incentive Mechanism within the Enterprise, In Proceedings of the Twenty-Sixth Annual SIGCHI Conference on Human Factors in Computing Systems, Florence, Italy, ACM, pp. 563-572.

Forrester, D & Jantzie, N. (1998). Learning Theories. Retrieved December 27, 2003 from http://tinyurl.com/5a5ut

Fredrickson, B. & Branigan, C. (2005). Positive Emotions Broaden the Scope of Attention and Thought-Action Repertoires. Cognition & Emotion, 19(3), 313-332. http://dx.doi.org/10.1080/02699930441000238

Gallup. (2013). Worldwide, 13% of Employees Are Engaged at Work. Retrieved from http://tinyurl.com/m7nvrmo

Gartner Group, Inc. (2012). Gartner Reveals Top Predictions for IT Organizations and Users for 2013 and Beyond. Retrieved from http://www.gartner.com/newsroom/id/2211115

Geelong. (2012). Proceedings of the 2012 Australian Collaborative Education Network National Conference. Melbourne: ACEN Inc. Retrieved from http://tinyurl.com/yc6p3k6n

Gerzon, J., Heuer, B., Kibbee, K., Nielsen, E., & Veal, L. (2006, December). MIT training Delivery Methods Survey Report.

Grant, H. & Dweck, C. (2003). Clarifying Achievement Goals and Their Impact. Journal of Personality And Social Psychology, 85(3), 541-553. http://dx.doi.org/10.1037/0022-3514.85.3.541

Griffiths, R., Chingos, M., Mulhern, C., & Spies, R. (2014). Interactive Online Learning on Campus: Testing MOOCs and Other Platforms in Hybrid Formats in the University System of Maryland (ITHAKA S+R Report). Retrieved from http://tinyurl.com/y85ckmxs

Hamari, J. (2013). Transforming Homo Economicus into Homo Ludens: A Field Experiment on Gamification in a Utilitarian Peer-To-Peer Trading Service, Electronic Commerce Research and Applications, 12(4), pp. 236- 245.

Hamari, J., Koivisto, J., & Sarsa, H. (2014). Does Gamification Work? – A Literature Review of Empirical Studies on Gamification. In proceedings of the 47th Hawaii International Conference on System Sciences, Hawaii, USA, January 6-9, 2014.

Harvard Business Review. (2015). Why Organizations Don't Learn. Cambridge: HBR.org. Retrieved from https://hbr.org/2015/11/why-organizations-dont-learn

Huotari, K., & Hamari, J. (2012). Defining Gamification: a Service Marketing Perspective, In Proceedings of the 16th International Academic MindTrek Conference, October 3-5, 2012, Tampere, Finland, ACM, pp. 17-22.

Israel, M. (2015). Effectiveness of Integrating MOOCs in Traditional Classrooms for Undergraduate Students. The International Review of Research In Open And Distributed Learning, 16(5). Retrieved from http://www.irrodl.org/index.php/irrodl/article/view/2222/3402

Jennings, C. 2013, 'The 70:20:10 Framework Explained', www.702010forum.com

Jones, D. (2015). Key Drivers for Employee Engagement and Productivity of GCC Nationals and Expatriates: A Longitudinal Study 2010-2012. In A. Kropf & M. Ramady, Employment and Career Motivation in the Arab Gulf States: The Rentier Mentality Revisited. (1st ed., pp. 122-157). Berlin, London: Gerlach Press. Retrieved from http://tinyurl.com/y9z4qwzk.

Jones, D. & Punshi, R. (2013). Unlocking the Paradox of Plenty. Dubai, Abu-Dhabi, London. Motivate Publishing.

Jones, D., Punshi, R., & Griffiths, L. (2015). Future of Learning in the GCC.

Jones, D., Le Ray, S., & Punshi, R. (2016). Game Changers. How Women in the Arab World Are Changing the Rules and Shaping the Future. Dubai, Abu-Dhabi, London. Motivate Publishing.

Koballa, T. R., & Glynn, S. M. (in press). Attitudinal and Motivational Constructs in Science Learning (Chapter 5). In S. K. Abell & N. Lederman (Eds.), Handbook for Research in Science Education. Mahwah, NJ: Erlbaum.

Krathwohl, D. (2002). A Revision of Bloom's Taxonomy: An Overview. Theory into Practice, 41(4), 212-218. http://dx.doi.org/10.1207/s15430421tip4104_2

Kular, S., Gatenby, M., Rees, C., Soane, E., & Truss, K. (2008). Employee Engagement: A Literature Review. Kingston University, 19.

Leahey, T. H. (2000). Control: A history of Behavioral Psychology. The Journal of American History, 87(2), 686-687.

Lyubomirsky, S., King, L., & Diener, E. (2005). The Benefits of Frequent Positive Affect: Does Happiness Lead to Success? Psychological Bulletin, 131(6), 803-855. http://dx.doi.org/10.1037/0033-2909.131.6.803

McAllister, M. and McKinnon, J. (2008) The Importance of Teaching and Learning Resilience in the Health Disciplines: A Critical Review of the Literature. Nurse Education Today. 29, 371 79

McDonald, G., Jackson, D., Wilkes, J. and Vickers, M. (2012). A Work-Based Educational Intervention to Support the Development of Personal Resilience in Nurses and Midwives. Nurse Education Today. 32, 378–84. [DOI:10.1016/j.nedt.2011.04.012]

McDonald, G., Jackson, D., Wilkes, J. and Vickers, M. (2013). Personal Resilience in Nurses and Midwives: Effects of a Work-Based Educational Intervention. Contemporary Nurse. 45(1) 134-143

McGurk, J. & Belliveau, V. (2013). Learning and Talent Development. Annual Survey Report. CIPD. Retrieved from http://www.cipd.co.uk/binaries/learning-and-talent-development_2013.pdf

Mill, C. (1960). Attitudes Affect Pupils' Learning. Educational Leadership, 212-216. Retrieved from http://www.ascd.org/ASCD/pdf/journals/ed_lead/el_196001_mill.pdf

Mills, J. A. (1998). Control. A history of Behavioral Psychology. New York, NY: New York University Press.

Nakamura, J., & Csikszentmihalyi, M. (2002). The Concept of Flow. In C. Snyder & S. Lopez (Eds.) Handbook of Positive Psychology. Oxford: Oxford University Press

Pflug, K., & Jara, J. (2014). Workplace Fun and Games Motivate Employees. Xerox. Workspan. Retrieved from http://tinyurl.com/y7c37ty4

Pohl, M. (2000). Learning to Think, Thinking to Learn: Models and Strategies to Develop a Classroom Culture of Thinking (p. 8). Hawker Brownlow Education.

Powell, S., & Tod, J. (2004). A Systematic Review of How Theories Explain Learning Behaviour in School Contexts, London: EPPI-Centre, Institute of Education.

Punshi, R., Mirza, C., & Gupta, G. (2015). A Strengths-Based Approach to Enhancing Youth Motivation and Employability: Research and Practice from the GCC, with a Focus on Bahrain. In A. Kropf & M. Ramady, Employment and Career Motivation in the Arab Gulf States: The Rentier Mentality Revisited. (1st ed., pp. 158-174). Berlin, London: Gerlach Press. Retrieved from http://tinyurl.com/y8o8w977

Ridge (2014). Education and the Reverse Gender Divide in the Gulf States: Embracing the Global, Ignoring the Local. Teacher's College Press.

Robertson-Smith, G., & Markwick C. Institute for Employment Studies. (2009). Employee Engagement A review of current thinking (pp. 23-31). Brighton: Institute for Employment Studies. Retrieved from http://www.employment-studies.co.uk/system/files/resources/files/469.pdf

Robinson, D., Perryman, S., & Hayday, S. (2004). The Drivers of Employee Engagement. Institute For Employment Studies, 408. Retrieved from http://www.employment-studies.co.uk/system/files/resources/files/408.pdf

Schuler, A. (2003). Overcoming Resistance to Change: Top Ten Reasons for Change Resistance. Retrieved from http://tinyurl.com/yd3kw92g

Schwab, S. & Sala-i-Martín, X. (2014). The Global Competitiveness Report 2014–2015. World Economic Forum, Insight Report. Retrieved from http://tinyurl.com/pt58scv

Scott, S. (2010). Factors Impacting the Selection of Training-Delivery Systems and Training Methodology of Virginia Training Professionals (Ph.D., Undergraduate). Virginia Polytechnic Institute and State University.

Skinner, B. F. (1968). The Technology of Teaching. New York: Meredith Corporation

Smith, J. (2012). Internships May Be The Easiest Way To A Job In 2013. Forbes.com. Retrieved 2 July 2016, from http://tinyurl.com/y76rgc5m

Staw, B. & Barsade, S. (1993). Affect and Managerial Performance: A Test of the Sadder-but Wiser vs. Happier-and-Smarter Hypotheses. Administrative Science Quarterly, 38(2), 304. http://dx.doi.org/10.2307/2393415

Staw, B., Sutton, R., Pelled, L. Employee Positive Emotion and Favorable Outcomes at the Workplace. Organization Science. 1994;5:51-71.

Thom, J., Millen, D., & DiMicco, J. (2012). Removing gamification from an enterprise SNS, In Proceedings of the ACM 2012 conference on Computer Supported Cooperative Work, February 11-15, 2012, Seattle, Washington, USA, ACM, pp. 1067-1070.

Truss, C., Soane, E., Edwards, C., Wisdom, K., Croll, A. and Burnett, J. (2006) Working Life: Employee Attitudes and Engagement 2006. London, CIPD.

Walter, W. & Malhotra, S. (2014). Varsity Blues. Time for Apprenticeships to Graduate? A Comparison of the Earnings, Employment, Productivity and Taxpayer Returns of Graduates to Ahose of Apprentices. Pera Training, Million Jobs Report. Retrieved from https://www.peratraining.com/varsity-blues.pdf

Watson, John B., and Rosalie Rayner. "Conditioned Emotional Reactions." Journal of Experimental Psychology 3.1 (1920): 1.

World Economic Forum. (2014). The Global Competitiveness Report 2014-2015. Geneva: WEF. Retrieved from http://www3.weforum.org/docs/WEF_GlobalCompetitivenessReport_2014-15.pdf

Zigarmi, P. & Hoekstra, J. (2008). Leadership Strategies for Making Change Stick. The Ken Blanchard Companies. Retrieved from http://tinyurl.com/y74q9rac

7

Building Life Skills Through Positive Education: Evidence from Ras Al Khaimah (UAE)

L. Lambert, N. Budhraja, C. A. Mullan and G. Gupta

Abstract

Positive education and positive psychology have made good strides in developing human excellence, in particular, the development of character strengths conducive to better employment choices, career success, workplace engagement, and overall life satisfaction. Yet, few schools, universities or organizations develop these strengths leaving school-aged youth and young adults bereft of skills in their transition to adulthood. This is especially the case in the GCC countries where governments are on a path to steer nationals away from the public sector toward the private arena where they will compete on an even playing field with international expatriate labour. Many issues exist in meeting this challenge: (1) educational reforms have not yet produced desired results, (2) there is a reluctance to leave the public sector where pay, benefits, and job security are higher, (3) graduate students are unprepared for the workforce, lacking the strengths, or soft skills needed to excel. To address this gap, a character strengths development program (Strengths Compass™) grounded in positive psychology and positive education, was developed and piloted to national and expatriate youth (aged 15 to 16) in Ras Al Khaimah (United Arab Emirates) to see whether the development of such a program is feasible and what lessons could be learned in delivery. Recommendations from this pilot are offered and suggest that character strengths can and should be taught to address the growing need for the mobilization and maximization of human capital in the GCC region.

Introduction

Across the Arab world, governments are recognizing the pressing employment needs of youth as they attempt to harness the human capital of this demographic group. How they respond to this challenge will determine their nation's political stability and successful economic growth over time. The development of youth capital is crucial given the demographic and social transitions now underway in the Middle East/North African (MENA) region, where the demand for jobs currently outstrips available opportunities. With government efforts, education also plays a role in these developments; however, current educational outputs do not provide for job skills such as critical thinking, initiative and persistence, the lack of which hamper the ability of youth to succeed in jobs undermining their development, as well as that of their nations.

To address these and other developmental challenges, positive education[1], a subset of positive psychology[2] combines best teaching practises with the identification and nurturance of character strengths and shows a promising foundation from which to tackle regional issues of employment and youth psychosocial development. From the perspective of positive education, schools are model settings in which to facilitate the development of social, emotional, and intellectual skill sets that promote individual and collective growth. The transition from a traditional educational paradigm focused on youth deficits to one centered on strengths and capacities emerged from the recognition that merely working on the negative and helping youth avoid or deal with problems did not result in the development of skills conducive to life and workplace success. As education is not only about teaching students to read and write, the inclusion of strengths facilitates the development and actualization of their full potential from which to attain a state of wellbeing and contribute to the development of a sustainable and stable society.

Yet, in spite of the propositions put forward by positive education, many learning institutions overlook their obligation in helping youth develop the skills for lifelong satisfaction, nurturing relationships, strong mental and physical health, and positive emotions[3], and neither attend to nor integrate character strengths education into curricula. This leaves youth at a disadvantage as they enter the realms of higher education, employment, relationships and parenting without the knowledge skills to navigate difficulties with potentially serious results when mistakes are made. Youth face further hindrances due to their developmental stage of near-adulthood; the supports in place to help them with their transition dwindles over time as universities for instance, provide for more independence and offer less guidance and security, but also the contexts in which youth could practise these strengths, i.e., sports, clubs, and volunteer positions become less frequently available[4]. As a result, by the time youth need help, it is unavailable or their strengths are deployed in the service of crisis management and problem solving rather than on growth opportunities. Consequently, in this paper, we present the efforts of a positive education program designed for youth to address the development of these very strengths.

Do We Need Positive Education?

This is a common question educators ask; are reading, writing and math not sufficient for success? In a stable environment with little competition and ample job opportunities these might suffice; but are sufficient and average all we want for youth? Even in the absence of problems, there is still a need to attend to wellbeing as the presence of resources as well as psychological and socioemotional assets are still needed for optimal functioning. Further, other regional and national issues prompt the need for a positive education program focused on the development of character strengths. Like its neighbors, the UAE is now well into what is called a youth bulge, a situation where nearly half of its population is currently under 30 years of age[5]. As a result, by 2020, UAE youth and their regional neighbors will need 85 million new jobs across the Arab World[6], as well as concurrent developments in education, post-secondary training, and employability skills across schools, universities and workplaces to ensure that the needs of these emerging knowledge-based economies are adequately met[7].

Further, across the Gulf Cooperation Council (GCC; Saudi Arabia, Qatar, Bahrain, Kuwait, Qatar, Oman, and the UAE) countries, significant numbers of youth are graduating from schools and universities, females in particular; however, the quality of this education has been questioned. Government schools especially rely upon expatriate teachers who are paid less, have little job security, and tend to come from nations where teacher training standards are poor[8] resulting in low teacher engagement, traditional forms of teaching focused on rote learning, as well as a focus on grades versus critical thinking and good character. This focus is unfortunate as the skills of team work, creativity, initiative, problem-solving, and leadership are really what account for success in life and the workplace and are what employers mistakenly assume new graduates possess[9]. To illustrate, a study[10] showed that almost one third of private sector respondents were unsatisfied with the quality of UAE graduates, adding that educational outputs were not aligned with what industry needed. Respondents also preferred foreign educated candidates as their skills, attitudes and behaviours were more conducive to the workplace. The regional lack of student jobs, summer employment, and few opportunities for internships also limited youth in this area and prevented them from competing with foreign peers who have access and exposure to such opportunities on a regular basis and at an earlier age[11].

As the composition of GCC countries relies heavily on expatriate populations, private organizations are also loath to spend time or resources on the development of workplace related character strengths as this pool of labour accounts for between 70% to 90% of the population and is considered a renewable resource[12]. Public service jobs in contrast account for almost 99%[13] of the positions reserved for and preferred by GCC nationals, which have greater entitlements[14] and focus more on the development of workplace skills, albeit sometimes at a remedial level. Unfortunately, the promise of public sector jobs has bred a sense of entitlement[15] that for some, has made the need for professional growth unnecessary. Public sector protections also largely preclude termination and render work ethics, self-efficacy, competitiveness, and the need for personal mastery redundant. The current climate of low oil prices, an unsustainably costly and saturated public sector, and the need for diversification towards greater competitiveness has forced GCC governments to steer nationals towards the private sector where more productive and competitive employment can be had[16].

In the government sector and across GCC youth populations, some of the lowest levels of workplace engagement in comparison to expatriates are also identified[17]. To illustrate, a report[18] showed that 60% of privately employed UAE nationals reported feeling engaged and satisfied with work, while only 34% in the public sector felt the same. The same study noted that private sector national employees were happier at work and gave as their reasons more opportunities for self-development, skills acquisition, and career progression, as well as more recognition for achievement despite lower pay and benefits[19] in comparison to the public sector. GCC youth may need to change their expectations of what constitutes acceptable pay and consider that other factors beyond financial considerations make a greater impact on life satisfaction as their peers report. The priority given to the public sector has resulted in high levels of voluntary unemployment[20] in the local population despite the world's highest rate of imported labour. As national youth prefer to wait for a public sector position rather than take a lower paying one in the private sector[21], they exclude themselves from the labour market and neither use, nor develop their workplace skills and waste their educational formation. Even the rate of entrepreneurship in the UAE only amounts to a mere 1% of youth and 3% of all UAE nationals (adults included)[22]. Others take public sector jobs in fields unrelated to their degrees for the pay or prestige and often see education as a tool for higher remuneration and not a means to achieve professional self-actualization.

Finally, the parents of GCC youth play a role in selecting the careers of youth with implications for their job and life satisfaction[23] and tend to favor professions with high prestige, job security and pay[24] over those that potentially produce happiness. Youth overlook their own desires opting for jobs that perhaps do not use their talents or strengths creating situations where youth who can excel in a given field do not, and those who cannot, remain in it. It is not a question of less parental involvement as youth want them to be involved[25], rather it is that parents need to expand their views of what success consists and provide their children with the skills and abilities toward greater independence, confidence, clarity about their chosen purpose in life, and with the relevant workplace attitudes and behaviors. Yet, parents feel this is the responsibility of schools, while schools feel the opposite, and underestimate the role they play in steering their children towards a good professional fit[26].

Despite these issues, the picture is not all gloomy. A recent survey highlighted that GCC youth also have faith in their nations with 81% believing that their country is heading in the "right direction" compared to only 57% in North Africa and 29% in the Levant area, while 39% of youth in the MENA region (the data were not available for the GCC) stating they are looking to start a business in the next five years suggesting that there is at least some recognition that individuals will have to be the solution to many of these long-term woes[27].

What are Character Strengths?

Interchangeably called 21st century skills, employability skills, or soft skills, these skills are not rooted in academics, but facilitate learning and long-term success in life, academic settings and workplace[28]. These skills are instrumental in many ways; for example, candidates with stronger skills are more successful in their job searches[29] and likely to be hired[30]. These skills overlap with what are known in positive psychology as character strengths[31], the stable[32] qualities used in thoughts, actions, and feelings that lead to functionality and excellence. In the Values in Action classification system (VIA[33]), 24 strengths are identified that include wisdom, self-control, and tolerance as examples, and which are considered universal as they were developed by identifying strengths noted across literary, philosophical and religious texts worldwide[34]. As an aside, the development of character strengths is not meant to change the character of youth towards an ideal, but to amplify existing strengths through the use of tools with which youth can achieve excellence on their own terms.

Problem-solving, collaboration, empathy, social responsibility, and self-control are examples of strengths; yet, each contributes to success in a unique way. Optimism, for instance, a positive expectation for the future was shown to predict job success, lifelong learning, and the planning associated with making good career decisions[35]. Alternatively, grit[36], the sustained passion, effort, and interest for long-term goals predicted success more than SAT scores, leadership potential and physical aptitude in a study of West Point training recruits, suggesting that success is not only about objective standards, but personality too. Self-control, the ability to control one's actions, thoughts, attention, and emotions in the pursuit of goals[37] predicted monetary savings, relational competence, attention and focus at school, as well as fewer criminal convictions and less substance use[38]. Finally, emotional intelligence, the awareness of social dynamics and the ability to adjust one's interaction style, also predicted job success beyond cognitive ability[39]. It has also been shown that the overall use of character strengths in the workplace for instance led to greater job satisfaction, positive affect, productivity and organizational citizenship behavior[40], improved coping with work stress[41], and higher engagement[42]. In fact, just being aware of one's strengths resulted in an almost 10-time higher likelihood of flourishing at work and an 18-time higher likelihood when these same strengths were used[43].

But, can character strengths be taught or are they innate? Teaching character strengths is possible and many examples exist[44] where they are introduced into existing curriculum or delivered as whole school approaches where teachers and parents learn and model the skills, or as stand-alone lessons[45]. It is not only in school that strengths can be taught; their development can also be nurtured within families, religion, communities, and activities[46] like sports, volunteerism, service learning and competitive settings[47]. School-based programs have produced increases in life satisfaction, positive affect and greater overall well-being[48], fewer symptoms of depression[49] as well as greater classroom engagement, social skills and stronger academic skills[50]. Other studies showed that greater immediate wellbeing also led to positive results in the future too, with individuals showing a lower prevalence of emotional disturbances, more frequent contact with family and friends, stronger social engagement, and higher satisfaction at work years later[51]. Finally, understanding one's character strengths seemed to be helpful in determining for which career one might be best suited with one study finding that intellectual strengths were associated with artistic and investigative careers, transcendence and people-oriented strengths to social careers, while strengths of leadership were closely aligned with entrepreneurial interest[52].

Given the successes of these programs, the Strengths Compass™ Program was developed by the primary author (Lambert) and The Talent Enterprise to determine whether the same positive benefits could be achieved in a mixed group of local Emirati and expatriate youth in the UAE. Given the absence of documented programs of this kind in the region, our endeavor was delivered as a pilot to determine how this program can best be implemented and what roadblocks might exist.

Method

Participants

The Talent Enterprise, a human capital consulting and research organization (Dubai), in collaboration with the Sheikh Saud bin Saqr Al Qasimi Foundation for Policy Research (Ras Al Khaimah), delivered the Strengths Compass™ program. The Foundation sponsors the Sheikh Saqr Student Enrichment Program, which seeks to develop the personal and academic skills of Emirati students attending public secondary schools in the city and prepare them for university studies overseas. Students were selected through a competitive application process in Grade 9 based on application materials, grades, and English proficiency. Admitted students begin the program in Grade 10 and may continue onwards based on successful completion of requirements and staff recommendation. Attrition is around 30-40% between Grades 10 and 11, as student commitment is considered for advancement. The pilot was conducted with Grade 11 students (ages 15-16). Participation was voluntary but highly encouraged as a way to complement students' existing English classes. The male-to-female ratio was about 2:3, similar to the gender ratio of the overall Grade 11 cohort. While expatriate students comprise one third of the Grade 11 students, 80% chose to be involved with the pilot compared to 42% of Emirati students. This trend was more pronounced when looking at the male Grade 11 students, as 81% of the expatriates were involved compared to only 33% of eligible Emiratis.

Materials

The Strengths Compass™ program was developed by reviewing the available positive psychology and positive education literature on character strengths and positive interventions for youth and young adults in the realm of work and life, as well as the literature on regional labour issues. The character strengths included in the Strengths Compass™ program were deliberately chosen for their relevance and associations with success in academics and the workplace like perseverance, social intelligence, and curiosity and explain why not all of the 24 VIA character strengths are represented such as appreciation of beauty, love, or spirituality[53]. The strengths were also chosen to overlap with the YTI (described below) so that assessing changes in one's habitual use of character strengths could be measured. The full range of strengths in the overall Strengths Compass™ program is outlined in Table 1. Overlapping psychological concepts, such as self-efficacy (not a strength yet a factor upon which to build strengths), were also included. Based on existing research, interventions, and teaching tools, activities were then devised to help introduce and develop each strength through assessment, written reflection, group discussion and activity, videos, role plays, and take-home exercises.

The Youth Thriving Index (YTI), designed, developed and validated by The Talent Enterprise, is an indigenous psychometric assessment tool used to evaluate youth strengths and work orientations, and results in a personalized report (complemented by small group debriefing sessions) to help identify and understand one's character strengths and best suited careers. The YTI includes 89 questions, is available in English and Arabic, and can be done online. It also has four items to verify the social desirability bias, the tendency to answer questions in a manner that is viewed favorably by others. It has 10 factors listed below, along with the sub-factors for each.

Mindset (Flexibility & Growth): Mindsets are theories of intelligence held by individuals that view ability as fixed or flexible. Individuals ascribe to a growth mindset, a belief that the mind can be developed, or a fixed mindset, and believe that the mind is resistant to change and effort[54].

Fortitude (Buoyancy & Determination): Individuals high on buoyancy are confident, driven and optimistic when confronting challenge, as well as creative and focused while finding solutions.

Efficacy (Control, Confidence, & Preparedness): Efficacy[55] refers to the belief individuals have in their own abilities. Individuals high in efficacy set tough goals and the required steps to reach them.

Vitality (Drive, Energy & Optimism): Optimists expect positive future outcomes[56], whereas individuals high in vitality enjoy a state of physical and mental energy along with a sense of aliveness, purpose, and meaning[57].

Achievement (Absorption, Ambition & Mastery): Individuals high on a need for achievement are ambitious, set difficult goals, and use their skills in challenging, absorbing activities and experience flow[58], a state described by total concentration, intrinsic motivation, a sense of control, and lack of self-consciousness and distortion of time. Individuals high on mastery exert effort towards the perfection of skills.

Accountability (Ambiguity, Conviction & Responsibility): Individuals take responsibility for their actions, emotions and thoughts, and are valued for their clarity in making moral decisions.

Affiliation (Autonomy, Empathy & Teamwork): Affiliation involves the ability to work with others, take initiative, and adjust their communication to meet the needs of others, while building trust and meaningful rapport[59].

Ingenuity (Analytical, Creativity & Curiosity): Curiosity is the recognition, pursuit, and desire for events that elicit active exploration and attention to new stimuli, and sparks creativity and greater analysis of situations.

Motivation (Extrinsic, Intrinsic & Extra Role Responsibility): Intrinsically motivated individuals are driven by internal rewards, such as a sense of pride or interest, while extrinsics pursue status, pay or prestige[60].

Integrity (Ethics & Values): Integrity involves acting upon moral principles and making decisions accordingly. Individuals with integrity are honest, accountable and true to their ethical and personal values.

Pre and post assessments also evaluated how participants felt about their lives. In this paper, we offer qualitative reflections obtained from parents and the primary group facilitator. Quantitative results are forthcoming.

Procedure

Participants taking part in the Strengths Compass™ Program attended five sessions of four hours every two weeks from January to March 2016. Only five modules from the Strengths Compass™ Program's 10 week complement were selected for this pilot (in Table 2), based on the Foundation's recommendations including grit[61], the passion, sustained effort and interest for long-term goals, as well as resilience, the ability to tolerate negative emotions, maintain a positive view of one's self, and deal with adversity[62]. Mindsets[63] highlighting growth (belief that intelligence and skill can be incrementally developed) and fixed (belief that they are resistant to change) types as well as self-efficacy[64], the conviction individuals hold to effect positive changes and prevent negative ones from occurring, as well as self-esteem and teamwork were also discussed. Locus of control (LOC)[65], where individuals place responsibility for what happens, was explored and considered appropriate as the influence of religion and family is significant in the GCC and may contribute to an external LOC, the belief that personal outcomes are determined by fate, luck, the supernatural, or locally called "wasta", the actions taken by influential others on one's behalf. Finally, capitalization[66], how individuals respond to others good news, and writing a gratitude letter[67], selected from the pool of positive psychology interventions effective in boosting positivity, were also used.

Results and Discussion

The primary author (Lambert) facilitated all sessions in conjunction with The Talent Enterprise, where a high level of interest in the program and desire to give of and improve one's self was evident in participants. Youth placed high value on academics, making their parents proud, as well as altruistic acts towards others with these contexts serving as the basis for many examples. For instance, when asked "Who are you are your best?," one female related the following: "I'm a caring human in my best. Last year, I did the most brave thing ever in my life. My brother was going through a complicated bone marrow transplant surgery and I donated my cell and blood to him by going through another surgery for me. Unfortunately, my dear brother passed away but I will always remember that I did my best just to see him happy." Similarly, a young male supplied the following: "I did not imagine that I would save a life one day. That actually happened last year when I was in a beach in RAK. My family and I went together to have fun. While my family were setting a tent, I went to walk near the beach. Suddenly, I heard someone shouting, "Help." I rushed into him and pulled him out of the water. Then, I took him to the nearest emergency unit to heal him. He thanked me after he got recovered." Outside of these singular events, home life also appeared to act as a backdrop for the practise of strengths: "I like to take care of people and kids. My mother always makes me responsible for the house and to take care of my little brothers and sisters." Examples like these showed that youth were motivated to help and were able to place the needs of others above their own.

In other components of the program, participants had greater difficulty relating to concepts given their lack of life experience; yet, participants who took part in sports seemed to have an easier time understanding the strengths required for success like grit and resilience as this setting acted as an arena in which they could practise these strengths, i.e., "I would like to be the first world champion in fencing because I tried how amazing is this feeling last year when I won the golden medal among all the UAE teams, specially that I used to be a very careful person in life but fencing freed me from the negative feelings I used to have" and "I feel that I am at my best when I play football because when I play football I feel that I do my best and the example of it when I got player of the school prize, I was sooo happy and felt proud of myself." Participants without access to extracurricular activities were limited to hypothetical scenarios and future judgements, i.e., "when I graduate and work, then I will..." To be fair, this lack of experience is perhaps not unlike youth of this age around the world who are preoccupied by school and a social life.

Planning and taking action also appeared difficult and many students remained at the wishful thinking stage; the most common strategy summarized by one student, 'think positive and hope for the best.' For example, in response to an exercise on goal development, students were asked to select a goal and outline the steps that would lead them to success over time with a plan for the day, week, month or year, as applicable. A lengthy explanation was given on the importance on establishing specific, time-dependent, incremental and measurable goals. A female student identified "math" as her goal with steps as follows: (day plan) "just thinking what I have to do"; (week) "organize my ideas"; (month) "start working harder"; (year) "I am awesome."

Tapping into the collective orientation of this group and making reference to parent's or grandparent's generations struck interesting notes. In talking about grit for instance and the need for difficult activities in which to labour and subsequently grow, several youth contested this assertion, declaring that 'easier is better.' When asked to consider their family name and what their grandparent's would say in response, many red faces appeared. We surmised that the link between effort and reward is neither unknown nor foreign, but appears to have been forgotten in this era of affluence for some. Yet, making parents proud was an evident theme: "I love it when I'm making my parents proud that's when I'm at my best and I'm so confident to say that, seeing them smile and happy because of me – it means the world. They have done a lot of uncountable things to me and I feel so good about myself when I make them proud with my grades since it's all I can do now." Using familial, historical as well as current examples of activities performed by family members as well as members of the UAE's ruling families provided excellent relevant proxies for experience and was one of the ways in which we adapted the program to the local culture.

Females tended to have a higher external locus of control in light of greater family oversight; yet, even in this context, peer to peer discussions (rather than facilitator-participant) proved effective in nudging this orientation to a more internal one where females recognized there were opportunities they could seize and in which they may already have been. An external locus of control further reflected the reality of life in the GCC. For instance, while some students expressed an internal locus of control, they still agreed with statements like, "it's better to have influential friends than be smart," or "I'll get the job someone decides to give me" highlighting the practise of wasta in obtaining employment or favors in society, or the degree to which public service jobs are anticipated.

The best success story was that of a young Egyptian male whose parents wanted him to become a doctor. His story resonated with others who felt pressured to make professional decisions to make the family proud, or out of concern for financial and professional security. We discussed how such a discussion might happen while recognizing the need to respect parental opinion and authority. By the next class, this same teen reported: "I told them I had no reason to be a doctor. My dad, he didn't talk to me all week and my mom crying, telling me to change my mind and show respect. I didn't want to change my mind. All week, my dad was angry; he didn't talk to me. Finally, they saw I wasn't changing my mind and my dad finally, he said, okay, do what you want, we will support you... I want to be an aviation engineer."

This conversation brought forth the need to understand that a range of careers exist beyond those prized by parents and society (i.e., engineer, doctor, CEO) and that the title of careers is less important than one's wellbeing in them. Out of curiosity, we asked youth how many wanted to be a leader or a follower and out of 33 participants, only two acknowledged wanting to follow. Yet, of those choosing leadership, few could advance convincing rationales for this preference other than for financial reasons or prestige. None had realistic views of what it meant to be a leader in terms of time commitment, stress, responsibilities, skills, and liability and after discussing a day in the life of a CEO as an example, most changed their minds. These conversations may seem trivial but are vital as youth make permanent decisions with consequences for their future work and life satisfaction, not to mention the consequences of an unengaged and uninterested workforce on the public's safety and wellbeing as well.

We also distributed questionnaires to parents to determine what changes they observed. Parents noted that their children were more confident (i.e., "the programme made my son more self-confident, I noticed the way he speaks is different, it's like he is sure of everything he does"), showed more responsibility for their actions (i.e., "she suddenly loves being organized"), took greater initiative in undertaking school work and were more focused on their studies as a way to meet goals (i.e., "my child started being ambitious recently and thinks a lot about her future, she speaks a lot about her major"). Parents also noted that their children seemed more mature (i.e., "more mature in his thinking style and I have noticed that he started to pick hard things to do"), optimistic (i.e., "she has become more positive and started to see things/people in a positive way"), and open (i.e., "he doesn't feel nervous when he speaks with other people – before he was shy and nervous").

Yet, when asked what other skills their children needed to attain a promising future, the majority of parents expressed the need for their children to have more practical life experience and general life skills versus academic skills. They identified to need to: "communicate more because she is so shy and gets nervous a lot"; "learn about how to be independent"; "deal with new people"; "understand others and the way they think, how to act/respond to others depending on their personality"; "deal with problems"; "be more social and believe in himself" and develop "social skills." Time management was also identified as parents felt their children were unable to structure or make appropriate decisions about where and in what activity their time should be spent. Yet, few of their children engaged in extra-curricular activities (especially females) that would have given them the means to do so.

Limitations and Future Directions

Limitations exist. Despite being chosen for their higher levels of English, it is possible that some participants did not understand concepts as they were intended despite frequent clarification and an Arabic speaking supervisor available for translation. Further, our small sample size limits the generalizability of our results; nonetheless, all research passes through initial phases of validation and our intention is to continue this process with samples of different ages and educational and employment contexts. Finally, the low number of male participants, especially Emiratis, is a cause for concern and may suggest that this group is already at risk for attrition prompting the need for even earlier intervention.

A number of suggestions for the future can nonetheless be made. As noted, while strengths are practised in families, religion and sports for example, the current scenario, i.e., lack of part-time jobs, few extra-curricular activities, and the lack of community opportunities for youth in general[68] preclude the deployment of these strengths. Responses from all parties signalled a lack of practise and meaningful interaction with a world outside of academics that precluded the integration of strengths in the lives of students. The needs noted by parents, of independence, learning to approaching people and deal with problems for instance are correctly identified, but necessitate present-day real life supportive environments in which to practise, succeed and fail versus waiting for youth to get to the workplace and already be at a disadvantage compared to others who have mastered them.

Consequently, until youth have access to and want to take on part-time jobs, responsibilities like volunteering, or engaging in sports, music, activism, or other learning, a parallel service or leadership[69] component to this program for youth to practise and understand their strengths is strongly advised. In fact, welcome news was received in July 2016, when a new ruling in the UAE accorded youth aged 12 to 18 the right to work on a part-time basis effective September 2016[70]. Further, a locally relevant character strengths program like ours would do well to incorporate career exploration and counselling as well as the development of workplace skills given that educational reforms have not yet produced these outcomes nor have these programs been incorporated into existing school and university curriculums or internships to date[71]. Educating youth about what jobs are available as well as what skills and education are required for these is critical, but so is the need for youth to develop realistic expectations away from the public sector and see that they can be successful in the private sector too. Redirecting their hopes would ensure that more are in careers that suit who they are and not what they feel others want them to be.

Given the scope of the available character strengths and the need for these to become lifelong habits and not mere time limited skills, we further advocate for this program to be offered over the course of a year across both school and university curriculums where many of the strengths as well as current issues like the economy and regional employment can be easily discussed. These can be embedded into English, History, Economics, Social Studies, Health, and Islamic Studies classes for example. The incorporation of strengths can further be done via a range of teaching modalities that encompass current events, news interviews, contemporary movies, classical literature, and other significant cultural or religious texts as applicable. A whole school approach where teachers can model desired behaviors, guide students in using skills, and support their practise across multiple contexts (i.e., sports, academics, work environment), as well as benefit from the changes in positivity themselves as professionals[72] will further serve to enhance the program's sustainability. Thus, incorporating positive psychology programs as part of teacher education programming is another suggestion we make for the Ministries of Higher Education across the GCC countries to consider when addressing educational reforms.

A necessary partner in the development of youth and even more so in a collective society, is parents. Education workshops for parents in the Arabic language should be provided on new curriculum developments and career options, as well as instruction in character strengths so that they can understand and nurture what is most valuable in their children. A final recommendation we make involves the need to do more to make character strengths education amenable to culture, religion and local conditions as well as develop and offer positive educational psychology programming in Arabic to speak to local values and practises around wellbeing, education, and learning and not merely offer imported Western models that are not contextualized and fall short of meeting local needs[73].

In sum, we feel that although the problems are well known, and in this edited volume at least, they have been repeatedly documented, they all have one thing in common, a lack of clear, practical solutions. It is our view that no amount of fast tracking, nationalization, private sector wage subsidies, quotas, policy or legislative changes or the plethora of other initiatives that have been tried so far, can be complete or successful without the inclusion of psychological factors. We do not promote a view on problems; instead, as has been the case in the paper, we propose adopting the tenets of positive education and positive psychology to capitalize, harness and mobilize the strengths of youth and young adults in the GCC region. These should be used to guide policy makers, educators and employers in bridging the education and employment skills gap currently faced in the UAE across all ministries. We anticipate that the nomination of a UAE Minister of Happiness earlier in 2016 will also spur more initiatives like this and promote these philosophies where youth and adults alike can actualize themselves fully and achieve both satisfaction in life as well as contribute to a much needed and promising state of national development across the region.

Table 1: Complete Strengths Compass™ Program Themes

Modules	Character Strengths
1	Introduction Program: What are Character Strengths; What is Positive Psychology? Youth Thriving Index
2	Mindsets: Fixed and Growth
3	Fortitude: What are Grit and Resilience?
4	Locus of Control and Self-Efficacy
5	Self-Control (Self-regulation)
6	Vitality: Optimism & Positive Attitude
7	Personal Accountability: Taking responsibility
8	Affiliation: Social Intelligence, Teamwork, Diversity
9	Prosocial Behavior: Good Deeds
10	Conclusion: Bringing it all together: Best Self

Table 2: Strengths Compass™ Pilot Program Themes

	Activity and Description of Strengths Compass™ Program
Pre-Session	Completion of the Career Perspective Index™ questionnaire
Session 1	Introduction to Positive Psychology and Strengths Gratitude Letter (Seligman et al., 2005)
Session 2	Icebreaker activity, getting to know you, expectations for program Introduction to Grit (Duckworth et al., 2007), resilience (Ungar et al., 2014), goal setting Understanding characteristics of grit and how to improve grit Self-reflection: How much grit do I have? Applying grit in my daily life and setting goals for the week
Session 3	Introduction to Mindsets (Dweck, 2006) Fixed and growth: What's the difference? Self-assessment and quiz. How to develop a Growth Mindset; self-reflection and group activity
Session 4	Character Strengths & Why They Matter Introduction to Career Perspective Index™ and review of individual reports highlighting strengths and suitable careers Locus of Control (Rotter, 1966) Self-efficacy (Bandura, 2008) and self-esteem In-class activities, assessment of internal/external locus of control Improving self-efficacy
Session 5	Team activity to summarize key learnings of Strengths Compass™ program Affiliation and Teamwork Capitalization (Gable et al., 2004) Practise response style

Notes

1 Martin E. P. Seligman et al., "Positive education: Positive psychology and classroom interventions," *Oxford Review of Education* 35, no. 3 (2009): 293-311.

2 Martin E. P. Seligman and Mihalyi Csikszentmihalyi, "Positive psychology: An introduction," *American Psychologist* 55, no. 1 (2000): 5-14.

3 Lindsey G. Oades et al., "Towards a positive university," *Journal of Positive Psychology* 6, no. 6 (2011): 432-39.

4 Margaret L. Kern et al., "A multifaceted approach to measuring wellbeing in students: Application of the PERMA framework," *Journal of Positive Psychology* 10 (2015): 262-71.

5 International Finance Corporation, "Education for employment: Realizing Arab youth potential", International Finance Corporation, 2011. http://tinyurl.com/yafyygkx

6 Ibid.

7 David Jones and Radhika Punshi, *Unlocking the paradox of plenty: A review of the talent landscape in the Arab world and your role in shaping it* (Dubai: Motivate Publishing, 2013); Wes Schwalje, "A conceptual model of national skills formation for knowledge-based economic development in the Arab world," Sheikh Saud bin Saqr Al Qasimi Foundation for Policy Research, July 2013. http://tinyurl.com/y9e8wx5r

8 Nabil M. Kronfol, "Demographics and the social reckoning in the Arab region," *Eastern Mediterranean Health Journal* 19, no. 4 (2013): 382-88; Natasha Ridge, *Education and the reverse gender divide in the Gulf states: Embracing the global, ignoring the local* (New York: Teachers College Press, 2014); Natasha Ridge et al., "Expatriate teachers and education quality in the Gulf Cooperation Council," The Sheikh Saud bin Saqr Al Qasimi Foundation for Policy Research, Policy Paper No. 11, November 2014. http://tinyurl.com/yd833n94

9 Abdulla Al Mutairi, Kamal Naser, and Muna Saeid, "Employability factors of business graduates in Kuwait: Evidence from an emerging country," *International Journal of Business and Management* 9, no. 10 (2014): 49-61; Kronfol, "Demographics", 382-88. Kevin Lowden et al., "Employers' perceptions of the employability skills of new graduates," Edge Foundation, London, UK, 2011. http://tinyurl.com/6y3gx8s

10 Ali Bhayani, "The market route to higher education in UAE: Its rationales and implications," *International Review on Public and Nonprofit Marketing* 11, no. 1 (2014): 75–87.

11 Mohammed Al-Waqfi and Ingo Forstenlechner, "Of private sector fear and prejudice," *Personnel Review* 41, no. 5 (2012): 609–629; Abhilasha Singh, David B. Jones and Nicholas Hall, "Talent management: A research based case study in the GCC region," *International Journal of Business and Management* 7, no. 24 (2012): 94-107.

12 Evangelos-Vagelis Dedoussis and Richard Rutter, "Workforce localisation and change management: The view from the Gulf," in *Organizational Change Management Strategies in Modern Business*, ed. Aslo Goksoy, (Hershey, PA: Business Science Reference, 2016): 301-27.

13 Alexander Cornwell, "Conference in Dubai highlights recruitment challenges," *Gulf News*, October 3, 2013, http://tinyurl.com/y7gsweq4

14 Al-Waqfi and Forstenlechner, "Of private sector," 609-629; Ingo Forstenlechner and Emilie Rutledge, "Unemployment in the Gulf: Time to update the "Social Contract"", *Middle East Policy* 17, no. 2 (2010): 38-51.

15 Al-Waqfi and Forstenlechner, "Of private sector," 609-629.

16 Ahmed Z. E. Ahmed, "The role of diversification strategies in the economic development for oil depended countries: The case of UAE," *International Journal of Business and Economic Development* 3, no. 1 (2015): 47-57; Al-Waqfi and Forstenlechner, "Of private sector," 609-629; Erogul, "Entrepreneurial activity," 195-211; Forstenlechner and Baruch, "Contemporary," 629-48.

17 Jones and Punshi, *Paradox.*

18 Aon Hewitt, "Aon Hewitt's Qudurat report reveals record levels of engagement among nationals working in the private sector" November 11, 2013, http://tinyurl.com/ycwjjump

19 Georgia Daleure and Zain Shareef, "Exploring under-representation of young Emirati adults in the UAE private sector by examining Emirati job satisfaction," The Sheikh Saud bin Saqr Al Qasimi Foundation for Policy Research, Policy Paper No. 9, April, 2015, http://tinyurl.com/yd7ham2o

20 Ola Salem and Haneen Dajani, "FNC would like Emiratisation to become law," *The National*, November 18, 2013, http://www.thenational.ae/uae/government/fnc-would-like-emiratisation-to-become-law

21 Al-Waqfi and Forstenlechner, "Of private sector," 609-629.

22 Khalifa Fund for Enterprise Development, "Youth and Entrepreneurship in UAE," 2015, http://tinyurl.com/y8q7lrt9

23 Samer Khasawneh, "Factors influencing the career planning and development of university students in Jordan," *Australian Journal of Career Development* 19, no. 2 (2010): 41–8; Sylvia C. Nassar-McMillan and Lynn Zagzebski-Tovar, "Career counseling with Americans of Arab descent," *Career Planning and Adult Development Journal* 28, no. 1 (2012): 72-87.

24 Al-Waqfi and Forstenlechner, "Of private sector," 609-629.

25 Alan Russell et al., "Youth in the United Arab Emirates: Perceptions of problems and needs for a successful transition to adulthood," *International Journal of Adolescence and Youth* 12, no. 3 (2005): 189-212.

26 Fiona Baker and Rida Blaik Hourani, "The nature of parental involvement in the city of Abu Dhabi in a context of change: Nurturing mutually responsive practice," *Education, Business and Society: Contemporary Middle Eastern Issues* 7, no. 4 (2014): 186-200.

27 ASDA'A Burson-Marsteller, "Arab Youth Survey 2015," 2015, http://tinyurl.com/ycmpwnnm
28 Laura H. Lippman et al., "Workforce connections: Key "soft skills" that foster youth workforce success: Toward a consensus across fields," Child Trends Publication #2015-24, June 2015, http://tinyurl.com/ycvjx58k
29 Selver D. Uysal and Winfried Pohlmeier, "Unemployment duration and personality," *Journal of Economic Psychology* 32 (2011): 980-92.
30 Madhu S. Mohanty, "Effects of positive attitude and optimism on employment: Evidence from the US data," *The Journal of Socio-Economics* 39 (2010): 258-70.
31 Christopher Peterson and Martin E. P. Seligman, *Character strengths and virtues: A handbook and classification.* (Oxford, UK: Oxford University Press, 2004).
32 Marta Ferragut, Maria J. Blanca and Margarita Ortiz-Tallo, "Psychological virtues during adolescence: A longitudinal study of gender differences," *European Journal of Development Psychology* 11, no. 5 (2014): 1-11.
33 Peterson and Seligman, *Character strengths.*
34 Katherine Dahlsgaard, Christopher Peterson and Martin E. P. Seligman, "Shared virtue: The convergence of valued human strengths across culture and history," *Review of General Psychology* 9, no. 3 (2005): 203-13.
35 Peter A. Creed, Wendy Patton, and Dee Bartrum, "Multidimensional properties of the LOT-R: Effects of optimism and pessimism on career and wellbeing related variables in adolescents," *Journal of Career Assessment* 10, (2002): 42-61; Roberta A. Neault, "Thriving in the new millennium: Career management in the changing world of work," *Canadian Journal of Career Development* 1, no. 1 (2002): 11-21.
36 Angela L. Duckworth et al., "Grit: Perseverance and passion for long-term goals," *Journal of Personality and Social Psychology* 92, no. 6 (2007): 1087-1101.
37 Angela L. Duckworth, "The significance of self-control," *Proceedings of the National Academy of Sciences* 108, no. 7 (2011): 2639-40.
38 Nancy Eisenberg et al., "Self-regulation, effortful control, and their socioemotional correlates" In *Handbook of emotion regulation,* ed. James J. Gross (New York, NY: Guilford, 2014), 157-172. Terrie E. Moffitt et al., "A gradient of childhood self- control predicts health, wealth, and public safety," *Proceedings of the National Academy of Sciences* 108 (2011): 2693-98. Daniel Romer et al., "Can adolescents learn self- control? Delay of gratification in the development of control over risk taking," *Prevention Science* 11, no. 3 (2010): 319-30. Elli Tsukayama, Angela L. Duckworth and Betty Kim, "Resisting everything except temptation: Evidence and an explanation for domain-specific impulsivity," *European Journal of Personality* 26 (2012): 318–34. Elli Tsukayama et al., "Self-control as a protective factor against overweight status in the transition from childhood to adolescence," *Archives of Pediatrics and Adolescent Medicine* 164 (2010): 631-35.
39 David L. Van Roy and Chockalingam Viswesvaran "Emotional intelligence: A meta-analytic investigation of predictive validity and nomological net," *Journal of Vocational Behavior* 65 (2004): 71-95.
40 Shiri Lavy and Hadassah Littman-Ovadia, "My better self: Using strengths at work and work productivity, organizational citizenship behavior and satisfaction," *Journal of Career Development* doi: 10.1177/0894845316634056. Marianne van Woerkom and Maria Christina Meyers, "My strengths count! Effects of a strengths-based psychological climate on positive affect and job performance," *Human Resource Management* 54, no. 1 (2015): 81-103
41 Claudia Harzer and Willibald Ruch, "The relationships of character strengths with coping, work-related stress, and job satisfaction," *Frontiers in Psychology* 6, no. 165 (2015). doi:10.3389/fpsyg.2015.00165
42 Claudia Harzer and Willibald Ruch, "The application of signature character strengths and positive experiences at work," *Journal of Happiness Studies* 14 (2013): 965–983. Steve Crabb, "The use of coaching principles to foster employee engagement," *The Coaching Psychologist 7, no.* 1 (2011): 27-31.
43 Lucy C. Hone et al., "Flourishing in New Zealand workers: Associations with lifestyle behaviors, physical health, psychosocial, and work-related indicators," *Journal of Occupational and Environmental Medicine* 57, no. 9 (2015): 973-983.

44 Terry Molony and Maureen Henwood, "Signature strengths in positive psychology," *Communique 38, no.* 8 (2010): 15-16.
45 Norrish, "Applied framework", 147-61.
46 Martin E. P. Seligman, *Authentic happiness: Using the new positive psychology to realize your potential for lasting fulfillment.* (New York, NY: Free Press, 2002).
47 Peterson and Seligman, *Character strengths.*
48 Carmel Proctor et al., "Strengths gym: The impact of a character strengths-based intervention on the life satisfaction and well-being of adolescents," *Journal of Positive Psychology* 6, (2011): 377-88. M. Oppenheimer et al., "Teaching to strengths: Character education for urban middle school students," *Journal of Character Education 10, no.* 2 (2014): 91-105.
49 Jane Gillham et al., "Character strengths predict subjective well-being during adolescence," *Journal of Positive Psychology* 6, no. 1 (2011): 31-44.
50 Martin E. P. Seligman et al., "Positive education," 293-311. Denise Quinlan et al., "How 'other people matter' in a classroom-based strengths intervention: Exploring interpersonal strategies and classroom outcomes," *Journal of Positive Psychology* 10, no. 1 (2015): 77-89.
51 Marcus Richards and Felicia A. Huppert, "Do positive children become positive adults? Evidence from a longitudinal birth cohort study", *The Journal of Positive Psychology* 6, no. 1 (2011): 75-87.
52 Rene T. Proyer et al., "A multi-method approach to studying the relationship between character strengths and vocational interests in adolescents," *International Journal for Educational and Vocational Guidance 12, no.* 2 (2012): 141-157.
53 Kevin Money, Carola Hillenbrand and Nuno Da Camara, "Putting positive psychology to work in organizations," *Journal of General Management 34, no.* 2 (2008): 21-26.
54 Carole Dweck, *Mindset: The new psychology of success* (New York: Random House, 2006).
55 Albert Bandura, "Reconstrual of "free will" from the agentic perspective of social cognitive theory," in *Are we free?: Psychology and free will*, eds. John Baer, James. C. Kaufman, and Roy F. Baumeister (Oxford, UK: Oxford University Press, 2008), 86-127.
56 Stephen Schueller and Martin E. P. Seligman, "Optimism and pessimism," in *Risk factors in depression,* eds. Keith Dobson and David Dozois, (New York, NY: Elsevier Inc., 2008), 171-94.
57 Richard M. Ryan and Edward L. Deci, "From ego depletion to vitality: Theory and findings concerning the facilitation of energy available to the self," *Social and Personality Psychology Compass* 2, no. 2 (2008): 702-17.
58 Mihalyi Csikszentmihalyi, *Flow: The psychology of optimal experience* (New York: Harper & Row, 1990).
59 Peterson and Seligman, *Character Strengths.*
60 Richard M. Ryan and Edward L. Deci, "Self-determination theory and the facilitation of intrinsic motivation, social development, and well-being," *American Psychologist* 55 (2000): 68-78.
61 Duckworth et al., "Grit", 1087-101.
62 Michael Ungar, Linda Liebenberg and Janice Ikeda, "Young people with complex needs: Designing coordinated interventions to promote resilience across child welfare, juvenile corrections, mental health and education services," *British Journal of Social Work* 44 (2014): 675-93.
63 Dweck, *Mindsets.*
64 Bandura, "Self-efficacy", 86-127.
65 Julian B. Rotter, "Generalized expectancies for internal versus external control of reinforcement," *Psychological Monographs* 80, (1966): 1-28.
66 Shelly L. Gable et al., "What do you do when things go right? The intrapersonal and interpersonal benefits of sharing positive events," *Journal of Personality and Social Psychology* 87 (2004): 228 -45.
67 Martin E. P. Seligman et al., "Positive psychology progress: Empirical validation of interventions," *American Psychologist* 60 (2005): 410-21.
68 Al-Waqfi and Forstenlechner, "Private sector," 609-629; Singh, Jones, and Hall, "Talent management", 94-107.

69 Shepherd Zeldin, Brian D. Christens and Jane Powers, (2013). "The psychology and practice of youth-adult partnership: Bridging generations for youth development and community change," *American Journal of Community Psychology* 51 (2013): 385-97.

70 Nadeem Hanif and Thamer Al Subaihi, "Youths welcome chance to get work experience in the UAE," July 13 2016, http://tinyurl.com/yamoxuqf

71 Al-Waqfi and Forstenlechner, "Of private sector," 609-629; Forstenlechner and Baruch, "Contemporary," 629-48.

72 Anat Shoshani and Sarit Steinmetz, "Positive psychology at school: A school-based intervention to promote adolescent's mental health and well-being," *Journal of Happiness Studies* 15, no. 6 (2014): 1289-1311.

73 Louise Lambert et al., "Developing an indigenous positive psychology in the United Arab Emirates," *Middle East Journal of Positive Psychology* 1, no. 11 (2015): 1-23; Rhea Owens, Jeana Magyar-Moe and Shane J. Lopez, "Finding balance via positive psychological assessment: Recommendations for practice," *The Counseling Psychologist* 43, no. 5 (2015): 634-70.

8

The Impact of Financial Rewards in Improving Students' Academic Results: The Case of Cadet Pilot Training within a Middle Eastern Airline

Wissam Hachem

Abstract

Financial rewards and merit pay plans are repeatedly used by organisations as a mean to reward employees for good performance and positive results. Linking performance reviews to compensation and rewards has become a common practice within organisations, aimed at improving the effectiveness of the system as well as providing an incentive to increase employees' motivation. On the other hand, this approach was also faced with much criticism from proponents who are calling for performance reviews to be decoupled from rewards. This paper seeks to investigate the impact of financial reward system on the overall academic results of the cadet pilot students within X-Air Airline (name kept anonymous). Consequently, the impact of P4P on students' performance and motivation is critically investigated. A combined qualitative and quantitative research approach was adopted to gather evidence through an online questionnaire, supplemented by face-to-face interviews with students and senior managers. This was accompanied by a thorough review of relevant literatures around the subject. Results from this research, revealed that students and managers alike, have positively associated the relationship between clear goal-setting with performance management system effectiveness, as well as the correlation between Pay-for-Performance and improved results. On the other hand, a modest correlation was identified between the impact of effective feedback on Performance and financial rewards on motivation. Finally, practical recommendations and limitations are presented in this paper to equip managers to address the findings revealed by this empirical research study.

Introduction

Rewarding employees for a job well done and for meeting the objectives of the role and ultimately the organisation, can come in various shapes and forms. Luthans (2000) describes two types of rewards, namely financial and non-financial, which could be used effectively by organisations to encourage positive behaviours and improve performance. Much controversy has surrounded the different types of motivation theories and the role of rewards in influencing the individuals' behaviours to improve job-related performance. However, the argument remains unclear in determining whether performance-related pay does actually imply an increase in motivation at work. If this is assumed to be correct, what needs to be determined is whether it remains the only decisive factor as the link between motivation and performance.

This research specifically looks at the case of X-Air's Cadet Pilot Students (CPS) in the Gulf region. X-Air has introduced an innovative and unique program for its CPS, where high school graduates are enrolled in a three-and-a-half year university program, and are provided with integrated academic courses and aviation classroom training. The university program is complemented by an eighteen-month of flight training programme, before finally graduating with a Bachelor degree in Aviation Science and a flying license. These cadets receive a monthly salary (stipend) for being on the program. Recently a Pay-for-Performance (P4P) solution has been introduced, whereby their academic performance, attendance, (amongst other key performance indicators) and overall performance determine their eligibility for the yearly bonus as well as salary increases.

The expected outcome of the research is to understand the impact of a performance reward system on the academic results and achievements of the cadet pilot students at X-Air. According to the researcher's knowledge, no similar study has ever been conducted in the region on this particular topic. The conventional training for Airlines' cadet pilots is usually restricted to the eighteen-month long practical and vocational training, as per the international regulatory requirements. Besides, performance management practices and particularly performance-related reward systems are not commonly known within the academic education system for students.

In order to ascertain whether the newly introduced P4P system for CPS at X-Air, has any effects on their academic performance, this empirical study will attempt to answer the following question: 'Does financial rewards system improve students' academic results?' The following sub-questions will attempt to further explore and investigate other factors associated with the highlighted subject in the central question: 1) 'What are the critical factors that play a major role in driving cadets' better performance?' 2) 'To what extent performance is impacted by financial rewards?' and 3) 'How does Pay-for-Performance contribute to students' motivation to achieve better results?'

Finally, within the context of students' education, this research aims to understand how students are expected to perform in relation to this phenomenon.

Literature Review

In modern times, the recipe for success for organisations is not just focusing on consumers or clients, but also looking within to maintain a motivated workforce for longer-term sustainability. The question in terms of the aspects that drive employee motivation remains open to many different interpretations. Deeprose (1994) claims that employees' productivity and their motivation could ultimately be improved through the introduction of effective reward and recognition system, which ensures improved organisational performance in return. According to Martin and Fellenz (2010) the purpose of any reward system is to attract, retain and motivate employees.

Rewarding employees' performance has become a widely utilised strategy and has also seen tremendous change in terms of approach, methods and forms. According to Luthans (2000), financial and non-financial types of rewards can be identified and positively adopted to improve performance behaviours of employees. Therefore, financial rewards could take the form of pay-for-performance (P4P), such as annual salary increase, yearly bonus, job promotion, commission incentives, gifts, etc. while non-financial rewards could take the form of social recognition such as appreciation awards, certificate, acknowledgement, etc. which Neckermann and Kosfeld (2008), refer to this type of non-financial rewards as materials award. Perry *et al* (2006) argue that financial rewards do not necessarily act as a motivating factor for employees, while Srivastava *et al* (2001) claim that financial rewards might have a de-motivating effects amongst employees.

Understanding the effectiveness of any reward system and its impact on motivation and performance would not be complete, unless the different types of motivations are explored. People are not all the same and therefore their motivational needs would vary significantly. Ryan & Deci (2000) claim that in relation to the self-determination theory, the type of work motivation that employees are driven by, influences the differences of how much energy is placed on work effort. As per the self-determination theory, intrinsic motivation represents self-directed motivation in its purest form while extrinsic motivation places more emphasis on the effects of the outcome of the activity, rather than the activity itself (Gagné & Deci, 2005).

Impact of Financial Rewards on Performance

It can be assumed that reward is amongst several human resource practices that play an important role in influencing the behaviours and attitudes of employees within an organisation. According to (Eisenhardt, 1989) aligning the interests of the organisation with employee behaviours can be achieved through reward mechanisms. P4P in particular has been identified as a reward practice linking individual's pay increase to performance results, as well as directing and motivating desirable behaviours. A view that was also ascertained by Stajkovic and Luthans (2001) that P4P supports both financial incentives and recognition of behaviours. It can help establish the allocation of rewards and recognition to specific behavioural criteria, which consequently aligns individual's behaviours with company values and strategic objectives. Simply explained, this approach would mean that pay increases are provided for employees who achieve and successfully meet their performance objectives. As a result, it would also mean that this type of recognition would reinforce positive and constructive work attitudes. So P4P has been one of the most adopted forms of incentives used by many organisations to foster value-added contributions of their employees, specifically when it is embedded into the performance management process within the organisation (Milkovich *et al*, 1991).

However, many still argue its effectiveness and question the simplification of this particular correlation, since little is known about the P4P perception and its link to work attitudes (Scott *et al*, 2008). Fama (1980) claims that employees and organisations are usually motivated by conflicting self-interests; therefore individual behaviours are not always directed to serve the interest and goals of the organisation. The role of P4P in this regard becomes important in eliciting expected and consistent performance behaviours from employees in the interest of alignment, in order to achieve employee-employer goal congruence (Eisenhardt, 1988). When linked to performance management, P4P can indicate what the organisation values the most in terms of priorities with regard to behavioural standards and performance objectives. And when employees establish a sense of trust and mutual understanding of the performance and reward culture, as well as the rationale behind it, then desired behaviours can be achieved effectively and efficiently.

Furthermore, when employees establish the trust that reward outcomes will be received as a result of desired behaviours, only then they will be motivated to demonstrate these behaviours (Porter and Lawler, 1968). It is therefore assumed that the perceived importance of such behaviours is encouraged by the reward results. More importantly, as stressed by Lawler (2000), employees need to be rewarded according to the value they bring to the organisation. This assumption leads us to believe that having incentives in place, greater effort is usually generated. But according to Deci and Ryan (1985), the cognitive-evaluation theory suggests that effort and task performance decrease as a result of a decrease in intrinsic motivation, due to the focus on the external reward when monetary incentives are associated with a task.

It would be difficult to argue, that P4P as a management practice seems to be a very logical strategy (Meyer, 1975), specifically when compensating and paying high performing employees more than their peers who are performing the same job at an average performance level. But despite its simplicity, it might not always work due to managers being inclined to differentiate in salary management between individuals performing the same job.

Despite the various arguments seen above about the effectiveness of monetary incentive practices in relation to performance management, many experts continue to criticise its application. Additionally, based on several examples mentioned earlier in this paper, it seems that a large number of employees are still not satisfied with this practice. On that basis, it can be argued that monetary rewards cannot be assumed as a critical factor impacting employees' behaviours although it is considered as a fundamental element of performance management effectiveness.

Impact of Financial Rewards on Motivation

The subject of motivation has been an area of interest for many researchers; therefore it is becoming crucial to learn more about the factors that impact employee motivation in the workplace. According to Lawler (2000), research indicates that individuals can very well be motivated to perform better if the Pay-for-Performance (P4P) is very well implemented. To better understand this phenomenon and despite the vast array of motivational theories that have been provided by psychologists over the years, the focus in this paper will mainly concentrate on work motivational theories that are directly linked to performance. To narrow the discussion on this matter, the 'Goal-Setting Theory' developed by Locke and Latham (2002) will be explored due to the significance of goals to performance management systems. Subsequently, as feedback plays a crucial role in performance management, the work of Carver and Scheier (1998) in terms of 'Control Theory' will also be reviewed. Finally, the social learning view of motivation will also be discussed in relation to the 'Social Cognitive Theory' developed by Donovan (2001).

Goal-Setting Theory

According to Locke *et al.* (1981), the extensive research of goal-setting and its effects on performance in 90% of their field and laboratory studies has been instrumental in identifying the validity, reliability and relevance across various work conditions. In their 35-year research of goal-setting theory, Locke and Latham (2002) have extensively studied and researched its effects on performance. Their work focused on understanding the primary properties of goals in terms of difficulty and specificity. They ascertain that the level of specific goals and their difficulty played a significant role in motivating individuals to improve and enhance performance when compared to unspecified and vague goals. Goals must be stretching rather than being easily attained, and for individuals to raise their level of performance; they have to fit within their level of capability. Bandura (1997) referred to 'self-efficacy' as the individual's internal belief concerning own level of job knowledge and skills. In addition to building and reinforcing employees' self-efficacy as a key enabler to setting goals successfully, employees must also accept such goals rather than simply having them assigned. Collaboration and participation in the goal-setting process enhance employee's commitment and motivation to perform towards achieving such goals. Locke and Latham also highlighted in their model the importance of feedback in helping and guiding employees attain their goals. Feedback is found helpful in letting individuals understand how well performance is trending and also allows for adjustments if performance towards achieving the goal is not quite on track.

The impact of goals generally increases when individuals are aware that their performance is being evaluated and measured.

Control Theory

As described above, goal-setting theory placed emphasis on the specificity and difficulty of the goal, and as a result, feedback was derived from the process as an essential factor in aligning behaviours to expected outcomes. Control theory, on the other hand, places feedback as a primary control mechanism to minimise the discrepancy between the expected thresholds for behaviours and the observed effects of actual behaviours (Carver and Scheier, 1998). Originally, the cybernetic theory was introduced to explain the functioning of self-regulating systems (Ashby, 1966) and is achieved through the negative feedback loop, which assesses variances between environmental input and internal standards and tries to reduce these discrepancies by either changing the environment or adapting standards, or both. This was also based on the assumption that people are self-regulating, and the elements of feedback are similar to the components of a thermostat that regulates the heat and temperature of a room. Therefore, the mechanical device acts similarly to the cognitive process in humans. In essence, this theory calls on individuals to take advantage of the feedback loop process to regulate own behaviours and their effects on performance, in relation to the expected outcomes.

Klein (1989), in his study discusses similarities between goal-setting theory and control theory. He points out that, within the goal-setting theory, individuals motivate themselves by setting certain goals in order to achieve a desired outcome. Similarly, the control theory has also a cognitive element composed of goals. Individuals aim at reducing any discrepancy that may deter the achievement of the goal, if such feedback is received. Based on the above, one can assume that a relationship can exist between goal-setting theory and control theory through its feedback loop. Such relationship explains that attaining a goal requires individuals to set multiple sub goals at the same time, since it is rare that people work toward attaining a singular independent goal at any given time (Campion and Lord, 1982).

Despite the broad advantage of the theory and its application to human behaviour, it has received many criticisms (e.g., Bandura, 1989, Locke, 1991, 1994). Despite the many adaptations of this theory to human behaviour, most criticisms against it argued its mechanistic approach. Additionally, since it focused mainly on reducing discrepancies, this can only be achieved by reducing standards, which is contradictory to the humans' behaviour in striving to attain goals by setting goals to minimize the discrepancies. Accordingly, Locke (1994) has called to abandon all the cybernetic theories of human behaviour.

Social Cognitive Theory

Bandura (1989) expanded on his earlier work of social learning theory and renamed his original theory 'social cognitive theory' to highlight the key role cognition plays in translating and performing behaviours. His argument was based on the fact that motivation or human behaviour is caused by the interaction between the work environment element, the personal actions and behaviours of the individual as well as the personal and human internal thought process. Bandura has identified the concept of self-efficacy as central to understanding how performers approach tasks, challenges and goals. The belief about one's capabilities helps performers identify what can or cannot be done in order to moderate own performance. Performers with high self-efficacy or positive self-beliefs are more likely to overcome challenges, moderate behaviours and enhance performance. In addition, employees with high level of self-efficacy are more likely to learn behaviours through observations (Bandura, 1989).

Bandura (1997) identified four influences to improve or increase self-efficacy. Mastery and experience have been identified very effective in shaping and influencing personality, as well as building efficacy as individual achievements can gradually progress from successfully completing simple to more complex tasks. Additionally, social modelling has also been identified as an influence on self-efficacy. Observing and watching peers and colleagues perform the same task, particularly if those had succeeded, can consequently increase confidence. Although it possessed limited and short-term impact, verbal persuasion, in the form of regular feedback, was another influence identified for managers to encourage employees to complete a task by convincing them that they possess the necessary skills to do so successfully. Finally, physiological reactions and its interpretation regarding work situations play a significant role in influencing self-efficacy.

Research Methodology

For the purpose of this empirical research, primary and secondary data will be obtained, using a mixture of qualitative and quantitative approach. As a first step, secondary data collection is conducted through a review of relevant literatures, using academic journals, theoretical frameworks, books and online materials, in order to create a deeper level of understanding of the P4P subject and help create sub-level research questions and arguments to answer the main question in this research.

The primary source of information is gathered and collected using the purposive sampling technique, as the preferred method, by conducting five semi-structured interviews with students of approximately one hour each and three senior management team members. These interviews aim to establish whether the adopted method of pay-for-performance has had any impact on students' motivation to strive to obtain better results and whether the difference in the level of performance has had any relation to the two types of intrinsic and extrinsic motivation. Furthermore, senior management interviews aim to gauge their perception and views on the approach and effectiveness of the methodology and whether any improvement of performance has been observed as a result of the implementation of the reward scheme. The two sets of qualitative questionnaires for students and senior managers were designed and divided into three parts and mapped against the three-sub questions of this research.

A larger population will also be studied, using an online questionnaire targeting 187 respondents, representing 61% of the total students' population, to obtain quantitative data required for the research. 39% of students were excluded, as they were new joiners in their second semester. The population for this research study included students who are currently enrolled in the cadet pilot training programme. CPS from Year 1 & 2 were admitted in the program after the P4P was introduced and this group has been referred to as the 'Post' sample in this report. Students from Year 3 & 4 were a part of the programme even before the P4P solution was introduced. After the four-year programme, graduates are enrolled for eighteen month flying at the Training College. Students from Year 3 & 4 along with the Training College have been referred to as the 'Pre' sample in this report.

SPSS has been used to calculate all descriptive statistics with various cuts such as pre/post, gender and age. For all descriptive statistics, ratings 1 and 2 have been combined to calculate 'Low', ratings 4 and 5 have been combined to calculate 'High' and rating 3 has been called 'Medium'. SPSS has also been used to calculate Pearson correlations. Finally, Principal Components Analysis (PCA) was also run to identify latent constructs in the items used in the questionnaire.

For performance data available from 2014 and 2015, coding was done to align performance ratings with the Likert scale items used in the online questionnaire and followed the classification of Outstanding (5), Exceeds Expectations (4), Meets Expectations (3), Improvement Required (2) and Unacceptable (1). In order to use a more consistent approach, performance ratings from 2014 and 2015 were aggregated to compute a new performance variable, which has been used for the analysis.

Data Analysis and Results of Online Questionnaire

The questionnaire was sent to 187 students where only 76 responses were returned, a response rate of 40%. However, 9 surveys were disregarded due to being incomplete, (the respondent did not finish the survey all the way to the end). Consequently, the final population sample for this study is considered as 67 students with usable completed questionnaire or 36% response rate. Visual breakdown is depicted in (figure 1)

Demographics

The 67 respondents to the questionnaire were divided into two groups of age cohorts. 56 belonged the age group of less than or equal to 24 years old and 11 respondents belonged to the age between 25 to 30 years of age, (figure 2). Additionally, 56 of the respondents were males while 11 were females (figure 3).

Moreover, respondents to the questionnaire represented all stages of the programme, spanning across the five-year duration with a mixture of 'pre' and 'post' introduction of the P4P solution. A total of 46 respondents had joined the programme before the introduction of P4P and 21 respondents had joined post introduction (figure 4). Following the coding of performance management data available for 2014 and 2015, in order to align with the Likert scale items used in the questionnaire, (figure 5) indicates the results of the analysis of the new performance rating variable used in the aggregated 2014 and 2015 performance ratings.

Pre and Post Groups Results

The group of students who have been a part of the programme before the P4P solution was introduced, had considerably higher agreement with the statement '*I receive appropriate recognition for my contributions and accomplishments at X-Air*', a significant majority of 95% for the pre-group and 72% for the post-group. Results also showed that 81% from the pre-group believe that they receive regular feedback from their line manager about their performance, while this was relatively lower for the post-group at 61%. Furthermore, 95% of the pre-group respondents believe that P4P is a good approach to drive better performance results, whereas 87% of the post-group students agreed with this. The pre-group respondents also showed considerably higher agreement levels of 86% with P4P being fair for cadet pilots, compared with only 67% with the post-group.

Interestingly, the post-group displayed a slightly higher preference for non-monetary rewards, with 83% confirming that they are encouraged to deliver better results if their work is recognized. The same resulted in only 76% of the pre-group respondents agreeing to this statement. Furthermore, 63% of the post-group respondents also believe that the management should introduce other rewards than money, compared with only 57% for the pre-group. On the other hand, the pre-group showed distinctly more motivation through monetary rewards with 95% versus 72% in the post-group. With regard to whether P4P motivated them to achieve higher grades, 90% of the pre-group positively associated their answers to the statement, while only 76% of the post-group agreed with this. In general, 86% of the pre-group also believed that their hard work and achievements are recognized at EA, compared to only 65% from the post-group.

General observations from the above results indicate that the pre-group respondents are more positively associated with seven out of nine questions representing a number of factors related to recognition, feedback effectiveness, P4P effectiveness and its impact on motivation. Consequently, respondents from the post-group population have demonstrated higher preference for other non-monetary rewards as recognition in two out of nine questions.

Age & Gender Wise Comparison

Students in the 25-30 years age cohort showed 100% agreement with items relating to role clarity asked in questions 1 to 3 "I understand what is expected of me in my role", "My performance objectives were discussed with my manager", "My performance objectives were agreed with my manager". Also, very interestingly one out of every four candidates in the 25-30 years cohort disagreed with the performance management system being fair and effective in measuring employee performance, while only 9% of respondents from the less than 25 years cohort disagreed with this. Furthermore, more than half the males confirmed that they are able to give feedback about P4P system to senior management and HR, only 27% of the females agreed with this.

Alternatively, 91% of the females said they are generally motivated by monetary rewards, whereas only seventy-seven percent 77% of the males agreed with this. Furthermore, 84% of the males believe that they are encouraged to deliver more if their work is recognized versus 64% of the females. Additionally, 91% of the 25-30 years age cohort also believed this, compared to 79% in the less than 25 years age cohort category. Finally, for the less than 25 years age cohort, there was considerably higher preference for other rewards than money, at 66% versus 36% for the 25-30 years age cohort.

For the pre-group, the Pearson Correlation for question eight '*I believe that Pay-for-Performance (salary increase/bonus) is a good approach to drive better performance results*' with performance ratings (combined for 2014 and 2015) was found to be positive and statistically significant at 0.05 level (0.31). Also '*I am usually encouraged to deliver better results if I am satisfied with my own work*' when correlated with performance ratings were found to be statistically significant at 0.05 level (0.33). While for the post-group, statements around role clarity found strong and positive correlation with performance ratings.

These results lead us to assume at this stage, that the introduction of P4P solution has had positive impact on the students' output, which was reflected in their performance appraisal results. These results also relate to one of the three sub-questions in this research, aiming to answer and support the hypothesis in terms of the positive association of P4P to performance improvements. Such association was also discussed previously, as various authors supported it. Specifically, in relation to the alignment of the organisation's interests with employee behaviours through the reward mechanism (Eisenhardt, 1989) and the link between performance results and reward practice (Stajkovic and Luthans, 2001) in directing and motivating desirable behaviours.

The rotated component matrix (Annex table 1) shows the results after the model was converged in seven iterations. This analysis has identified the following latent constructs, which are also highlighted in bold in table 1.

1. Social and Learning Cognition
2. Role Clarity
3. Drive and Self-Efficacy
4. Financial Rewards

On the other hand, there were two items that did not theoretically nor statistically align with any of the factors and therefore, they have been dropped from this model. These are highlighted in bold in the same below table.

Many aspects of students' responses to the online questionnaire were brought to light based on their views, perceptions and beliefs in relation to the impact of P4P on their overall performance results. The results of their data were analysed using SPSS 15.0 for Windows. The four factors emerging from the descriptive statistics were grouped into four latent constructs, which were aligned and mapped to the main sections of the questionnaire and ultimately to the three sub-questions of the research in the attempt to answer the main question posed by this study.

Data Analysis of Interviews

Following the analysis of respondents' answers during the interviews and the coding of themes into categories, the following four categories emerged as factors playing a key role in the influence of performance management application and effectiveness, as well as the performance of the students in the programme.

5. Clarity of expectations
6. Feedback effectiveness
7. Reward and recognition strategies
8. Motivational drivers

Despite the slight variations in the type and number of questions in the two different sets of interview guides, the above framework indicates to a certain degree the alignment between management and students, in terms of outlook regarding the PMS, reward strategy and motivational factors. Commonalities and contrasts of their answers are presented next, in relation to each main category identified above.

Clarity of Expectations

The first common theme that was consistently mentioned amongst all interviewees, apart from Student #4 (S4), was the appreciation from both parties, regarding the role of objectives in enhancing the level of understanding and clarity in terms of expectations. From the managers' perspective, when asked about the students' objectives and how they react to them, Senior Manager #2 (SM2) stated: "*the criteria put has really made it easier for them to benchmark their progress against our expectations*". Furthermore, SM2 added "*these objectives are also important for us as managers to guide our discussion and feedback with cadets*". Moreover, Senior Manager #1 (SM1) mentioned "*we have a routine follow-up and meetings with cadets twice a month through visits to the university. Our performance managers meet regularly with cadets to discuss their progress and try to identify if help is needed.*"

From students' perspective, when asked about how the system has improved clarity of cadets' performance expectations, Student #2 (S2) responded "*I got clearer picture, understood my KPIs about minimum acceptable GPA*". Similarly, Student #1 (S1) viewed that the introduction of clear and specific goals created an opportunity to aim higher and attain better results. S1 added: "*it made it clearer for me and since it was announced, I am trying to achieve the 36 credit hours per year as a minimum*". This is also in line with the views of the goal-setting theory (Locke and Latham, 2002), which was discussed earlier in chapter 2, in relation to the role of specific and difficult goals in motivating individuals to enhance and improve performance.

In terms of students' participation in the goal-setting process, in relation to the earlier topic on employees' self-efficacy (Bandura, 1997); senior managers were asked about their approach to ensuring students are clear about what is expected from them. All three senior managers shared information about a 'letter of consent' provided to all students at the beginning of each academic year in addition to verbal and email communications. According to SM1, all cadets are issued with a consent letter that contains information about objectives, expectations and standards. This was also confirmed by SM2 and added, "*...They read it, and sign it and they keep a copy while another copy is put in their file. They exactly know what is expected from them*". When the researcher probed further in terms of students' involvement, SM1 reiterated that these objectives are decided by the management, while Senior Manager #3 (SM3) responded: "*since they all have similar objectives, our online performance management system does allow us to mass-assign the objectives into the system*".

Based on the above responses, it was obvious that the applied objective-setting process is a top-down approach with no involvement from the students. Lawler *et al.* (2012), stress that effective performance management is very much dependent on the use of goals. Goals that are jointly set have demonstrated stronger relation to the effectiveness of PMS. A view that was also supported by Buchner (2007) in terms of the constraints the top-down approach might entail.

Feedback Effectiveness

Feedback effectiveness refers to the communication process between senior managers and students and the amount of guidance and learning taking place during this process. As previously discussed, feedback usually stimulates motivation and performance (Luis, 1990) in shaping performers' behaviours. When asked about the role of the system in improving the frequency and quality of feedback between the two parties, SM3 confirmed that the system

"*...encouraged two-way feedback between CPS and performance managers*" "*...this was also part of performance managers' objectives to conduct regular one-to-one meetings, if performance issues arise*". Accordingly, SM2 stated: "*the new system allows us more structure in how to direct feedback to CPS*". From the management's perspective, it was clear that the new system added value to the process and helped develop a structured relationship, aimed at finding solutions and remedial interventions to enhance performance. SM1 stated: "*when students became aware of a shortfall after feedback, they raised their concern and worked hard to improve*". This feedback from senior managers, endorses claims by supporters of the previously discussed control theory, that feedback influences individuals to reduce discrepancies that could prevent the attainment of the goal (Klein, 1989).

Surprisingly, three out five students, including Student #3 (S3) did not completely agree with their managers' views mentioned above. Although S4 and Student #5 (S5) agreed with the importance of feedback, they mentioned that "*the feedback mainly focused on what is wrong and what to do and rarely about the good job*". On the other hand, two of the high-performing students expressed their satisfaction with regard to the structure and follow-up received from respective performance managers. S2 stated "*this helped put some standards for us, the performance manager was able to give specific feedback about expectations. Consequently, I was able to understand better what to do*". Furthermore, S1 was particularly satisfied with the regular feedback received at the end of each semester.

Such lack of alignment in the perception and the divergent views indicates that although the process is strongly seen relevant, some issues in terms of implementation and execution were observed. As discussed earlier in this paper, feedback has been identified as a key factor in enhancing the implementation of any performance management system. Luis (1990) considers feedback as a powerful instrument in improving satisfaction at work and enhancing performance. At the same time, he stresses that managers might not realise at times, how their subordinates' behaviours are constantly shaped by their performance feedback style. DeVries *et al.* (1981) advise managers to develop their performance appraisal skills through training and specifically focus on how to provide constructive feedback.

Reward and Recognition Strategies

During the interviews, several questions were designed to elicit respondents' views on the role of rewards and its impact on driving better performance. Strong correlation was observed from all interviewees. From the managers' perspective, there was a belief that the introduction of P4P was a good decision to reward and recognise those doing well. SM3 stated "because we are targeting a young population in their early twenties, extra cash is an attractive tool for them". SM3 further explained and elaborated that most students during the interview stage, attempt to negotiate their salaries, which indicates the association they have with financial rewards. SM2 quoted Madonna's famous song "living in a material world" to illustrate the point and agreement with the approach.

From the students' perspective, satisfactory responses were also received and the introduction of P4P was positively welcomed. S3 shared a personal example of dissatisfaction, prior to the introduction of P4P, when all students used to receive salary increases and bonuses, irrespective of GPA results. S4 called it a fair process and said: "*if you come to work and finish your work, you get paid, otherwise you don't*".

When senior managers were asked about the impact the reward system has had on cadets' performance, all three responses showed high level of satisfaction and were able to share specific examples indicating changes in students' behaviours. SM2 used the example of the first batch in the programme to illustrate the point and added, "*When the reward system was introduced, 6 out 40 cadets were not performing up to standards. After it was applied, it took them two semesters to score GPA 2.0 and above*". Moreover, as per SM3, more students are now contacting their respective performance managers, well in time before the end of the year, asking for support and guidance in order to ensure performance is met before it is too late. This feedback from senior managers does imply that individuals are showing signs of behavioural change regarding their performance. Additionally, the P4P system has prompted them to exert some extra efforts towards meeting the objectives set for them and ultimately getting the reward.

These assumptions have been ascertained, earlier in this paper, under the social cognitive theory (Bandura, 1989). Provided that performers have positive self-beliefs and high self-efficacy, challenges can be overcome by moderating behaviours to improve performance. Furthermore, students expressed some gratitude towards what the company is trying to do through differentiation in performance to recognise high achievers. S3 mentioned: "*... because we are sponsored by the company, this gave us better push to raise self-esteem compared to self-sponsored students*". The impact of reward on performance was also observed amongst low performing students. S5 admitted that learning about the opportunity of getting bonus as a result of good grades, prompted additional efforts in meeting the objectives.

Motivational Drivers

In order to understand what motivates the cadets' population, senior managers were asked "How do you usually motivate cadets to perform better?" interestingly; the three of them consistently mentioned other factors than financial rewards. Their answers were aligned in terms of providing good performers the opportunity to participate in external events, exhibitions, air shows and in-company programmes. SM2 and SM3 responses were also aligned with regard to the continuous and open channels of communications between both parties, ensuring permanent availability of support. Accordingly, when students were asked "what motivates you the most to perform better?" the majority referred to non-financial rewards. S4 considered "*...encouragement from my line manager*", while S2 mentioned: "*... being able to obtain my flying license*".

Accordingly, students were asked to list in terms of priority, their top three and most important motivators. Four out of five respondents did not refer to monetary rewards amongst their top motivators, except S4 who stated '*money*' as a second choice. However, when asked about their views if money is seen as a motivator, all five agreed with this as an important factor for motivation, but none has seen it as a priority. Consequently, when senior managers where asked the same question, financial rewards featured in their answers but none considered it as a primary factor.

One can conclude form the above answers, that despite the various literatures around the subject, respondents in this particular intervention of the research, agreed, to some extent, that money plays a role in the fairness and recognition process of cadets, but it is simply not a key factor nor a priority in motivating and influencing their drive towards achieving better results.

Discussion and Conclusion

Based on the earlier reviews of the three different types of motivational theories, it is assumed that the type of goal-setting (Locke *et al.* 1981) in terms of difficulty and specificity and the extent of buy-in from the individual in relation to one's capability coupled with performance feedback do in fact influence the level of commitment and motivation in attaining the desired goal. Additionally, the mechanism of feedback as part of the Control theory (Carver and Scheier, 1998) is identified as a key factor in helping individuals regulate own behaviours in the pursuit of attaining the expected results. Finally, as part of the Social Cognitive theory (Bandura, 1989), self-efficacy and positive self-beliefs about one's capability as a result of observation and feedback have also been identified as important factors in influencing and motivating individuals' positive behaviours.

Additionally, the above mentioned conditions need to be fulfilled or considered, before any human resources or management policy is introduced in order to increase the effects of pay or rewards on employees' motivation. Consequently, Deci *et al.* (1999), in their reference to the existence and continuous interface of 'Intrinsic and Extrinsic' as the two types of motivation, claim that intrinsic motivation to perform a task can be reduced by the introduction of monetary rewards. Therefore, this is explained in relation to the perception obtained by the individual that reward is only associated with the control of the work and thus affecting the feelings of capability and autonomy, or in other words their intrinsic motivation. Such an approach would eventually lead for intrinsic motivation to be replaced by extrinsic motivation. Subsequently, it can be concluded at this stage that most theorists agree that motivation is required for employees to improve their desire to perform better; however, considerations in terms of the different monetary incentive tools adopted must be carefully planned in order to avoid any counter productivity.

In relation to the CPS and senior managers' input and views about the role of objectives in enhancing the effectiveness of PMS, it was found that both have strongly expressed the benefits of role clarity and clear expectations in the system. The three first questions in the online survey had significantly high satisfaction response rate from all demographics but particularly unanimous agreement (100%) from the pre-group (n=46) and the '25 – 30' age group (n=11). All other responses were also significantly higher than 90%. This also leads us to believe that the culture of performance management is evolving amongst the students and they are becoming more familiar and integrated into the system over time, given that higher scores are mainly driven by the pre-group and this particular age group.

Subsequently, senior managers have also indicated high-level of satisfaction of the system and particularly the structure it brought to the interaction between them and the students, in relation to the clarity of expectations provided through the consent letter and the frequency of the face-to-face meetings. 'Clarity of expectations' factor emerged strongly from the qualitative interviews as a theme being associated with almost all respondents. Equally, 'Role Clarity' has been identified as strong factor in the quantitative analysis of the survey with strong correlations amongst all the respective items included in the survey. These views are also strengthened by the literature and the use of secondary data in this paper. According to Locke and Latham (2002), specific goal-setting mechanism is usually included in PMS to strengthen the influence on employees' behaviours. Despite the findings seen earlier with regard to the top-down approach of goal-setting currently used with this particular group of students and the arguments around its negative impact, the findings from this study seem to support the importance of objectives' clarity and its positive association with the effectiveness of performance management.

In terms of students' views in relation to 'feedback effectiveness', data from the responses indicate relatively low satisfaction in its application, except from the pre-group students. Again, this might suggest that due to the tenure and maturity of this group in the programme, they could have become more familiar with the system and more independent, though requiring less support and guidance. Despite the positive outlook projected during the interviews with senior managers and their beliefs in the structure of feedback being provided to students as a result of the new system, some of CPS interviewees expressed some concerns about the content and approach to feedback by their line managers. S3 and S5 highlighted the fact that feedback is mainly received "*...when something is wrong*".

P4P as a reward strategy plays a key role in many organisations' strategic vision (Appelbaum and Shapiro, 1991) and it is critical to the success of the performance management process (Milkovic *et al.*, 1991). Equally, both senior managers and CPS responses to the question on whether the P4P has had any impact on cadets' performance, was positively associated with this assumption. Senior managers in terms of students' GPA improvements highlighted specific examples of behavioural changes. Similar question in the online survey also provided evidence of high satisfaction from respondents across different demographics. Specifically, more than ninety-percent (90%) of males, the pre-group and the age group of 25 to 30 have demonstrated a level of trust in the P4P solution and agreed to this.

Furthermore, in terms of the Pearson Correlation for the same question above with the combined performance ratings for 2014 and 2015, was found to be positive and statistically significant at 0.05 level (0.31). Such results certainly support the views expressed by Porter and Lawler (1968) that employees tend to be motivated to change behaviours and enhance performance, if trust is established about receiving rewards as a result. One can conclude, on the basis of the results' findings from the above, that P4P is seen to be positively associated with improved performance.

Interesting findings have been identified from both quantitative and qualitative data in relation to motivation. Based on the online survey results, the pre-group respondents showed distinctively more motivation through monetary rewards. Results from all other groups and demographics have also shown moderately high percentage. These results lead us to believe that that the P4P solution is widely accepted amongst the students.

Alternatively, contrary to the above responses, all three senior managers during the face-to-face interviews, when asked about "*how do you usually motivate employees*?" they interestingly shared various motivation strategies not related to money. Accordingly, when all CPS were asked to list their top three motivators in terms of priority, 'money' did not feature on the list. More importantly, similarity in the responses was observed between managers and students. The common top motivators were more related to additional responsibilities, participation in external event and promotions, self-satisfaction and making family proud. According to Jones and Punshi (2013), research indicate that nationals within the Gulf region, are highly motivated by various artefacts such as office size, job title and status rather that purely financial rewards, however recognition and career progression have been identified as more important drivers for motivation.

Further to the above, Lawler, (2000) claims that if P4P is effectively implemented, employees can be very well motivated to perform better. Alternatively, in his research on the effects of reward on intrinsic motivation, Deci (1972) shares strong evidence to demonstrate that money should not be focused on as the primary motivator. He further explains that intrinsic motivation decreases if money is directly linked to the performance of the task. Given the contradictory perceptions, views and beliefs about the association of money with the cadets' motivation in these findings, it can be concluded that money, in the case of the students surveyed in this study, does not have strong and positive association with motivation.

Overall, numerous patterns have emerged from this research in relation to the effectiveness of reward system when linked to performance management within the context of CPS. Firstly, in relation to 'clarity of expectations', it is evident that almost the majority of CPS are satisfied with the clarity of objectives with regards to their roles and the expectations of output in their performance. Secondly, in relation to 'feedback expectations' despite the beliefs from the majority of respondents in this study, that the newly introduced system has enabled more frequent and regular feedback discussions and interventions between managers and students, many areas for improvement have been identified, specifically in relation to its quality and application. Thirdly, in relation to 'rewards strategies', the evidence in the study indicates that there is a positive correlation between the reward solutions and the improvement of CPS' performance. And finally, in relation to 'motivational drivers', contradictory findings have been identified in this research and led us to conclude that despite the modest views and opinions regarding the positive relationship between the P4P solution and cadets' motivation, other non-monetary incentives have been identified as strongly desired in driving motivation.

Limitations and Recommendations

This research has only focused on a small sample size of students and results cannot be generalized to represent a wider population. Additionally, given the young experience of cadet pilot students in the performance management system due to it being newly introduced, responses and results of the data need to be further strengthened. Therefore, further research on the topic is highly recommended to include a bigger sample size and more representation.

Rewarding employees' performance has become a widely utilised strategy and has also seen tremendous change in terms of approach, methods and application. Considering the age group of participants in this research, more focus could have been placed on linking this research to the wider studies about young talent within the Gulf region and particularly millennials, in order to better understand their engagement and motivation level. According to Crowly (2016), millennials value accountability and their accomplishments must have a sense of significance, they are more inclined to take ownership for their successes and want to hold themselves accountable as they aim for higher goals. Moreover, national talent in the Gulf region have reportedly shown lower levels of engagement and motivation, when compared with expatriates (Jones and Punshi, 2013) and consequently, the Gulf region continues to use monetary incentives as rewards to attract and retain national talent.

Millennials need to feel emotionally connected to their place of work. Retention is founded on their employer respecting them for who they are, developing and coaching them, providing a flexible working environment and having a clear shared purpose. Therefore, it would be important to link future researches to the kind of environment created by employers in the region and specifically identifying performance management practices and strategies in place in order to cater to these needs and drive engagement and retention.

Additionally, Contributing to the greater good is critical to Millennials, as they expect to make the world a better place by working for an organization with a strong vision and a clear purpose. Understanding, how other organisations in general and X-Air in particular define and communicate their purpose and vision when attracting and recruiting Millennials, would contribute to validating and identifying best practices in adapting talent management strategies to respond to the new generations' changing needs.

The workforce is changing rapidly. Baby Boomers are staying in the job market longer than anticipated, Gen Z is struggling to move up the corporate ladder, Millennials are now making up more than 50% of the workforce and Generation Z is on its way. Therefore, further research to understand future and relevant performance management practices and motivation strategies to respond to people's changing needs is key in order to retain top talent and ensure success in the workplace.

References

Appelbaum, S.H. and Shapiro, B.T. (1991) Pay for Performance: Implementation of Individual and Group Plans, *Journal of Management Development*, Vol. 10, Iss: 7, pp. 30-40

Ashby, W.R. (1966) *An introduction to cybernetics*. New York: Wiley

Bandura, A. (1989) Human Agency in Social Theory, *American Psychologist*, Vol. 44, Iss: 9, pp. 1175-1184

Bandura, A. (1997) *Self-efficacy: The exercise of control*. New York, NY: W.H. Freeman

Bryman A. and Bell E. (2007) *Business Research Methods*, 2nd ed, Oxford: Oxford University Press

Buchner, W.T. (2007) Performance Management Theory: A Look from the Performer's Perspective with Implications for HRD, *Human Resources Development International*, Vol. 10, Iss: 1, pp. 59-73

Campion, M.A., and Lord, R.G. (1982) A Control Systems Conceptualisation of Goal-Setting and Changing Process: *Organizational Behaviour and Human Performance*, Vol. 30, Iss: 2, pp. 265-287

Carver, C.S. and Scheier, M.F. (1998) *On the self-regulation of behaviour* (Cambridge: Cambridge University Press)

Crowly, M. (2016) *Millennials Don't Want Fun; They Want You To Lead Better*, available online at: https:// http://tinyurl.com/zryjchl (accessed on 04.06.2016)

Deci, E.L. (1972) The Effects of Contingent and Non-contingent Rewards and Controls on Intrinsic Motivation, *Organisational Behaviour and Human Performance*, Vol. 8, Iss: 2, pp. 217-229

Deci, E.L., and Ryan, R.M. (1985) *Intrinsic Motivation and Self-determination in Human Behaviour*. New York, NY: Plenum Press

Deci, E.L., Koestner, R. and Ryan, R.M. (1999) A Meta-analytic Review of Experiments Examining the Effects of Extrinsic Rewards on Intrinsic Motivation, *Psychological Bulletin*, Vol. 125, Iss: 6, pp. 627-668

Deeprose, D. (1994) *How to recognize and reward employees*. Newyour: AMACOM

Denscombe, M. (2010) Ground Rules for Social Research: *Guidelines for Good Practice* (2nd ed.), Berkshire: Open University Press

DeVries, M.L., Morrison, A.M., Shullman, S.L. and Gerlach, M.L. (1981) *Appraising Managerial Performance: Current Practices and Future Directions*, The Conference Board, New York

Donovan, J.J. (2001) Work Motivation, in: N. Andereson, D. Ones, H. Sinangil and C. Viswesvaran (Eds) *Handbook of Industrial, Work and Organisational Psychology*. Vol. 2, pp. 53-76 (London: Sage)

Eisenhardt, K.M. (1988) Agency- and Institutional-Theory explanations: the Case of Retail Sales Compensation. *Academy of Management Journal*, Vol. 31, Iss. 3, pp. 488-511

Eisenhardt, K.M. (1989) Agency Theory: an assessment and review. *Academy of Management Review*, Vol. 14, Iss.1, pp. 57-74

Fama, E.F. (1980) Agency problems and the theory of the firm. *The Journal of Political Theory*, Vol. 88, Iss. 2, pp. 288-307

Gagné, M., & Deci, E. L. (2005). Self-determination theory and work motivation. Journal of Organizational Behavior, 26(4), 331-362.

Greener, S. (2008) *Business Research Methods*, Bookboon

Jones, B.D. and Punshi, R. (2013), *Unlocking the Paradox of Plenty: A Review of The Talent Landscape in the GCC and Your Role in Shaping Its Future*, Dubai: Motivate Publishing

Kaiser, H.F. (1974) *An Index of Factorial Simplicity*, Psychometrika, vol. 39, Iss: 1, pp. 31-36

Klein, H.J. (1989) An Integrated Control Theory Model of Work Motivation, *The Academy of Management Review*, Vol. 14, Iss: 2, pp. 150-172

Lawler, E.E. (2000) *Rewarding excellence: Pay strategies for the new economy.* San Francisco: Jossey-Bass

Lawler, E.E., Benson, G.S. and McDermott, M. (2012) What makes Performance Appraisals Effective? *Compensation & Benefits Review* Vol. 44, Iss: 4, pp. 191-200

Locke, E.A., Shaw, K.N, Saari, L.M. and Latham, G.P. (1981) Goal Setting and Task Performance: 1969 – 1980, *Psychological Bulletin*, Vol. 90, Iss: 1, pp. 125-152

Locke, E.A. (1991) Goal Theory vs. Control Theory: Contrasting Approached to Understanding Work Motivation, *Motivation and Emotion*, Vol. 15, Iss: 1, pp. 9-28

Locke, E.A. (1994) The Emperor is Naked. *Applied Psychology: An International Review*, Vol. 43, Iss: 3, pp. 367-370

Locke, E.A., and Latham, G.P., (2002) Building a practically useful of goal setting and task performance: A 35-year Odyssey, *American Psychological Association*, Vol. 57, Iss: 9, pp. 705-717

Luis R. Gomez-Mejia (1990) "Increasing Productivity: Performance Appraisal and Reward Systems", *Personnel Review*, Vol. 19, Iss: 2, pp. 21-26

Luthans, K. (2000) Recognition: A Powerful, but often Overlooked, Leadership Tool to Improve Employee Performance, *The Journal of Leadership Studies*, Vol. 7, Iss: 1, pp. 32 - 39

Martin J, and Fellenz M. 2010. Organizational Behavior and Management. Cengage Learning EMEA: Hampshire.

McClelland, S.B. (1994) Training Needs Assessment Data-gathering Methods: Part 1, Survey Questionnaires, *Journal of European Industrial Training*, Vol. 18, Iss: 1, pp. 22-26

Meyer, H.H. (1975) The Pay-for-Performance Dilemma, *Organizational Dynamics*. Vol. 3, Iss: 3, pp. 39-50

Milkovich, G.T., Widgor, A.K. and Broderick, R.F. (1991) *Pay for Performance: Evaluating Performance Appraisal and Merit Pay*. National Academies Press

Neckermann, S. and Kosfel, M. (2008) *Working for Nothing? The Effect of Non-Material Awards on Employee Perfromance*, Goethe-University Frankfurt, Germany

Perry, J.L., Mesch, D., & Paarlberg, L. (2006) 'Motivating Employees in a New Governance Era: The Performance Paradigm Revisited', *Public Administration Review*, Vol. 66, pp. 11-32

Porter, L.W., Lawler, E.E. (1968) Managerial Attitudes and Performance. *Richard D. Irwin Inc.*, Homewood

Ryan, R. M., & Deci, E. L. (2000). Self-determination theory and the facilitation of intrinsic motivation, social development, and well-being. American Psychologist, 55(1), 68-78.

Scott, K.L., Shaw, J.D., Duffy, M.K., (2008) Merit pay rises and organisation-based self-esteem. *Journal of Organisational Behaviour*, Vol. 29, Iss. 7, pp. 967-980

Srivastava, A., Locke, E.A. and Bartol, K.M. (2001) ' money and Subjective Well-Being it's Not the Money, it's the Motives', *Journal of personality and Social Psychology*, Vol. 80, pp. 959-917

Stajkkovic, A.D. and Luthans, F. ((2001) Differential Effects of incentive motivators on work performance, *Academy of Management Journal*, Vol. 44, Iss. 3, pp. 580-590

Strauss, A. and Corbin, J.M. (1990) *Basics of Qualitative Research: Grounded Theory Procedures and Techniques*, Newbury Park, Calif.: Sage

Appendix

Figure 1: Composition of Population Sample

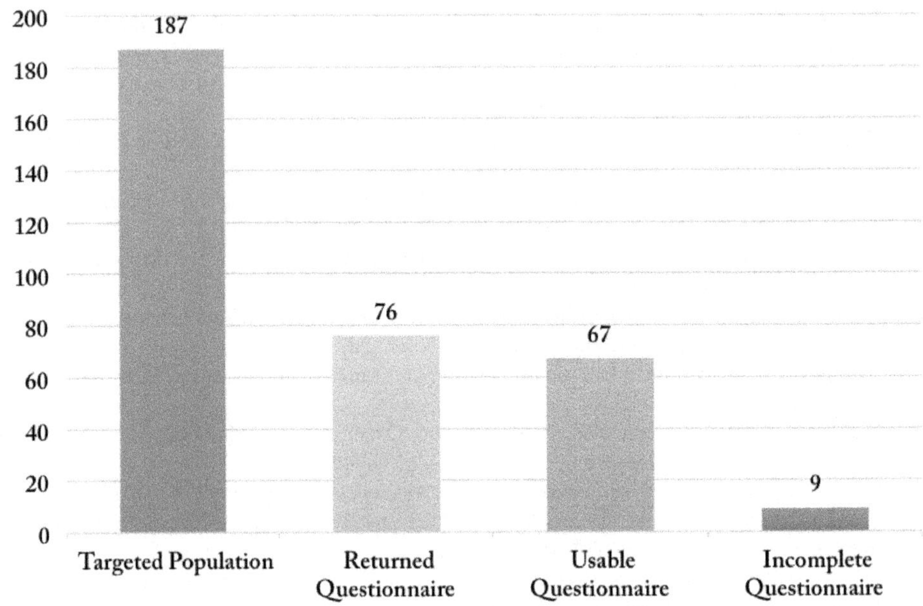

Figure 2: Age Group of Respondents

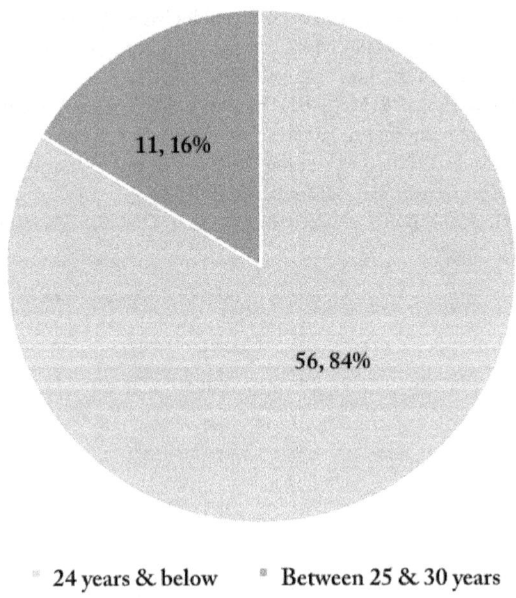

Figure 3: Gender Demographics

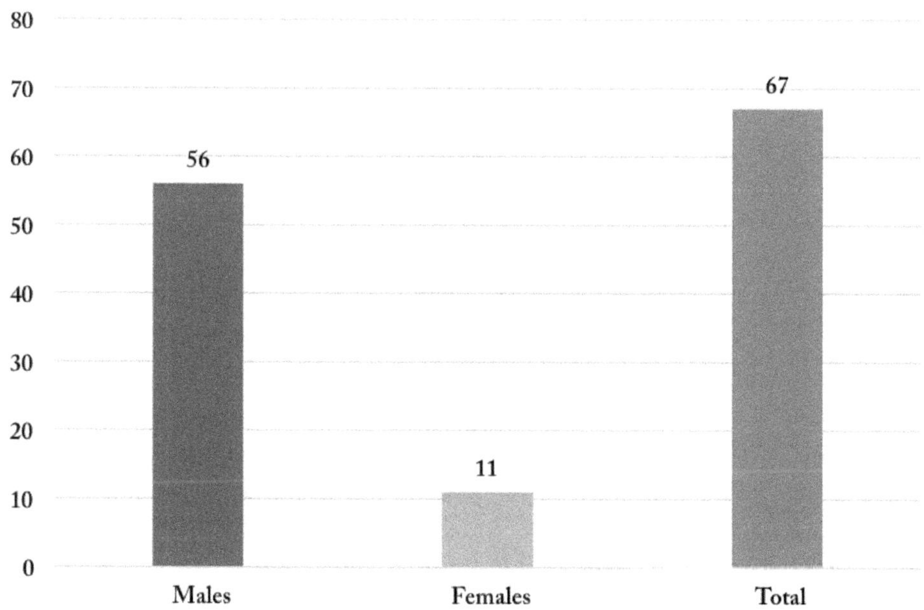

Figure 4: Stages of the Programme

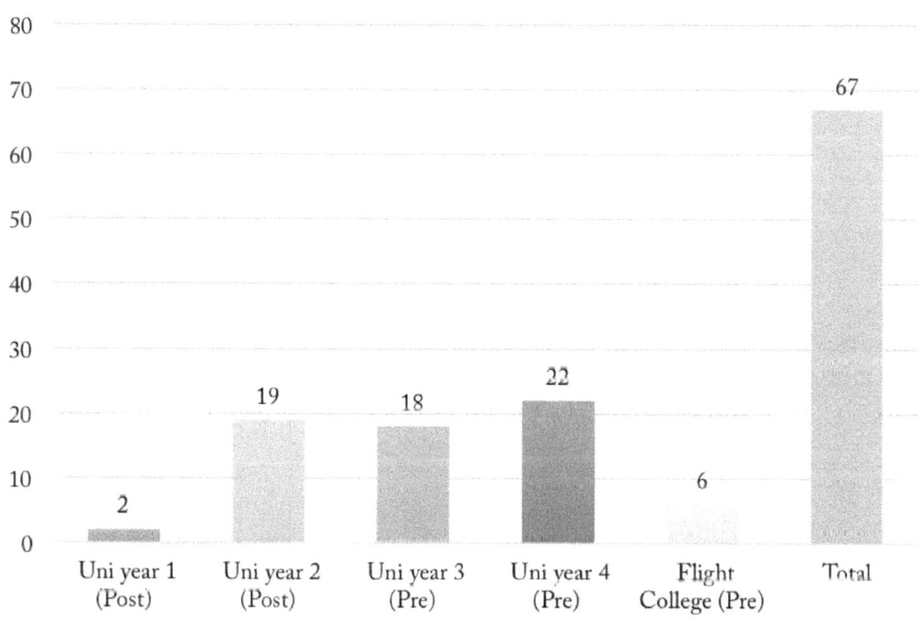

Figure 5: Aggregated Distribution of Performance Rating (2014-2015)

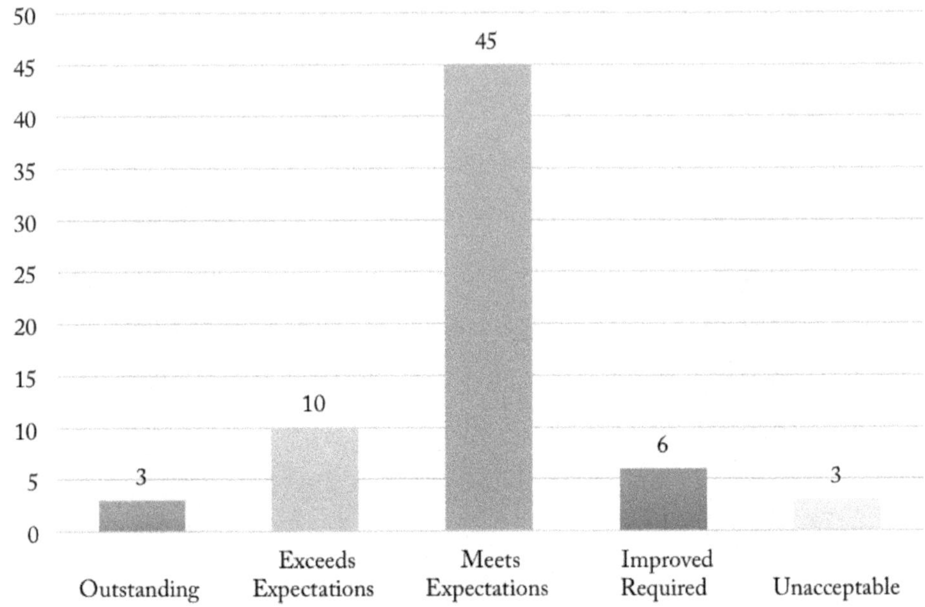

Table 1: Rotated Component Matrix from PCA

Rotated Component Matrix	1	2	3	4	5
Social Cognition					
I believe that performance management system for cadet pilots at Etihad is fair and effective in measuring employee performance	**0.74**	0.21	-0.09	-0.02	0.01
I receive appropriate recognition for my contributions and accomplishments at Etihad	**0.77**	0.17	0.13	0.08	0.03
I receive regular feedback from my line manager about my performance	**0.54**	0.48	0.25	-0.07	-0.26
I believe the Pay-for-Performance system (salary increase/bonus) for cadet pilots at Etihad is fair	0.66	0.02	0.03	0.37	0.21
I was fully briefed by my manager about the Pay-for-Performance (salary increase/bonus) strategy related to my role	**0.76**	0.24	0.05	0.10	-0.13
I believe Pay-for-Performance has improved the feedback mechanism between cadets and line manager	**0.79**	-0.05	0.11	0.37	-0.08
I am able to give feedback about the Pay-for-Performance system to my senior management and HR	**0.80**	0.15	0.12	0.25	-0.05
My hard work and achievements are recognized at Etihad Airways	**0.78**	0.14	0.09	0.19	0.11

Role Clarity					
I understand what is expected of me in my role	0.15	**0.75**	0.14	0.31	0.22
My performance objectives were discussed with my manager	0.28	**0.84**	0.05	0.01	-0.02
My performance objectives were agreed with my manager	0.16	**0.81**	0.22	0.14	-0.01
Drive, commitment & Self-Efficacy					
I am usually encouraged to deliver better results if my work is recognized	0.16	0.00	**0.83**	0.21	0.17
I am usually encouraged to deliver better results if I am satisfied with my own work	-0.16	0.27	**0.70**	-0.19	0.15
I perform better if my performance goals are clear	0.09	0.10	**0.76**	0.04	-0.19
My role gives me a personal sense of achievement to do better	0.19	0.49	**0.58**	0.21	0.06
I am willing to go over and above my normal job expectations to achieve better results	0.25	0.12	**0.50**	0.38	0.37
Financial Rewards					
I believe that Pay-for-Performance (salary increase/bonus) is a good approach to drive better performance results	0.07	0.29	0.24	**0.70**	0.21
I am generally motivated by monetary rewards	0.31	0.10	0.04	**0.76**	-0.05
The Pay-for-Performance motivated me to achieve higher grades	0.28	0.06	-0.02	**0.81**	-0.15
No Statistical nor Theoretical Alignment					
I believe that feedback process between line manager and cadets should be improved	-0.17	-0.11	-0.01	0.08	0.77
I believe the management should introduce other rewards than money	0.18	0.30	0.18	-0.19	0.68

Table 2: Detailed Descriptive Results

		Stage		Gender		Age	
		Post	Pre	Females	Males	Less than 24 years	25 to 30 years
Items	N	21	46	11	56	56	11
1. I understand what is expected of me in my role	High	93%	100%	91%	96%	95%	100%
	Medium	7%	0%	9%	4%	5%	0%
2. My performance objectives were discussed with my manager	High	89%	95%	91%	91%	89%	100%
	Medium	7%	5%	9%	5%	7%	0%
	Low	4%	0%	0%	4%	4%	0%
3. My performance objectives were agreed with my manager	High	87%	100%	91%	91%	89%	100%
	Medium	13%	0%	9%	9%	11%	0%

4. I believe that performance management system for cadet pilots at Etihad is fair and effective in measuring employee performance	High	70%	76%	73%	71%	73%	64%
	Medium	20%	14%	9%	20%	20%	9%
	Low	11%	10%	18%	9%	7%	27%
5. I receive appropriate recognition for my contributions and accomplishments at Etihad	High	72%	95%	82%	79%	80%	73%
	Medium	13%	0%	18%	7%	11%	0%
	Low	15%	5%	0%	14%	9%	27%
6. I receive regular feedback from my line manager about my performance	High	61%	81%	64%	68%	68%	64%
	Medium	24%	10%	27%	18%	20%	18%
	Low	15%	10%	9%	14%	13%	18%
7. I believe that feedback process between line manager and cadets should be improved	High	57%	48%	64%	52%	55%	45%
	Medium	24%	43%	27%	30%	32%	18%
	Low	20%	10%	9%	18%	13%	36%
8. I believe that Pay-for-Performance is a good approach to drive better performance results	High	87%	95%	82%	91%	89%	91%
	Medium	13%	5%	18%	9%	11%	9%
9. I believe the Pay-for-Performance system (salary increase/bonus) for cadet pilots at Etihad is fair	High	67%	86%	64%	75%	75%	64%
	Medium	17%	14%	36%	13%	14%	27%
	Low	15%	0%	0%	13%	11%	9%
10. I was fully briefed by my manager about the Pay-for-Performance strategy related to my role	High	76%	95%	73%	84%	84%	73%
	Medium	15%	0%	18%	9%	11%	9%
	Low	9%	5%	9%	7%	5%	18%
11. I believe Pay-for-Performance has improved the feedback mechanism between cadets and line manager	High	70%	81%	64%	75%	73%	73%
	Medium	24%	19%	36%	20%	23%	18%
	Low	7%	0%	0%	5%	4%	9%

1. I am able to give feedback about the Pay-for-Performance system to my senior management and HR	High	48%	62%	27%	57%	54%	45%
	Medium	37%	29%	64%	29%	36%	27%
	Low	15%	10%	9%	14%	11%	27%
2. I am generally motivated by monetary rewards	High	72%	95%	91%	77%	79%	82%
	Medium	22%	0%	0%	18%	14%	18%
	Low	7%	5%	9%	5%	7%	0%
3. The Pay-for-Performance motivated me to achieve higher grades	High	76%	90%	73%	82%	80%	82%
	Medium	20%	5%	9%	16%	16%	9%
	Low	4%	5%	18%	2%	4%	9%
4. I believe the management should introduce other rewards than money	High	63%	57%	64%	61%	66%	36%
	Medium	26%	33%	27%	29%	25%	45%
	Low	11%	10%	9%	11%	9%	18%
5. I am usually encouraged to deliver better results if my work is recognized	High	83%	76%	64%	84%	79%	91%
	Medium	17%	19%	36%	14%	20%	9%
	Low	0%	5%	0%	2%	2%	0%
6. I am usually encouraged to deliver better results if I am satisfied with my own work	High	83%	86%	82%	84%	84%	82%
	Medium	17%	14%	18%	16%	16%	18%
7. I perform better if my performance goals are clear	High	93%	100%	100%	95%	95%	100%
	Medium	4%	0%	0%	4%	4%	0%
	Low	2%	0%	0%	2%	2%	0%
8. My role gives me a personal sense of achievement to do better	High	89%	100%	82%	95%	95%	82%
	Medium	11%	0%	18%	5%	5%	18%
9. I am willing to go over and above my normal job expectations to achieve better results	High	91%	100%	91%	95%	95%	91%
	Medium	7%	0%	9%	4%	5%	0%
	Low	2%	0%	0%	2%	0%	9%
10. My hard work and achievements are recognized at Etihad Airways	High	65%	86%	73%	71%	73%	64%
	Medium	15%	14%	9%	16%	16%	9%
	Low	20%	0%	18%	13%	11%	27%

9

A Predictive Model of Outbound Sales Performance at a Large UAE Based Bank

Jonas Harring Boll

Abstract

Organisations have become increasingly aware that a key driver of sustainability is the ability to attract, retain and manage talent effectively. Objectively assessing and effectively managing high performing employees has been the focus of much research and debate, yet many organisations still struggle when it comes to implementing an effective talent management system. This is particularly evident within developing nations and economies such as the UAE where these approaches are still in their infancy. Ironically the UAE, and the Gulf region in general, has a vast pool of young talent just waiting to be developed and engaged for current and future job demands. At Tanfeeth we have tried to approach this challenge from a scientific and evidence-based perspective, with the UAE's specific demographic and cultural features in mind. So far we have had success with creating a highly predictive organisational talent model mainly focusing on leadership and management and we have now turned our attention to sales and customer service. The main aims of the research presented in this paper was (1) to understand the potentials, talents, competencies and skills which separates high performing sales employees from the rest. (2) To use this understanding to create a predictive model of sales performance which can help assessing to the extent to which someone will perform at an outstanding level within our sales teams. (3) To use the model to aid the identification of training, development and engagement activities that will develop and sustain high performance and (4) create a set of effective IT supported tools to manage sales employees across the talent life cycle. Initially 120 sales employees were selected to take part in this research but after a number of resignations and 'reshuffling 'of the sales team we ended up with a group of 79 participants. We divided this group into three sub groups based on whether they were top, medium or low performers. Each employee completed a number of assessments including potential, strength, mental ability and competency questionnaires in order to (1) identify core performance differentiators between the groups and (2) explore the predictive qualities of these differentiators. (3) Create a competency and skills framework for the department to further improve overall talent management processes and (4) develop a situational judgement test to be used for hiring and development purposes. Our results showed that a number of factors were predictive of sales performance and these factors were integrated into a set of tools and talent management methods to be used with our sales teams.

Introduction

Organisations have increasingly realised that in order to compete in a modern, global economy they need to be able to manage their talent effectively. Because of this focus on talent management there is an increasing recognition that employees need to be positioned and empowered to use their core strengths and talents. The old command and control style of management is becoming increasingly obsolete and is being replaced by a more sophisticated approach to managing people, an approach that is based on the assumption that talent is important in all roles and that all employees have the potential to develop certain talents which can be optimised and utilised in the work place.

Yet, despite of the fact that most organisations understands the power of having the right people in the right jobs many are still struggling to apply talent management successfully. This is evident globally as well as in developing economies such as the UAE. Besides a large expat population, the UAE, like the rest of the gulf countries, have a very large population of young nationals with talent just waiting to get tapped into and it must be tapped into if Emiratisation targets are to be met and the economy is to remain stable and sustainable (Jones & Punshi 2013). The problem is that though Talent Management has been around for quite a while, most organisations in the UAE (like their global counterparts), don't seem to be very good at it. Or as Conaty & Charan stated: "If businesses managed their money as carelessly as they manage their people, most would be bankrupt"[1]. As such we face a 'double challenge' in the sense that we both have to manage talent effectively in terms of the general multicultural workforce and more specifically in terms of the national population. We have to do so in an environment where managing talent is still in its infancy but if we meet the challenges and successfully make talent management a mature practice, the future looks bright indeed.

The reason for why talent management has not been more successful both globally and locally is down to a number of factors including general unawareness of how you get the right people in the right roles, lack of senior management support, and ineffective assessment tools or people management processes. But most importantly it is down to a misconception of what human talent is and how it is measured, managed and developed. If one does a literature scan and note the number of books, journals and articles that have been written on talent, often using very different concepts and definitions, you can't really blame organisations for finding it difficult to create a shared and practical understanding of talent and talent management.

So what is talent? According to The Oxford English Dictionary it was used to refer to "an ancient weight, a money of account" in early days which is probably the root of our association of talent with something valuable. A later definition from the same source describes it as "a special natural ability, usually for something expressed or implied; a natural capacity for success in some department of mental or physical ability". Other common definitions include "A capacity for excellent, outstanding, competitively advantageous performance" and "the ability and personality attributes leading to outstanding performance"[2]. According to Clifton & Nelson (1992) it can be defined as "a capacity for almost perfect performance". In this paper we will refer to talent as "the individual attributes that leads someone to consistently perform above a specific performance standard". The reason for creating this definition is that it explains three important things about talent: (1) talent is characterised by consistency. That is, if you can only occasionally perform at an outstanding level you are not displaying a talent, (2) it involves performance and (3) it sets a standard for measurement, as only performance above a certain standard can be considered a sign of talent. Whether we talk about talent in arts, organisations, schools or sports, we only refer to something as talent when it consists of performance which is above the standards which we consider normal or average. Do note that we do not use the 'strength 'concept in the same way that has been popularised by writers such as Clifton, Buckingham and Rath[3], which essentially is similar to how much of the literature defines talent. Rather we use it as a term for potentials which have been cultivated through experience or practice to the extent where they can be productively applied in a job. A strength does not lead to outstanding performance but rather allows someone to meet required performance standards. In other words, talents are strengths which has been cultivated to a point where they lead to outstanding performance.

Having defined what talent means we need to understand where it is coming from and how it is developed. We have already briefly touched upon potential which we consider as an inborn predisposition for doing well in a certain field or area of performance. But how are these potentials transformed into talent? To answer this question, we need to challenge some of the previous definitions and more traditional views of talent which states that talent is something inborn, something some people just have and others don't. Like intelligence research much of the early research on talent was based on the assumption that it was innate and unchangeable, either you were born with talent or you were not. However, a more recent line of research seems to indicate that talent is as much a result of psychological and environmental factors as it is a result of genetics. For example, one line of research has highlighted how consistent practice[4] at the edge of one's current capacity (deliberate practice) plays a key role in talent development. Another line of research has explored how our mindset and attitudes[5] (such as grit) affect talent development and yet another source of research has looked into how environmental factors such as being presented with certain opportunities affects subsequent levels of talent[6]. What all these lines of research have in common is that they confirm that talent is something that can be developed and cultivated. However, there are limits to the extent to which we can develop talents. Some of the limits are biological in nature such as physical make-up or our inborn potentials others have to do with age. Is we grow older our neurology becomes increasingly 'crystallised' and our brain starts to do away with weak neural connections and instead focus on preserving those which are related to the behaviours, skills, thoughts and emotions we most often engage in or experience[7]. To be more specific, our brain starts preserving our strengths for further optimisation while leaving our weaker areas to wither, explaining why it becomes increasingly difficult to develop our areas of weakness while being able to capitalise increasingly on our strengths.

Our response to the misconceptions and disagreements discussed above was to develop a sophisticated talent model which was not only empirically justifiable but also capable of explaining and predicting key talent and business outcomes. In addition, we wanted a common language for explaining and understanding talent as well as a set of unified evidence-based organisational practices that could break down any 'silos' existing between departments in terms of how they selected or managed talent. The first step was to tailor the basic definition of talent mentioned earlier to the requirements of Tanfeeth. We chose "the ability to consistently engage in outstanding performance which is beneficial to the objectives and values of Tanfeeth" and then develop a model around that definition.

Our model consists of three core elements: potential, strengths and talent and a number of facilitators including learning agility, motivation/aspirations, fit and resilience/risk. All the factors have been mapped unto our psychometric tools so, for example, in the case of 'fit' we have calibrated our behavioural assessment to the behaviours we see as expression of our values, making it possible already during the hiring phase to say something about how likely someone will act in accordance with them or not. We are fully aware that other facilitators such as relationships with managers and co-workers are important as well, however these relationships are either explored through 360 degree evaluations (for mid-managers and above) or through our engagement surveys (for all positions and grades) and as such these results will find a way into our model as well.

The potential part of the model is mainly used as an initial input for the rest of the factors. That is, we use potential indicators in recruitment situations where we may have little evidence for the individual's capacity to perform (beyond what the CV indicates) or when we want to make assumptions regarding which jobs an employee could do in the future. Strength consists of those potentials which have been developed far enough to be productively applied in a given role. To be precise, those potentials which have manifested themselves in skills and behaviours relevant to the job at hand. When those skills and behaviours reach a sophistication that allows the employee to consistently perform outstandingly we mark that individual as having a talent for the domain in which the performance take place (leadership, accounting and so forth). In order to help our employees, grow and develop or for managers to make informed decision about their people we consider the various facilitator factors and how they will impact development activities. For example, if we want to develop a new line of future leaders, we would want to consider whether the candidates have the agility required to take on a new set of skills and learnings and if so, how much effort is required. We would look at how well they "fit" with our values, we would look at whether or not their motivations and aspirations are in line with a leadership role and finally we would consider their overall resilience and potential risk behaviours. All of these factors would be put together to create a 'leadership quotient' score. Note that all the facilitators are weighted differently across grades so the requirements for a mid-manager is different from that of an executive, except for our 'fit' (or values) score which is the same for all.

As we finished our core talent model, we started to look towards the future and how we could create a series of smaller talent models for each critical job area or department within the organisation. Sales and customer service roles were a natural place to start due to their criticality in affecting overall business results. Quality of customer service and sales volumes are one way a bank like ours can differentiate itself from its competitors. It is therefore crucial that our sales and customer service staff are highly skilled in both areas. Though we are looking only at sales roles in this study, customer service skills are still of relevance as the modern sales role requires both the ability to sell a product and doing so in a way that the customer is satisfied with. Sales performance and the underlying traits and skills that produces it has received major attention by researchers over the years. Some of these studies have focused on single traits and characteristics such as Explanatory Style, Conscientiousness, and Achievement Strivings[8]. Other studies have looked at how different personality types affect the seller-buyer relationship[9] or how different competencies and skillsets impact sales performance[10]. What most of these studies have in common is that the individual characteristics underlying effective sales and customer service performance can be empirically studied and defined. What is lacking from many of these studies is an exploration of how these different characteristics affect different parts of the sales cycle and how predictive each characteristic is of actual performance outcomes. In addition, very few studies have successfully defined a 'complete sales model' which can be applied across that the talent life-cycle within an organisation.

Though many assessment companies supply their tests and questionnaires with optional sales profiles or sales reports, most of these products were made to be valid on a global scale, across industries or organisational size, and as such were designed around what great sales forces have in common. From a validity and reliability standpoint such tools have great value. However, the generalizing nature of the test design means that the small idiosyncrasies that makes one company different from another may sometimes "get lost in translation". Our interest is in having a model that defines what makes *us* great, what make our sales and customer service agents standout and have a set of tools that can manage this excellence from before the agent joins until he or she leaves.

As we started our study the creation of such a model was our main purpose. However, by the end of 2015 falling oil prices started to create a new set of challenges for us. Along with the oil industry itself and the property industry, regional banks have been among the most affected, including ours. One strategy we have pursued in order to deal with these changes has been to focus on digitisation and automation of work processes and procedures, whilst another has been exploring ways to optimise people performance in the face headcount reduction and hiring freezes. Both of these strategies are intimately tied in with our Talent Management practices and as such became part of the purpose of this study. As a result, the focus for this paper has been on:

- finding ways to optimise sales hiring and selection processes
- finding better ways to identify current pools of sales talent
- enhancing sales performance management and development activities
- increase, or at least, sustain sales employee engagement
- develop a set of tools supporting the above objectives that are easily optimised or automated through digitisation

Methodology

Please refer to the appendices for additional details on the methodology.

Sample Selection

We initiated the study by selecting random samples of top, medium and low performers, which resulted in a pool of 45 sales agents, this was later increased to a total of 101 agents. Performance in this case consisted of an annual performance ratings and an average PES[11] rating for the year which were combined for a final overall performance rating. We then created three experimental groups based on top, medium and low performance ratings. We chose to use an average of the last three years of performance to increase the reliability and validity of our later analyses. We also made sure that the sample included people from different sections of the sales team (such as credit cards, insurance and so forth).

Secondly, we took a random sample of 34 new joiners from the CCO sales department (around 6 months of experience within Tanfeeth) and also grouped them according to whether they could be considered top, medium or low performers after 6 months. In this case we were did not have an annual performance rating so we took the average of 6 months of PES scores. This group was going to act as an experimental group for our examination of the impact of talent facilitators on improved performance over time. In addition, this group would be used to reconfirm the predictive validity of the model by examining actual performance rating after one year of service.

Thirdly, we were given access to recorded sales calls for a selection employees participating in the study which would be used to explore any significant difference in language patterns and communicational strategies between the three groups and lastly, we created a group of SME's consisting of 12 top performers, 15 team leaders, 5 assistant managers and 1 manager.

Job Analysis

The first step in the modelling process involved defining the critical steps in the sales cycle so we had a framework to "hang" our findings on. We involved managers and assistant managers in a Repertory Grid Analysis[12]. In addition, we listened to recorded sales calls to see if the sales process followed a logical series of steps. From this process we identified six critical stages: (1) Planning the Sale, (2) Creating Rapport, (3) Engaging Emotions, (4) Dealing with Objections, (5) Closing the Sale and (6) Customer Care. This framework would allow us to sort potentials, strengths, skills and knowledge according to the specific steps in the sales process which they related to.

Identifying Sales Potentials, Abilities and Strengths

The first thing we wanted to do to meet the objectives of the study was to understand which potentials (traits and mental abilities) would explain high levels of performance within the sales teams. More precisely we wanted to understand which potentials, when they have become strengths through experience and learning, would predict high levels of actual performance. The purpose for examining this relationship was to meet a number of our objectives: (1) by understanding the strengths predicting high performance we could optimise our recruitment and selection efforts where potential assessments play a major role. In addition, we could develop interview guides to help us explore these strengths further doing job interviews. (2) We could improve our development processes by focusing our training and coaching efforts on only those strengths that have a direct impact on performance and (3) we could improve engagement efforts by understanding the most dominant motivators underlying high performance. In other words, we could get a glimpse into what is really engaging our top performers.

Test Administration

To meet these objectives, we administered a strength questionnaire and a set of mental ability tests. The strength questionnaire was the ETI (Employee Thriving Index) developed by the Talent Enterprise. This questionnaire measures respondents on 10 strength dimension and 27 sub-dimensions. Our mental ability tests came from Mindmill and included verbal and numerical ability, general reasoning, and error detection abilities. In total 79 individual test batteries were administered and out of those all respondents completed. The raw data and scores from each respondent (variable and sub-variable scores from the ETI and raw scores from the mental ability assessments) were downloaded as an excel document for further processing in SPSS.

Data Analysis

First we summarised the data and looked for any significant differences between top, medium and low performers. We then checked any significant correlations between assessment scores and performance ratings and these relationships were further analysed using Regression and Automatic Linear Modelling. These procedures would give us information on the predictability of each strength or mental ability and also its overall contribution (weight) to performance ratings.

Performance Predictors

The strengths that were found to predict performance were kept and a predictive model was built in excel based on the results from the predictive analysis. This model would then be used to predict the most likely annual performance rating of a candidate or employee based on his or her potential, strength or mental ability ratings.

Building the Sales Skills Framework

When we initially decided to create the sales performance framework we aimed to identify a set of competencies, but due to the "fuzziness" of the traditional definition of competencies (often a mix of behaviours, knowledge and skills) we had to create a more effective way of distinguishing between potentials, behaviours and knowledge or skill. The problem with the traditional competency approach is that it makes it hard to differentiate between what can easily be learned (knowledge), what can be trained for (skills) and what is difficult to change such as behavioural style. In addition, many competency models ignore the fact that people with different behavioural styles but who have the same set skills can often achieve the same results. In other words, more than one behavioural style can lead to a great result if the appropriate skills are in place.

Since we had already identified which potentials and behaviours were related to high performance, our next step was to focus on the specific skill sets that, when combined with certain strengths, would lead to outstanding performance. We did so for two reasons (1) behaviours cannot easily be trained due to their strong links to traits but skills can, and as such being able differentiate between behaviours and skills would help us decide what to hire for and what we could develop.

Having models and assessment tools that can tell us something about the extent to which an employee or candidate has the potential to succeed in a sales role and if so, what aspects of the sale process each employee is most likely to be successful in and to what extent, is in itself of great value to any sales department. But to get to where "the rubber meets the road" we had to understand the specific skills and knowledge underlying performance. This would not only help us fine tune the skills and knowledge aspects of our model but also help us focus our training interventions on the actual skills and domain knowledge that would really make a difference. In addition, it would give us yet another area to explore during our hiring, selection and talent mobility practices.

So to get a complete picture of a top sales employee's talent we also needed to consider their current level of skill, knowledge and expertise. It was only through this exercise we could completely determine where on the 'talent scale' an employee belonged. As mentioned in the introduction, the way Tanfeeth define talent is "The ability to engage in consistent outstanding performance which is beneficial to the objectives and values of the organisation".

Critical Incident Analysis

At this stage we wanted explore the specific knowledge and skills that would exemplify outstanding performance at each step of the sales cycle. This would help us differentiate between performance related behaviours and skills. We did so using Critical Incident Analysis[13] with managers and assistant managers, as well as examining recorded sales calls of top performers. This exercise resulted in six distinct groups including: (1) Product Knowledge, (2) Contact Building, (3) Information Gathering, (4) Customer Adaptability, (5) Sales Closure and (6) Maintaining Relationships.

Rating Skills

We created a skills rating sheet that team leaders could use to rate their agents and that the agents could use to rate themselves. This was not done to examine current skill levels within the department (though that was an informative by-product) but to have some quantifiable data we could use to explore performance predictability and any strength-skills relationships that might exist.

Data Analysis

Like in the previous exercise we first explored significant differences in skill ratings between each performance group and we examined the validity and reliability of the ratings that were provided. We then set out to do two things: (1) first we wanted to explore performance predictability and (2) we wanted to examine significant relationships between our identified sales strengths and skills. This would help us integrate the two models.

Completing the skills framework successfully would help us meet further objectives: We would have an additional tool to use during recruitment and selection processes, and we had a meaningful way to discuss development and coaching needs during our Personal

Development Plan process. Furthermore, we could use the skill clusters as part of our talent pool creation activities by being able to identify current sales skill levels and future skill potential within a department as well as explore if people within other departments would have the skill sets or strengths needed for a current or future sales role.

Examining the Role of Talent Facilitators

In order to understand how much each talent facilitator would impact an employee's performance over time we examined the data for our new employees (6 months of experience) and collected their PES performance ratings for each month since they joined. Our purpose was to see if there were any significant relationship between improvement of performance over six months and various facilitator factors. These findings would be an important addition to our recruitment, training and career development processes.

Development of Situational Judgement Tests

Outstanding performance requires outstanding levels of skill and knowledge and one of the best ways to capture those features is through a Situational Judgement Test[14]. In addition, and in contrast to potential assessments, SJT's measure those things which can be learned and developed either through training or on-the-job experience.

To be more precise, an SJT measures an individual's reasoning ability, level of knowledge and skill proficiency within a specific field or role and compares his or her results with those of an expert or very talented performer within the same field in an objective and scientific manner. It does so by presenting respondents with hypothetical but job-related situations and then present them with a number of response options which represent different ways to respond to the situation, with some being more effective or ineffective than others[15]

Generating Hypothetical Situations

From our previous work on behaviours, knowledge and skill we had already identified the key steps of work involved in the sales role. For the SJT's we needed to develop a number of critical and realistic situations for each step in the sales cycle. We approached this part of the puzzle in three ways:

1. Team leaders, assistant managers and managers were are asked to consider what would be the most critical situation an employee could experience during a given step of the sales cycle.
2. Top performers from the sales team (experimental group 1) were asked the same question as above.
3. A sample of recorded sales calls with people from all three experimental groups were analysed for situations that appeared particularly challenging to most employees.

In total 28 hypothetical situations were identified across the entire sales cycle.

Generating Response Items

The first step involved designing a rating scale for the response items. We chose a standard 6-point scale which is commonly used with SJT's. This scale has no neutral point and captures both what can be considered effective responses and non-effective responses.

The second step involved:

1. Asking team Leaders, assistant managers and managers to provide what they deemed to be the most effective behaviour and ineffective response to a given critical situation.
2. Top performers were asked the same question as above.
3. Recorded sale calls with top performers were analysed for responses that created positive results to a specific critical situation.

The positive response examples given by the SME's were initially treated as "highly desirable responses", whereas negative response examples were treated as "highly undesirable" responses. Thirdly, the responses were subjected to a qualitative content analysis to identify similarities or differences between responses.

Lastly, we shared the remaining response items with all team leaders, assistant managers and managers as well as top performers to reach consensus on where on the measuring scale each item belonged (for example did a highly undesirable response really belong where it was or was it more of an undesirable response?). The way we did this was by collecting all responses belonging to a critical situation and have each SME rate the responses, so what may be a +3 for one top performer may be a +1 for an assistant manager. We then took the mean of responses as a guide for where to place each on the rating scale.

The final response set was mapped unto the sales competencies identified earlier in the study. In total 58 individual responses were identified.

Pilot Testing and Future Work

We piloted SJT's with the sales teams and the results were used to:

- Generating norm groups and tackling issues around fairness
- Examine various types of reliability and validity
- Explore the relationship between scores on the SJT and other parts of the sales talent model
- Identify any predictability of SJT item scores and sales performance

Integrating the Sales Model with TM Processes

Having finished the model (except for the final SJT) we started designing the tools that we could use with our Talent Management processes. This step involved producing a sales talent calculation model in excel and design tools for recruitment, performance management, training and development and talent mobility. Finally, we produced a manual explaining the model and its features for sharing with the sales management teams.

Creating a Database of Action and Development Items

This part of the study included a review of action items from OPQ assessments, the ETI assessments, The StrengthFinder, The Standout Assessment and interviews with our top performers. We had planned to do a meta-analysis on the effectiveness of action and development items but had to abandon that due to lack of availability to such data. Instead we qualitatively selected items that we, through consensus, felt belonged to a certain potentials, strengths or skill sets.

Results

The following sections will highlight the results from our study and present core statistics related to those results. Additional details can be found in the appendices. Overall, we found that significant differences existed between performance groups, particularly in terms of three broad areas we labelled People Orientation, Domain Expertise and Personal Resilience.

Potentials, Strengths and Mental Abilities

We first conducted an analysis for the entire sample which revealed significant relationships between performance and *Energy, Ambiguity and Ambition*, but since we want to understand what our best performers do, we ran another correlation for that group. The correlation analysis showed a number of significant relationships between ETI dimensions and the annual performance ratings of top performers. The top 5 included: *Mastery, Buoyancy, Preparedness, Fortitude, and Determination.*

Correlations can show relationships but not causes. So we moved unto our predictive exercise. Regression Analysis and Automated Linear Modelling showed us that the following strengths and abilities had the highest predictive values in rank order: *Ambiguity, Mastery, Empathy, Buoyancy, General Reasoning, Absorption, Verbal Reasoning, Vitality, and Number Fluency.* The predictive ability of the model was 79.5%.

For practical reasons, we grouped these findings into three broad talent dimensions: (1) People Orientation, including Empathy, (2) Domain Expertise, including mental abilities,

Mastery and Absorption and (3) Personal Resilience, including Ambiguity, Buoyancy and Vitality. The reason for including Mastery and Absorption within the Domain Expertise cluster was that they relate to the successful acquisition and application of skills and knowledge. Mastery is an indicator of the desire to master a domain and Absorption has to do with how engaged someone becomes in a given activity.

Skills Framework

As in our previous analysis we first wanted to explore if proficiency on any of the skill clusters differed significantly between the performance groups using one-way ANOVA. We found that significant differences existed ($p<0.05$) between groups in terms of all skill clusters: Product Knowledge, Contact Building, Information Gathering, Customer Adaptation, Sales Closure and Maintaining Relationships. This finding confirmed our repertory grid exercise and our analysis of recorded sales calls.

Our regression analysis and Automated Linear Modelling revealed the following ranking of the skills dimensions from top to bottom: *Sales Closure, Customer Adaptation, Product Knowledge, Information Gathering, Contact Building and Maintaining Relationships.* The resulting model could predict annual performance ratings with 86.5% accuracy. All the skills clusters where added to the Domain Expertise Dimension.

Despite the differences in the predictability of the various skills, they must all be considered important to the sales process. It wouldn't make sense from a practical perspective to only emphasize those skills that has the highest predictability. For example, Customer Adaptability has a higher predictability than Product Knowledge but expertise is needed in both to close the sale. Being able to explain the details of a product as well as being able to adapt that knowledge to the needs of the customer is important for success even if Customer Adaptation is more predictive of performance than Product Knowledge. The ANOVA and predictive analysis showed us that all the skills clusters must be mastered for successful performance, though some may have a more significant impact than others.

Model Integration

The last stage of our analysis was to integrate our findings and optimise our final sales talent model. We initiated this stage by trying to establish relationships between potentials, strengths and skills. The reason being that understanding such a relationship would help us make decisions regarding the extent to which someone would find it easy to develop the skills required for a sales role. This would greatly aid us in developing sales talent pools and it could also help us assess to what extend a new hire, in absence of actual skills ratings, has what it takes to develop his or her sales skills-set to a level where top performance would be the result.

However, we found that the relationships between potentials, strengths and skills was quite complex. For example, Empathy was associated with skills ratings across various stages of the sales process including Contact Building, Information Gathering, Customer Adaptation and Maintaining Relationships. From a modelling perspective this was not an issue but one of the aims of our endeavour was to create a model that would be easy for sales managers and agents to understand and apply on a day-to-day basis.

So to aid ease of use and ease of comprehension we examined the impact of the three major talent dimensions (People Orientation, Domain Expertise and Personal Resilience) on annual performance and based our final predictive model on these results. At the end of our analysis we could predict the annual performance rating of a sales agent with 82.5% accuracy based on his or her scores on the three talent dimensions.

The Operational and Financial Benefits of Using the Model

Two test the business impact of the model we designed two scenarios (please note that the examples here are generalized examples for confidentiality reasons). The first involved the impact using the SJTs would have on selection ratios in recruitment. This is done using the 'Taylor Russel Approach', which aims to identify the least number of candidates you need to assess or interview while retaining the highest level of probability that you will select the best individual. If the current success rate for hiring a top sales performer is 60%, then implementing the SJTs as part of the hiring process will increase the success rate to 88%.

The second scenario involved exploring the cost-benefits of applying the model in a sales department. We hypothesised that if 80 top performing sales agents are hired out of a total 500 applicants annually and that the average annual salary of each sales agent is 85000 dirhams, then the utility gain would be roughly 1.2 million dirhams.

Talent Facilitators

In order to examine our talent facilitation model, we used the new joiners sample in order to see which variables, if any, would predict improvement in performance over a 6 months' period. Our analysis of the impact of the talent facilitators revealed that 'fit' and in particularly 'learning agility' were predictive of increasing performance over time. The regression analysis and the following automated linear modelling exercise generated a framework that can predict performance improvement with 76.5% accuracy. The following ETI dimensions related to learning agility had a significant impact on performance improvement: Mindset, Growth, Mastery and Preparedness.

Situational Judgment Test

Reliability and validity studies of the SJTs were conducted with original sample of employees. A total of 95 employees completed the SJTs. Chi-square tests and Cronbach alpha results were examined and showed relatively high validity and reliability for all the major sales skills clusters.

Discussion

General Discussion

Overall, our study met the majority of our objectives. The results clearly show that potentials such as strengths and mental abilities (in this case ETI dimensions) and job critical skills are important when it comes to on-the-job sales performance. More specifically we found that three broad dimensions (People Orientation, Domain Expertise and Personal Resilience) could account for the differences seen between top and bottom performers. People Orientation says something about the extent to which someone is empathic and sensitive to the needs of other people. Sales agents who had high People Orientation scores, tended to better at connecting with customers at the beginning of calls and also spend considerable more time on understanding the customer's needs during the information gathering phase. In addition, they were more likely to explain to the customer what to do or whom to contact if they experienced any issues with their product. In terms of Domain Expertise, we found that a number skills underlie successful sales performance, a finding that is hardly surprising. However, what was interesting was that strength indicators such as mastery and absorption seemed to have an impact on how effectively skills were applied on the job. Mastery is an indicator of how driven someone is to master the skills of a certain field and top performers generally scored higher than average and low performers on this indicator. Similarly, agents who reported experiencing higher levels of absorption (engagement, flow) on the job tended to have better end of year ratings. Finally, Personal Resilience was crucial to overall job success. Personal Resilience or the willingness to persevere and overcome setbacks and rejections was generally higher in top performers. This dimension seemed particularly important during the "Customer Adaption" phase, where top performers tended to challenge customer objections for longer periods of time than average or low performance. Agents scoring high on Personal Resilience where generally less likely to back down or give up when confronted with objections or negative responses for customers. It could be interesting in future research to see how this dimension relates to the number of calls agents make during a day. Based on our findings it could be hypothesised that agents with higher levels of Personal Resilience would be more persistent in completing the target set for them in terms how many calls they need to make.

In addition to the above findings, we discovered that various agility factors accounted for improvements in performance over time (in this case over a six-month period). Learning agility and employee fit has been of interest to researchers for many years now and our findings seems to be in line with that research. Agents with a strong belief in their ability to learn and master the sales role tended to have monthly performance ratings that increased over time. This was also the case with agents who showed good fit with our culture and values. This result highlights the importance of considering fit and agility as part of the overall employee assessment process. Someone may have the skills and strengths required for a job, but if they do not fit in with the culture of an organisation or do not believe in their ability to succeed and master a given role, they are not likely to deliver top performance.

Implementation of Our Findings

Developing a comprehensive model of talent as we have done with this study provides an organisation with a number of opportunities for optimising their talent practices. Having a clear idea of the potentials and, more specifically, strengths which are facilitative of performance or the execution of certain skills can be a great aid in identifying the right candidate both during the hiring process and within the organisation itself. For example, psychometric assessments can be calibrated to measure the potentials which have been found to be predictive of performance and help a hiring manager determine whether someone has enough of a potential for it manifest as a strength. With the predictive model we have created we can roughly say with 80% accuracy what someone's performance rating is going to be after a year, even before they are hired. Furthermore, we can look across the bank for people who may possess the right strength or talent profile required for openings within our sales departments. In addition, having identified both the potentials and skills sets needed for effective sales performance makes it possible to create tailored interview questions which can effectively probe a potential candidates previous experience and current proficiency. This investigation can be further enhanced by applying SJTs.

In terms of performance management and talent development, having a clear understanding of what drives performance makes it easier to create interventions and training programs to facilitate performance and aid employee development. It makes it possible for managers and training departments to create customised training programs or on-the-job activities that can target the specific skills or behaviours that will improve performance. It is possible to go further than we did in this study an examine the relationship between talent indicators and very specific performance measures such as number of calls made in a day, number of errors made during order confirmations and so forth. Such insights would make it possible for operational managers to make some very precise decisions in terms of which skills should be prioritised in order to deal with performance deviations.

Lastly, being aware of what drives performance across various functions takes out a lot of the complexity and guesswork that is often involved in moving people from one area of work to another. This is particularly useful in times of economic uncertainty where an organisation may not be able to hire outside talent and is therefore extra vulnerable to the negative effects of letting go of the wrong people or placing unqualified people in vacant positions during restructuring efforts.

Methodological Issues

Since this study relied heavily on psychometrics to provide the majority of the input for the model, a number of considerations must be taken into account.

The first issue is related to the reliability and validity of the psychometric tools being used. The quality of your results will be directly related to the psychometric properties of your assessments. Psychometric assessments, though effective have their flaws and couple of things must be kept in mind when using them. One of the only ways test designers can increase validity and reliability of their instruments is to increase the number of items used in the test. However, this may have a detrimental impact on the length of the test as increased number of items means increased amount of time for test takers to complete the test. Raising Cronbach's alpha through increasing the number of items removes degrees of freedom within in a scale and may have a negative impact on content validity and in some cases criterion validity. This leaves test-designers with the dilemma of compromising between reliability and test-efficiency. When doing the type of research presented in this paper, a compromise must always be sought between maintaining reliability and avoiding exhausting participants with large test batteries.

Secondly, since we used a "home-made" questionnaire when we assessed the perceived skill levels of our agents and did not have the time to assess the reliability or validity of the questionnaire, it is possible that the data may not be as "clean" as one could wish for. Secondly, we did not give team leaders any formal training on how to rate people and how to avoid any of the biases that may be involved when making judgements about others. It is also possible that skills set which were not identified during our critical incident exercise may play a role in high performance.

Lastly, it could be argued that the number of participants in our study may have affected the power of some of the statistics that we used. Particularly correlations and regression methodologies greatly benefit from large sample sizes.

Conclusions

Despite the potential weakness involved in psychometric research of this type, our study met our core objectives and made it possible for us to develop and implement more effective ways of identifying and manager our sales talent. By being able to manage our talent better and document the positive effect this has on our organisation we help make talent management a respected and credible practice that can help increase the sustainability and longevity of Tanfeeth and the Emirates NBD banking group. We also hope that by setting a high standard for our people management and assessment practices we can serve as an example and an inspiration to other organisations in the UAE and help create a nation where raising the skills, educational levels and contribution of people are a main priority.

We believe that the UAE has the will to do so, but may need a clearer understanding on how to do so. We believe this paper serves as a small contribution to this challenging, yet exciting task.

The Author would like to thank Kazim Jezza, Nithin Kalinda, Vijay Prataj, Lovesh Miranda and the entire CCO and Tawasal teams for their cooperation and support. This paper would not have been possible without you.

Appendices

1. The Sales Cycle and Related Skill Clusters

Sales Cycle	Skill Clusters	Description
1. Planning the Sale	Product Knowledge	In-depth understanding of the product and how to position it to the customer and/or specific market segment.
2. Creating Rapport	Contact Building	Has the ability to 'break the ice' and make the customer feel comfortable.
3. Engaging Emotions	Information Gathering	Can build desire in the customer probing their needs and engaging their emotions
4. Dealing w. Objections	Customer Adaptability	Understands how to reposition a product or offer another product in the face of objections.
5. Closing the Sale	Sales Closure	Can close the sale and check for customer satisfaction.
6. Customer Care	Customer Care	Follows up with the customers and/or can generate new leads.

2. Core Sales Talent Drivers

Core Talent Drivers	Description
1. People Orientation	Top performers show high levels passion when it comes to engaging with customers. They enjoy meeting customer needs and/or solve their problems. They can handle difficult conversations with an optimistic mindset. They also excel at talking to the customers 'heart' rather relying on rational argumentation alone.
2. Domain Expertise	Top performers have a deep understanding of their products and knows how to link product features to customer needs. They are capable of dealing with customer objections in a creative and flexible manner. They pay attention to customer satisfaction and make sure to follow through on promises given. In addition, they work hard continuously improving their ability to sell.
3. Personal Resilience	Top performers show high levels of resilience towards customer objections and work pressure. They are more likely than mid or low performers to bounce back from a customer rejection. They tend to show higher levels of optimism in relation to their own abilities to meet their target.

3. SJT Excerpt: Production Knowledge

Question: A customer is asking you for information about a new product. Since you were on sick leave for the last few days, you haven't had a chance to read up on the product. Which of the following actions would you take?

1. I would try to read up on the information while speaking to the customer
2. I would ask the customer to stay on hold while I ask a colleague for help
3. I would apologize to the customer and ask them to call another agent who might know more
4. I would explain to the customer that I may not have all the information he or she needs and then tell him or her that I will call back shortly with right answers

***Scoring Key: Answer 1:** 2 points, **Answer 2:** 3 points, **Answer 3:** 1 point, **Answer 4:** 4 points*

4. Example of Development Items Related to Strengths

Area of Potential	Example Items	Area of Impact
Mastery	1. Provide the employee with increasingly challenging targets or objectives. 2. Set up additional (non-impact) performance measures or games to challenge the employee 3. Provide the employee with additional opportunities to master his or her skills 4. Provide them with books or learning material on high performance concepts 5. Give them the opportunity to shadow the very best performers	Domain Expertise

5. Example of the Predictive Power of The Model

Employee	Actual Annual Performance*	Predicted Annual Performance
Employee 1	4.00	4.23
Employee 2	3.50	3.53
Employee 3	4.40	4.90
Employee 4	3.73	3.39
Employee 5	2.00	2.00
Employee 6	3.00	2.95
Employee 7	3.66	3.53

* The average reflects a combination of performance rating and PES

6. Validity and Reliability of SJT Dimensions

Skill Clusters	Cronbach Alpha	Chi-Square Significance
Product Knowledge	.76	.023
Contact Building	.69	.012
Information Gathering	.64	.001
Customer Adaptability	.79	.000
Sales Closure	.68	.003
Customer Care	.64	.008

References

Aspenlund, J., Lopez, S.J., Hodges, T. & Harter, J. *The Clifton StrengthFinder 2.0.* Technical Report. The Gallup Organisation 2007.

Bruer, John T. *The Myth of the First Three Years: A New Understanding of Early Brain Development and Lifelong Learning*. New York: Free Press, 1999.

Buckingham, M. *StandOut 2.0: Assess Your Strengths, Find Your Edge, Win at Work.* Nashville: Thomas Nelson, 2011

Buckingham, M. & Clifton, D. Now, Discover Your Strengths. London: Simon & Chuster 2004

Conaty B., and Charan R. *The Talent Masters: Why Smart Leaders Put People before Numbers.* New York: Crown Business, 2010. P.1

Cook, W. & Hababou, M. *Sales Performance Measurement in Bank Branches.* Volume 29, Issue 4, August 2001, Pages 299-307

Coyle, D. *The Talent Code: Greatness Isn't Born: It's Grown, Here's How.* New York: Bantam Books, 2009.

Dweck, C. S. *Mindset: The New Psychology of Success.* New York: Random House, 2006.

Edenborough, R., and Edenborough, M. *The Psychology of Talent: Exploring and Exploding the Myths.* Toronto: Hogrefe Pub., 2011.

Flanagan, John.C. *The Critical Incident Technique.* Psychological Bulletin, Vol 51(4), Jul 1954, 327-358.

Fransella, F., Bell, Richard & Bannister, D. *A Manual for The Repertory Grid Technique.* 2nd Ed. Chichester: Wiley & Sons, 2004.

Musch, J., and Grondin, S. *"Unequal Competition as an Impediment to Personal Development: A Review of the Relative Age Effect in Sport."* Developmental Review 21, no. 2 (2001): 147-67.

Motowildo, S.J. & Tippins, N. Further studies of the low-fidelity simulation in the form of a situational inventory. Journal of Occupational Psychology, Vol. 66 (1993), 337-583

Parasuraman, A., Berry L.L. & Zeithaml. *Refinement and reassessment of the SERVQUAL scale.* Journal of Retailing, Vo. 67 No.4 1991, p.55-68

Rath, T. *Strengthsfinder 2.0.* New York, NY: Gallup Press, 2007.

Seligman, M. E., & Schulman, P. *"Explanatory Style as a Predictor of Productivity and Quitting among Life Insurance Sales Agents."* Journal of Personality and Social Psychology 50, no. 4 (1986): 832-38.

Notes

1 Bill Conaty, and Ram Charan. *The Talent Masters: Why Smart Leaders Put People before Numbers.* New York: Crown Business, 2010. P.1

2 Robert Edenborough, and Marion Edenborough. *The Psychology of Talent: Exploring and Exploding the Myths.* Toronto: Hogrefe Pub., 2011.

3 Tom Rath. *Strengthsfinder 2.0.* New York, NY: Gallup Press, 2007.

4 Daniel Coyle. *The Talent Code: Greatness Isn't Born: It's Grown, Here's How.* New York: Bantam Books, 2009.

5 Carol Dweck. *Mindset: The New Psychology of Success.* New York: Random House, 2006.

6 Jochen Musch and Simon Grondin. *"Unequal Competition as an Impediment to Personal Development: A Review of the Relative Age Effect in Sport."* Developmental Review 21, no. 2 (2001): 147-67.

7 John T. Bruer. *The Myth of the First Three Years: A New Understanding of Early Brain Development and Lifelong Learning.* New York: Free Press, 1999.

8 Seligman, Martin E., and Peter Schulman. *"Explanatory Style as a Predictor of Productivity and Quitting among Life Insurance Sales Agents."* Journal of Personality and Social Psychology 50, no. 4 (1986): 832-38.

9 A. Parasuraman et al. *Refinement and reassessment of the SERVQUAL scale.* Journal of Retailing, Vo. 67 No.4 1991, p.55-68

10 Wade D. Cook & Momi Hababuo. *Sales Performance Measurement in Bank Branches.* Omega Volume 29, Issue 4, August 2001, Pages 299-307

11 A PES rating is a monthly rating consisting of scores gained from various sales related KPI's such as 'number of calls made' or 'number of sales targets met' and so forth.

12 Fay Fransella et al (2004). A Manual for the Repertory Grid Technique. 2nd Ed. (Chichester: Wiley & Sons 2004)

13 John C. Flanagan. *The Critical Incident Technique.* Psychological Bulletin, Vol 51(4), Jul 1954, 327-358.

14 Marcus Buckingham. StandOut 2.0: Assess Your Strengths, Find Your Edge, Win at Work. Nashville: Thomas Nelson, 2011

15 Stephan J. Motowildo & Nancy Tippins, N. *Further studies of the low-fidelity simulation in the form of a situational inventory.* Journal of Occupational Psychology, Vol. 66 (1993), 337-583

About the Contributors

Iram Fatma Al Ansari is an Assistant Professor of Accounting at Sultan Qaboos University in Muscat Oman and along with her teaching responsibilities, her research activities have led her to specialize in the operations, investment and financial issues related to both European Family Firms and Omani small and medium size enterprises.

Elinor Bajraktari is a former United Nations staff member who has worked on public-sector reform and development issues in a number of countries, including Bahrain, Egypt, Belarus, Canada, Kosovo, Albania, Mozambique, Myanmar and Ukraine amongst others. He has a Master of Public Administration in International Development from Harvard University and is currently a PhD-candidate at the University of Alberta in Canada.

Bamrata Budhraja is Senior Manager Consulting at The Talent Enterprise. After gaining experience as an entrepreneur, she completed her Master's in Business Administration, specializing in strategy formulation and execution, from HEC, Paris. Namrata has worked extensively on creating The Talent Enterprise's Strength's Compass program, aiming to foster critical life-skills and employability amongst the GCC region's youth. She has completed extensive research on the impact of positive education and has recently co-authored a paper on 'Building Life Skills Through Positive Education: Evidence from Ras Al Khaimah (UAE).'

Gauri Gupta is the Co-Founder and Director of Analytics at The Talent Enterprise. Based in Toronto, Gauri leads the research strategy at The Talent Enterprise, with a focus on labour market challenges, talent management, happiness and well-being. Gauri is also responsible for developing and delivering innovative assessment and employee engagement solutions, with an expertise in advanced statistical analysis, predictive modeling and psychometrics, working on large, complex datasets. Gauri has co-authored a number of whitepapers and journal articles, including on "Predicting Attrition Risk" and her latest chapter contribution to the book 'Employment and Career Motivation in the Gulf States', also published by Gerlach Press.

Wissam Hachem is a senior HR professional with more than 25 years' experience in aviation. He is currently the Vice President Learning and Development working for a major Gulf Airline. He holds an Executive MBA from the University of Leicester in the UK. He is responsible for the design and implementation of the people development strategy across the business, where he focuses on building airline-specific capabilities among the company's talent pool, providing business-aligned leadership development solutions, best-in-class performance management, talent succession strategies and company-wide career development to over 27,000 employees. He has played an instrumental role in setting-up local talent initiatives for the airline, which placed an emphasis on attracting talented nationals into the company. This has laid the foundations for a successful company-wide nationalisation.

Jonas Harring Boll is a seasoned Talent and HR executive with more than 17 years of experience in Talent Management, HR and people development roles across several organisations in the EU, UK and GCC. He is a Kings College Alumni with an MSc in Organisational Psychology, as well as holding a number of professional certifications in Psychometrics, Coaching, Counselling and HR Management. Jonas is currently serving as the Head of Talent and Performance Management with Tanfeeth – Emirates NBD in Dubai, UAE.

Louise Lambert is a Canadian registered psychologist and Associate Professor at the Canadian University Dubai (United Arab Emirates). With over 15 year's experience in mental health, primary healthcare and higher education and a concentration in positive psychology, she has developed and delivered several evidence-based intervention programs in Canada and the GCC region. She leads many research projects in collaboration with local and international researchers and has published in a number of peer – reviewed academic journals. She is currently editing the region's first textbook in positive psychology and an introductory psychology textbook written exclusively for a GCC audience. She is also the founder and Editor-in-Chief of the Middle East Journal of Positive Psychology.

Jacqueline McGlade is an Associate Professor of Political Science at Sultan Qaboos University in Muscat Oman and specializes in International Political Economic and Business development, International relations, and International Trade and Technology Transfer. She is the author of several publications on the impact of U.S. foreign aid programs on post-1945 world business and technology development.

Caitrin Mullan is the Director of Community Engagement and Outreach at the Sheikh Saud Bin Saqr Al Qasimi Foundation in Ras al Khaimah, UAE. Previously, she held several positions at the University of Minnesota (College of Food, Agricultural and Natural Resource Sciences), including Chief of Staff to the Associate Dean, where she helped lead a strategic planning effort to embed experiential and interdisciplinary teaching strategies into the curriculum. Caitrin's background also includes work in admissions, advising, student leadership development, study abroad, strategic communications, and diversity and inclusion capacity building. A Minnesota native, Caitrin holds three degrees from the University of Minnesota-Twin Cities campus: Journalism (BA), Environmental Science (BS), and Water Resources Science (MS). She also spent a year studying at the University of Queensland in Australia as a Rotary Ambassadorial Scholar.

Anastasia Nosova recently completely a PhD at the London School of Economics on Kuwait's business elite and parliamentary politics. She was also involved in an ESRC research project on

'State-Business Relations and Reforms in the Gulf', a joint initiative of the University of Exeter and Georgetown University, Qatar. Anastasia's work on Gulf business and politics has been previously published in a number of edited volumes and academic journals, including the British Journal of Middle Eastern Studies and Journal of Arabian Studies. She currently works in the field of business intelligence and corporate investigation.

Sophie Olver-Ellis is a political economist and recent PhD Graduate from the University of Bath. Her most recent research is a comparative study on the transforming governance of the labour market in Saudi Arabia, Kuwait and Qatar and identified how they are situated within the debates of late rentierism. She also holds two Masters degrees during which her research focused on international migration, international development, governance and the international political economy, the reproductive labour of Filipina domestic workers in the case of Saudi Arabia and nationalisation policies in the case of Saudi Arabia, Kuwait and Dubai. She has over nine year's research experience on the Arabian Gulf.

Radhika Punshi is the Co-Founder and Managing Director at The Talent Enterprise, a human capital 'think' and 'do' tank focused on the MENA region. As an organisational psychologist, she is a senior advisor to policy makers and organisational leaders on their people priorities, with a key focus on youth and female inclusion. With an Ivy League education, and two Masters Degrees in Organisational Behaviour, Radhika is the first person from the MENASA region to be awarded a degree in Positive Psychology. She served on founding Board of Directors of the prestigious International Positive Psychology Association and is a Visiting Scholar at the University of Pennsylvania. She is a prolific speaker and published author of two books, 'Unlocking the Paradox of Plenty' and 'Game-Changers' by Motivate Publishing, in addition to contributing to several leading publications on GCC labour markets.

Ali Salman Saleh is a United Nations developmental programme analyst, who leads the portfolio of social development and government efficiency at UNDP, Bahrain. He develops projects in the areas of youth, health, childhood, disability, and public administration. He holds a Master Degree in "Methods of Training English Language Teachers", from Murray State University, Kentucky USA and Bachelor Degree of English Literature from University of Bahrain. In the past 14 years, he participated in many national and international conferences, seminars and forums as a speaker, commentator, and/or participant; covering various human development-related subject areas, including within the broader Middle East region.

Mark C. Thompson is Assistant Professor of Middle East Studies at King Fahd University of Petroleum and Minerals (KFUPM), Dhahran, Saudi Arabia. He is also Senior Associate Fellow at King Faisal Center for Research & Islamic Studies (KFCRIS), Riyadh, Saudi Arabia. His principal research areas are Saudi socio-political development and societal transformation and he has published on topics such as Saudi youth issues and challenges facing Saudi women leaders in publications such as the Journal of Arabian Studies; Asian Affairs; Middle Eastern Studies; and Diplomacy and

Statecraft. In addition, he has published books with I.B. Tauris on "Saudi Arabia and the Path to Political Change: National Dialogue and Civil Society" (2014) and "Policy-Making in the GCC: State, Citizens and Institutions" (2017) with Dr. Neil Quilliam.

Elizabeth Topolskaya is a consultant at the Talent Enterprise, after recently graduating from the Canadian University of Dubai. She has been furthering her research skills, including collaborating with Dr. Louise Lambert on the application of Positive Psychology concepts to the modern workplace. In addition, she has also written her own article targeting HR professionals, conveying the deterministic importance of taking "soft skills" into consideration within talent management decisions. She also collaborated with Radhika Punshi on another article revealing the trends of online learning in the GCC, followed by her partnership with Dr. Ahmed Okasha on a medical trial study, intended to reveal the difference in effectiveness of two well-known medicines against ASD. Most recently, she has lead a research project on testicular cancer awareness being tested amongst UAE residents, which is due for imminent publication.